RABBI HAIM DAVID HALEVY

GENTLE SCHOLAR AND COURAGEOUS THINKER

Modern Jewish Lives
volume 2

Rabbi Shlomo Goren: Torah Sage and General (MJL, volume 1)

RABBI HAIM DAVID HALEVY

GENTLE SCHOLAR AND COURAGEOUS THINKER

by
MARC D. ANGEL
with HAYYIM ANGEL

URIM PUBLICATIONS
Jerusalem • New York

Rabbi Haim David Halevy: Gentle Scholar and
Courageous Thinker
by Marc D. Angel with Hayyim Angel
Series: Modern Jewish Lives – Volume 2
Series Editor: Tzvi Mauer

ISBN 965-7108-82-9

Urim Publications, P.O. Box 52287, Jerusalem 91521 Israel

Lambda Publishers Inc.
3709 13th Avenue Brooklyn, New York 11218 U.S.A.
Tel: 718-972-5449 Fax: 718-972-6307
E-mail: mh@ejudaica.com

www.UrimPublications.com

Contents

Guide to Abbreviations of Rabbi Halevy's Books

ALR= Asei Lekha Rav
BYL= Bein Yisrael la'Ammim
DM= Dat uMedinah
DVM= Devar haMishpat
MH= Mayyim Hayyim
MKH= Mekor Hayyim
MZR= Maftehot haZohar veRa'ayonotav
NM= Netzah Moshe
TH= Torat Hayyim

INTRODUCTION

Early in the 1980s, my colleague Rabbi Michael Azose invited me to give a lecture to his congregation in Chicago. While at his home, I had the opportunity to look through his bookcases and came across a small volume, *Asei Lekha Rav*, volume one. I had not heard of this book of responsa, nor had I known of its author – the Sephardic Chief Rabbi of Tel Aviv – Rabbi Haim David Halevy.

As I leafed through the book, I immediately had an overwhelming feeling of elation. The book was written with such clarity and erudition! It dealt with questions of such pressing importance! I knew that I wanted to study this volume at length, and also to find every other book written by Rabbi Halevy. When I returned to New York, I contacted my book dealer, Mr. Samuel Gross, and asked him to send me whatever books he could find by Rabbi Halevy. I soon was studying *Mekor Hayyim* and other volumes of *Asei Lekha Rav*. As is the case with so many others who have studied the writings of Rabbi Halevy, I became his devoted student. In his books, I found a remarkable depth and breadth of Torah knowledge, a willingness to confront the most problematic questions, a profound traditionalism blended with intense sensitivity to the challenges of the modern world. Rabbi Halevy was the quintessential Sephardic rabbinic sage.

In 1984, our family spent the summer in Israel. I had the privilege of meeting with Rabbi Halevy in his office and his home. I visited him on subsequent trips to Israel, and also maintained a written correspondence. In the summer of 1995, when our son Hayyim received rabbinical ordination from the Rabbi Isaac Elchanan Theological Seminary of

Yeshiva University, both of us visited Rabbi Halevy. Hayyim, too, had become an enthusiastic student of Rabbi Halevy's writings, and was eager to meet him. At the conclusion of our meeting, Rabbi Halevy gave his blessing to Hayyim, wishing him success in his Torah study and teaching, and in his work on behalf of the Jewish community.

In one of my early meetings with Rabbi Halevy, I asked him if he would establish a yeshiva that would promote his style of Torah scholarship. After all, the Jewish world needed rabbis and educators trained in the classic Sephardic approach – in the pattern of Rabbi Halevy and his mentor Rabbi Benzion Meir Hai Uziel. Rabbi Halevy, in a voice of quiet resignation, indicated that he did not think it possible for him to establish such a yeshiva in the current religious climate. He stated: "my books are my yeshiva."

If his books are indeed his yeshiva, then his yeshiva has many students scattered throughout the world. Yet, in spite of the impressive success of his books, Rabbi Halevy was – and remains – an under-appreciated and inadequately recognized Torah luminary of our time. He was a public figure, who was essentially a private person. He was a prolific author of books and articles, and he had a popular radio program for a number of years; and yet, he was surprisingly unknown to large segments of the religious and general Jewish community. He scrupulously avoided controversy and confrontation; and yet his career was not untouched by controversy and confrontation. He was a man who loved the public and worked tirelessly for the public; and yet, he clearly felt the pangs of isolation.

In 1999, I published a book, *Loving Truth and Peace: The Grand Religious Worldview of Rabbi Benzion Uziel* (Jason Aronson). The book presented the essential teachings of Rabbi Uziel, the pre-eminent Sephardic sage of the first half of the twentieth century. Upon completing that book, I had in mind to write a similar study of the teachings of Rabbi Halevy – the pre-eminent disciple of Rabbi Uziel. This idea was given encouragement by Tzvi Mauer of Urim Publications, who expressed his interest in publishing such a book. We agreed that I would write a book on

Rabbi Halevy and that my son Hayyim would write several of the chapters. We thank the Almighty for having given us the privilege of preparing this volume and presenting it to the public. We pray that it will redound to the honor of Rabbi Halevy's memory.

In preparing this volume, a number of friends in Israel were of singular importance. Dr. Zvi Zohar, who had arranged a conference of papers on the teachings of Rabbi Halevy, was kind enough to share those papers with us. He himself has written important essays on modern Sephardic sages, including Rabbi Halevy.

Rabbi Halevy's daughter Gila and her husband Rabbi Achia Amitai have been of inestimable help and encouragement. They provided considerable information about the life of Rabbi Halevy, and also assembled the photographs that are part of this book.

Rabbi Halevy's brother, Nissim, offered his reminiscences of growing up in the Ohel Moshe neighborhood of Jerusalem, and shed important light on his brother's childhood years.

Mr. Sholem Hurwitz interviewed a number of individuals in Israel who had known Rabbi Halevy in different contexts. Among those interviewed were Rabbi Shlomo Levi, son-in-law of Rabbi Halevy; Rabbi Yitzhak Shlinka, former chairman of Rishon Letzion's religious council; Rabbi Shmuel David, Chief Rabbi of Afula; Rabbi Binyamin Aviad, a lifelong colleague of Rabbi Halevy; Rabbi David Shloush, Chief Rabbi of Netanya and an in-law of Rabbi Halevy; Rabbi Yisrael Meir Lau, Ashkenazic Chief Rabbi of Tel Aviv and former Ashkenazic Chief Rabbi of Israel; Rabbi Sharvit, Chief Rabbi of Ashkelon, a former student of Rabbi Halevy. I express appreciation to each of these distinguished scholars for sharing of their time and knowledge.

My son, Rabbi Hayyim Angel, wrote four of the chapters of this book: Dealing With Conflicting Sources; Jewish Education; Metaphysical Issues; *At'halta deGe'ulah*. I wrote the remainder of the book. I thank Hayyim not only for the chapters he prepared, but also for reviewing the chapters I wrote and giving his insightful suggestions.

Rabbi Halevy's books – what he called his yeshiva – have touched the lives of thousands of people, many of whom have come to view Rabbi Halevy as a genuine *gadol hador*, great sage of the generation. I believe that his books will become increasingly important with the passage of time. For many generations to come, students thirsty for the truth of Torah will become part of Rabbi Haim David Halevy's extended yeshiva.

Chapter One

BIOGRAPHICAL SKETCH

A story is told of a married couple that came to the office of Rabbi Shalom Hedaya in Jerusalem in 1923. They had been married for many years but had not been blessed with children. They came to the rabbi for a divorce. They thought that if they would marry other spouses, they perhaps would be able to have children.

The rabbi saw that the couple was distraught. The husband and wife obviously loved each other, and were heartbroken to have reached the decision to end their marriage. Rabbi Hedaya did not grant them a divorce, but gave them a blessing that they would have children together. The couple returned home. The next year, a baby boy was born to them. The Hedaya family reports that the barren couple that had sought the divorce was Moshe and Victoria Levy; the child born as a result of Rabbi Hedaya's blessing was named Haim David.[1]

Moshe Levy, born in Bursa (known among Sephardim as Brussa) Turkey in 1882, migrated to the land of Israel with his parents when he was sixteen years old. Several years later, he married his wife, also of Turkish Sephardic background. He was a shoemaker. Having a pleasant

---

[1] The story was told by Gila Amitai, Rabbi Halevy's daughter, in a biographical paper about her father. This paper is included in the volume of essays about Rabbi Halevy being prepared for publication by Zvi Zohar and Avi Sagi. Much of the following biographical information is drawn from Gila Amitai's paper, and from material from interviews with her and her husband. The family name was originally "Levy," but Rabbi Haim David later adopted "Halevy" as his family surname.

voice and a good knowledge of the Sephardic style of worship, he also served as hazzan (leader of prayer services) at the Taranto synagogue in the Ohel Moshe neighborhood of Jerusalem, a position he held for many years.[2]

Two years after the birth of Haim David, Moshe and Victoria Levy had a second son, Nissim. The two boys grew up together, and attended the Talmud Torah in the vicinity.

In those days, many parents believed that their children could advance academically and professionally only if they attended the French-speaking school sponsored by the Alliance Israelite Universelle. Even in the Ohel Moshe neighborhood, where most of the residents were religiously observant Jews, the pressure to educate children in "progressive" schools was strongly felt. It would have been natural for Moshe and Victoria Levy to send their sons to a school that offered a broad program of general studies, not merely Torah studies.

Yet, when Haim David was nine or ten years old, his parents enrolled him in a traditional yeshiva, Porat Yosef. Mr. Nissim Levy explained this decision: "In our surroundings resided a number of famous rabbis of the Sephardic community. One of them, a very distinguished rabbi, Benzion Cuenca, who served as *Av Beth Din* of the Rabbinical High Justice Court of Jerusalem, followed and watched carefully after the behavior of my brother at the synagogue and with his friends. He came to the conclusion that the boy is a genius. Therefore, he advised my father and rather urged him to send him to a yeshiva and not to a general school."

So Moshe and Victoria Levy, heeding the advice of Rabbi Cuenca, placed their son in the Sephardic yeshiva Porat Yosef. They incurred the extra expenses as their investment in Haim David's Torah education. Some of the Levy's neighbors thought this decision was wrong. "Send him (Haim David) to the Alliance school, there he will learn; he might even

---

[2] Information about Haim David's childhood is drawn from information provided to me by his brother, Nissim, of Jerusalem.

become a postal clerk." But, fortunately, the Levys did not follow the advice of their "progressive" neighbors.

Haim David was predisposed to the life of a yeshiva student from his earliest childhood. He was a serious, highly intelligent boy, who preferred to sit in the Beth Midrash with elder men rather than to play childhood games with his peers. His classmates thought he was a saint; they respected him. A rumor circulated among them that he knew the mysterious Divine Name *(shem hameforash)* – so holy was he. Mr. Nissim Levy recalls: "I remember that he always loved to read Zohar. I still see him in my imagination, a thin and pale boy, seated with elders at the Beth Midrash, listening with thirst to Zohar lectures."

The mother tongue in the Levy household was Judeo-Spanish, the language of the Jews of Turkey. Hebrew came to predominate when the boys entered school, but they continued to speak with their parents – especially their mother – in Judeo-Spanish.

Nissim Levy attended general schools and went on to become an accountant. Meanwhile, his older brother was proving himself a remarkably dedicated student at Porat Yosef.

At Porat Yosef, Haim David studied under the tutelage of Rabbi Yosef Tawil, and under the guidance of the head of the yeshiva, Rabbi Ezra Attiyah. Both of these scholars were of Syrian Sephardic background, and Haim David picked up their Aleppan pronunciation of Hebrew. The yeshiva was under the official presidency of Rabbi Benzion Uziel, and he would visit from time to time to test the students and to give lectures. Yet, Rabbi Uziel's relationship with the yeshiva's administration was not altogether smooth. Rabbi Uziel was an outspoken Zionist, identified with the Mizrachi movement; the yeshiva's administration tended to be more closely aligned with Agudat Israel, and was not enthusiastic about religious Zionism. Moreover, Rabbi Uziel stressed the importance of Jewish thought and philosophy, while the yeshiva's administration favored the study of Torah, Talmud and halakhah, without wanting students to become involved in philosophical studies.

Rabbi Halevy upon his election as rabbi of the Sephardic community of Rishon LeZion, 1952. Courtesy of the Halevy family.

Rabbi Halevy in photo dated July 1962. Photo by Naftali Rothschild.

Rabbi Halevy and Rabbi Yitzhak Greenberg (Chairman of the Religious Council of Rishon LeZion and author of *Iturei Torah)* in Rishon LeZion, 1967. Courtesy of the Halevy family.

Rabbi Halevy with the saintly Rabbi Yitzhak AbuHatseira, head of the Sephardic Rabbis Association, on a trip to the Golan Heights after the Six Day War of June 1967.
Courtesy of the Halevy family.

Rabbi Halevy with Rabbi Aryeh Levin (2nd from right), c. 1970.
Courtesy of Ezra uBitsaron of Rishon LeZion.

Rabbi Uziel taught classes in his home on Jewish thought, especially on the *Kuzari* of Rabbi Yehudah Halevy, to a select group of students. Among them were Haim David Halevy and David Shloush, who were to become lifelong friends – and in-laws. (Rabbi Halevy's daughter Ronit married Rabbi Shloush's son Shlomo.) Rabbi Uziel also instructed his students to learn chapters of the Bible by heart, and led them in serious discussions on various aspects of Jewish thought.[3]

Rabbi Uziel impressed upon his students the need to attain general knowledge along with Torah knowledge. He also stressed the importance of learning foreign languages. His urgings had an impact on Haim David Halevy, who studied English language at a Berlitz school, and pedagogy at a school under the auspices of Mizrachi.

Haim David excelled in his Torah studies and ultimately was one of a group of students who studied with Rabbi Attiyah, head of the yeshiva. Among the other students in this group were David Shloush, Ovadya Yosef, Zion Levi, Benzion Abba Shaul, and Avraham Barukh. Each of these students went on to important positions of leadership in the rabbinical world. Rabbi Halevy became Chief Rabbi of Rishon Letzion and then Tel Aviv; Rabbi Shloush became Chief Rabbi of Netanya. Rabbi Yosef became Chief Rabbi of Tel Aviv, Sephardic Chief Rabbi of Israel, and spiritual head of the Shas party; Rabbi Levi became rabbi of the community in Panama; Rabbi Abba Shaul became the head of the Porat Yosef yeshiva; and Rabbi Barukh served as rabbi in New York.

Rabbi Halevy received his rabbinic ordination from Rabbi Attiyah and Rabbi Uziel. For a short time, he then taught in Rabbi Uziel's yeshiva, Shaarei Zion, headed by the illustrious Rabbi Eliezer Waldenberg. During Israel's War of Independence in 1948, Rabbi Halevy served in an army unit comprised of yeshiva students and graduates. After the war, he married Miriam Vaknin, granddaughter of Rabbi Meir Vaknin, Chief Rabbi of Tiberias. Immediately after his marriage, he was appointed rabbi of the Romema neighborhood of Jerusalem. Shortly thereafter, he served as

---

[3] From interview with Rabbi David Shloush, June 11, 2002.

secretary to Rabbi Uziel, a position he held for nearly two years. He referred to his time with Rabbi Uziel as "the best years of his life."[4]

In the summer of 5711 (1950), Rabbi Halevy began his service as rabbi of the Sephardic community of Rishon Letzion, where he remained until his appointment as Chief Rabbi of Tel Aviv in 1972. In Rishon Letzion, he was on good terms with the Ashkenazic Chief Rabbi, Rabbi Zevulun Charlop.

Rabbi Halevy, unlike so many other rabbis of that time, did not take fees for performing weddings or for other rabbinic functions. He and his family lived simply, on little income; he felt it was inappropriate and degrading for a rabbi to take gifts and handouts. During his tenure in Rishon Letzion, three daughters were born to him and his wife, in addition to their eldest child, Raphael, who had been born in Jerusalem.

Many of the residents of Rishon Letzion were storekeepers, farmers, and workers in the wine trade. Rabbi Halevy devoted himself to teaching them Torah and raising their level of commitment to religious observance. He was especially active in strengthening the religious education offered to the children of the city. He would frequently visit the schools, meet with teachers and students, and generally demonstrate his concern for Torah education.

Rabbi Yaakov Yitzhak Shlinka, head of the religious council of Rishon Letzion and vice-mayor of the city during Rabbi Halevy's tenure there, reports that Rabbi Halevy won the admiration and respect of the community very early in his career. His public lectures were impressive and well attended. Sephardim and Ashkenazim alike viewed him as an idealistic, dedicated Torah personality. He was dignified, modest, and serious; he hated to waste time. Whether Jews were religiously observant or not, they felt they could approach Rabbi Halevy and study with him. Rabbi Halevy was respectful to the public and was vitally concerned with

---

[4] The influence of Rabbi Uziel on Rabbi Halevy will be discussed in chapter three.

Rabbi Halevy at home in Rishon
LeZion, 1967.
Courtesy of the Halevy family.

Rabbi Haim David Halevy.

A group of rabbis with Chief Rabbi Yitzhak Nissim, summer 5732 (1972),
celebrating the graduation of students from Rabbi Nissim's dayanut program.
Right to left: Rabbi Aviad, Rabbi Avraham Abuhatseira, unknown, Rabbi Halevy
(standing), Rabbi Mordechai Eliyahu, Chief Rabbi Nissim,
Rabbi Amram Aburabia, Dayan Rabbi Abbu. Photo by Aharon Zuckerman.

their welfare. He prayed and taught in the main Sephardic synagogue, Mekor Hayyim.[5]

While in Rishon Letzion, Rabbi Halevy wrote his first books. They reflected his concern for deepening the religious character of the Jewish State, and his belief in the primacy of Torah education and observance. *Bein Yisrael laAmmim* appeared in 1954; *Devar haMishpat* (three volumes), 1963–65; the first two volumes of *Mekor Hayyim*, 1967–68; and *Dat uMedinah*, 1969.

Rabbi Halevy also concerned himself with the spiritual well being of the many new immigrants who were pouring into Israel from Muslim lands. He served on the rabbinic council of the Po'el haMizrachi, in which capacity he provided rabbinic leadership to the *moshavim* Kefar Uziel and Ge'ulei Teiman. He would travel to the moshavim each week to give Torah lectures, and to deal with their religious issues and halakhic questions.

For many years, Rabbi Halevy gave classes in halakhah to young men studying for the rabbinate. The classes were given in Even Shmuel, and drew students from Lachish, Safir and Ashkelon. In teaching the *Yoreh Deah*, Rabbi Halevy would first cover the relevant sections in the *Tur*, with commentaries, especially the *Bet Yosef*. Then, the class would study the same sections as codified in the *Shulhan Arukh*.[6] Rabbi Halevy derived much satisfaction from his years teaching rabbinical students.[7]

In 1955, he traveled to North and South America in order to raise funds for Torah institutions in Israel. This journey lasted nearly a year. In visiting the various communities in the Diaspora, he was pained by the weakening of religious life. He saw first hand the impact of assimilation and interfaith marriage on the Jewish communities. His travels reinforced his view that the future of the Jewish people was in Israel – not in the Diaspora. He often told Diaspora Jews that they should consider moving to Israel, or at least sending their children to settle in the Jewish State.

---

[5] Interview with Rabbi Shlinka, June 20, 2002.

[6] From interview with Rabbi Binyamin Aviad, June 22, 2002.

[7] From interview with Rabbi Shlomo Levi, July 1, 2002.

Rabbi Halevy and Rabbi Ovadya Yosef, when Rabbi Yosef was Chief Rabbi of Tel Aviv, 1973. Photo by Yitzhak Freidin.

Rabbi Halevy and Rabbi Shlomo Goren, 1974.
Photo by Zvi Friedman.

Rabbi Halevy with Rabbi Vaknin,
Chief Rabbi of Tiberias, at a family
occasion in 1974.
Courtesy of the Halevy family.

Rabbi Halevy wearing the traditional
garb of the Sephardic Chief Rabbi –
the only time he dressed in this outfit,
1973. Photo by Tsalmania Peri-Or.

Blessing of Rabbi Halevy by his wife's grandfather, the saintly Rabbi Meir Vaknin,
Chief Rabbi of Tiberias, at Rabbi Halevy's installation as Chief Rabbi of Tel Aviv,
July 4, 1973. Photo by Yitzhak Freidin.

When he traveled throughout South America again in the late 1960s, under the auspices of the Jewish Agency, his main goal was to encourage Jews to move to Israel.

Between 1953 and 1959, Rabbi Halevy was actively involved in an association of Sephardic rabbis known as Agudat haRabbanim haSephardiyim beYisrael. The president of the organization was Rabbi Yaakov Moshe Toledano, then Sephardic Chief Rabbi of Tel Aviv. Although normally Rabbi Halevy eschewed involvement in political or ethnically based activity, he was an important voice in this organization. In those years, the rabbinic establishment in Israel was dominated by Ashkenazim. It ignored the emergence of a new generation of Sephardic rabbinical leaders and the dramatic increase in Israel's Sephardic population. The situation of Sephardic rabbis was so bad that they were not allowed to sign simple documents attesting that a person was married or single. While Ashkenazic rabbis were appointed as chief rabbis of cities (and received commensurate compensation), Sephardic rabbis, for the most part, were only appointed as rabbis of communities (*rabbanei ha'eidah*) – and received lower salaries. Rabbi Halevy, Rabbi Shloush and Rabbi Aviad – together with other young Sephardic rabbis – were outraged by the discriminatory practices. They organized this Sephardic rabbinic organization to fight for justice and equality in the rabbinate so that Sephardic rabbis would be entitled to the same rights, responsibilities and salaries as Ashkenazic rabbis. Once these goals were achieved (and by 1959 they were largely achieved), the organization of Sephardic rabbis faded away.[8]

In 1964, Rabbi Halevy was chosen to serve on the rabbinic council of the Chief Rabbinate, and he remained a member of this council for the rest of his life. In 1972, the Chief Rabbinate authorized him to serve as a judge on the rabbinic court of appeals (*Beth Din haGadol le'Ir'urim*).

---

[8] Information about the Agudat haRabbanim haSefardiyim beYisrael was provided in interviews with Rabbi Binyamin Aviad, June 22, 2002; and Rabbi David Shloush, June 11, 2002.

Rabbi Halevy speaking at Rabbi Ovadya Yosef's coronation ceremony for Chief Rabbi of Israel, at the Ben Zakai Synagogue, 1974.
From right to left: Dayan Rabbi Masud ben Shimeon, Dayan Rabbi Abbu, Rabbi Halevi (standing), a government official, Chief Rabbi Yosef, Chief Rabbi Goren, unknown, Religious Affairs Minister Dr. Yitzhak Refael, Pinchas Sheinman, IDF's Chief Rabbi Gad Navon. Photo by Aharon Zukerman.

Right to Left: Chief Rabbi Ovadya Yosef, Minister of Religious Affairs Aharon Abuhatseira, Chief Rabbi of Jerusalem Bezalel Zolti, Rosh Yeshiva of Porat Yosef Rabbi Benzion Abba Shaul, Chief Rabbi Navon of the Israel Defense Forces, Rabbi Halevy (standing), Rabbi Yeshayahu Goldshmit, head of the Tel Aviv Rabbinical Court, Fall, 1978. Photo by Photo Weiss.

But around that time, he was invited by Rabbi Ovadya Yosef to become Chief Rabbi of Tel Aviv.

When Rabbi Halevy was installed as Sephardic Chief Rabbi of Tel Aviv, many of his friends and admirers from Rishon Letzion attended the ceremony. While they were sorry to lose him as their rabbi, they were pleased that he had been elevated to such a lofty rabbinic office.

In Tel Aviv, he served with the Ashkenazic Chief Rabbi Yitzhak Yedidya Frankel. Rabbi Frankel's son-in-law, Rabbi Yisrael Meir Lau, noted that Rabbis Halevy and Frankel worked together for fourteen years in amity and cooperation. After Rabbi Frankel died, the office of Ashkenazic Chief Rabbi remained vacant for two years, after which Rabbi Lau was appointed to succeed his father-in-law. He worked with Rabbi Halevy for five years, before being elected Ashkenazic Chief Rabbi of Israel.[9]

In describing Rabbi Halevy's qualities, Rabbi Lau stated: "He was a very noble person. He was one who conceded to everybody, and was never one to stand up for his own honor or flaunt his worth. I don't mean that he would not stand up for his moral values. When it came to that, he was a fighter who would never concede or surrender. Rabbi Halevy had honor and respect for everyone. He strongly believed in the holiness of the Jewish nation and in the honor of the Torah."

In Tel Aviv, Rabbi Halevy prayed at the Ohel Mo'ed synagogue that had been established by Rabbi Benzion Uziel. He also made it a point of visiting all the other Sephardic synagogues so that he could maintain a direct and personal relationship with his constituents. Moreover, he had a particularly warm relationship with the congregation Ihud Shivat Zion, established by German Jews.

While in Tel Aviv, he continued his impressive literary production. He published his comprehensive index to the Zohar, the remaining volumes of *Mekor Hayyim*, the abridged *Mekor Hayyim*, the responsa

---

[9] From interview with Rabbi Lau, June 23, 2002.

Rabbi Halevy and Rabbi Frenkel at the dedication of the HaShalom Synagogue in 1978. Standing on the right is Mayor Y. Rabinovitch of Tel Aviv. Appearing between Rabbi Halevy and Rabbi Frenkel but one row back is Rabbi Issar Frankel (son) and two rows back is Rabbi Israel Meir Lau, later to become Chief Rabbi of Tel Aviv and Chief Rabbi of Israel. Courtesy of the Halevy family.

כב' עוזן להשתתף בעיעד החגיגי

של הכתרת מרנן ורבנן הגאונים

הרב יצחק ידידיה פרנקל שליט"א   הרב חיים דוד הלוי שליט"א

לרבנים ראשיים לתל-אביב-יפו

מעמד ההכתרה יתקיים בעיעת ה'
ביום רביעי, ד' בתמוז תשל"ג (4.7.73), בשעה 4 אחה"צ.
באולם "היכל התרבות", רחוב הוברמן, תל-אביב.

בהשתתפות:
הרבנים הראשיים לישראל, שרי הממשלה, ראש העיר וראש המועצה הדתית

Invitation to the installation of the two new Chief Rabbis of Tel Aviv, 4 Tamuz 5733 (July 4, 1973), Rabbi Haim David Halevy and Rabbi Yitzhak Yedidya Frenkel.

Rabbi Halevy receives the Rav Kook Prize, 1984.
Photo courtesy of the city of Tel Aviv, Department of Events.

Rabbi Halevy receives the Israel Prize for outstanding contributions to Torah
scholarship, 5757 (1997). Right to Left: Dr. Goldberg, head of the *Pras Yisrael*
committee, President Ezer Weitzman, Prime Minister Netanyahu, Supreme Court
Chief Justice Barak, Minister of Education Zevulun Hammer, Rabbi Halevy.
Photo by Muki Schwartz.

volumes of *Asei Lekha Rav* and *Mayyim Hayyim*, as well as homiletical volumes *Torat Hayyim* and *Netzah Moshe*. Aside from these books, he wrote literally hundreds of articles for learned Torah journals as well as the popular Israeli press.

When the term of office of Sephardic Chief Rabbi of Israel, Rabbi Mordechai Eliyahu, was concluding in the early 1990s, Rabbi Halevy was offered as a candidate by the Mafdal party (Mizrachi). Rabbi Halevy, though, was not one to engage in political maneuvering or campaigning for office. Rabbi Ovadya Yosef, although a colleague of Rabbi Halevy's from their days together at Porat Yosef, was interested in having a Sephardic Chief Rabbi affiliated with and loyal to his Shas party. Given Rabbi Yosef's vast influence in the process of selecting the Sephardic Chief Rabbi, it was almost a foregone conclusion that Rabbi Halevy could not win – unless he became a member of the Shas party. Having been a longtime member of Mizrachi, and having a general aversion to the ethnic politics of Shas, Rabbi Halevy would not consider sacrificing his principles and integrity to join the Shas bandwagon. Consequently, he did not win the office of Sephardic Chief Rabbi of Israel; rather, the office went to Rabbi Eliyahu Bakshi-Doron, a follower of Rabbi Ovadya Yosef.[10]

Rabbi Halevy seemed not to have been upset by the results of the election. He may even have been relieved. He could continue to devote himself to his Torah study and writing, without having to be involved in the multifarious administrative and ceremonial tasks expected of a Chief Rabbi of Israel.

His monumental achievements as a Torah scholar and leader were recognized by various awards and prizes. In 1982, he won the Rabbi Y.M. Toledano prize from the city of Tel Aviv. Mossad haRav Kook awarded him the Rabbi Y.L. Maimon prize that same year. In 1984, he won the Rabbi Kook prize for Torah literature, awarded by the city of Tel Aviv.

---

[10] Information about Rabbi Halevy's candidacy for the position of Sephardic Chief Rabbi of Israel was drawn from interviews with Rabbi D. Shloush (June 11, 2002); Rabbi Lau (June 23, 2002); and Rabbi Shmuel David (June 13, 2002).

Reception for the new Chief Rabbis of Israel with the Chief Rabbinate Council at the home of President Herzog, 1983. Right to Left: General Manager of the Israeli Religious Courts Rabbi Bendahan, Chief Rabbi of Haifa Eliyahu Bakshi Doron, Chief Rabbi of Netanya Israel Meir Lau, Chief Rabbi of Ashkelon Yosef Sharvit, Chief Rabbi Mordechai Eliyahu, President Hayim Herzog, Chief Rabbi Avraham Shapira, Chief Rabbi of Tel Aviv Halevy, Chief Rabbi of Haifa Shear Yashuv Cohen. Courtesy of the Halevy family.

Photo from the reception at President Herzog's home, 1983.
Courtesy of the Halevy family.

הרב חיים דוד הלוי זצ"ל
יח שבט התרפ"ד - יב אדר התשנ"ח
הרב הראשי וראב"ד לתל אביב יפו
מחבר שולחן ערוך מקור חיים השלם

Israel Prize picture of Rabbi Halevy, 5757/1997. Photo by Muki Schwartz.

In 1997 he was given the Israel Prize by the State of Israel, in appreciation of his contributions to Torah scholarship. In 1998, he received an honorary doctoral degree from Bar Ilan University. For a rabbinic sage – who had never attended university – to receive an honorary doctorate from Bar Ilan was a testimony to Rabbi Halevy's profound intellectual capacities and interests.

On March 3, 1998, Rabbi Halevy attended an assembly of rabbis at the home of the President of Israel. As the elder scholar of the group, he spoke about the role of the rabbi, and the need to follow in the ways of Aharon the high priest, loving peace and pursuing peace. He was then planning to give an address at the Israel Center for Democracy (*Makhon haYisraeli leDemocratia*), but felt heart pains on the way and was unable to give the lecture. A week later, on 12 Adar 5758 (March 10, 1998), he passed away.[11]

He left behind his beloved wife, Miriam, who had been a great source of strength to him. She devoted herself to her family and household, enabling Rabbi Halevy to study and teach Torah and to serve the community. Their children and grandchildren were great sources of pride and happiness to him. Their son, Dr. Raphael Halevy – married to Limor – serves as Vice Principal of the children's department in haEmek Medical Center in Afula. Rabbi Halevy's daughter Nitzhia – married to Rabbi Shlomo Levi, head of the rabbinical program of Har Etzion yeshiva – is a medical secretary in Efrat. His daughter Ronit – married to Rabbi

---

[11] Rabbi Halevy was eulogized, orally and in print, by a number of rabbinic leaders, including his son-in-law Rabbi Shlomo Levi (*Shanah beShanah*, 5759, pp. 549–554); Chief Rabbi Eliyahu Bakshi-Doron (*haTzofeh*, 13 Adar 5758); Rabbi Ratzon Arousi (*haTzofeh*, 18 Adar 5758). Rabbi Shlomo Levi and Rabbi Yehudah Amital eulogized Rabbi Halevy at a memorial service held 9 Adar 5759. Many other rabbis in Israel and throughout the world said and wrote words of eulogy on the passing of Rabbi Halevy. In Congregation Shearith Israel in New York, we not only spoke words of eulogy, but also led classes in which we studied the writings of Rabbi Halevy.

Rabbi Halevy delivering an address at the Great Sephardic Synagogue
(Ohel Moed) of Tel Aviv, c. 1976. Courtesy of the Halevy family.

Rabbi Halevy delivers a lecture at Bar Ilan University on women's status in
halakhah, *Adar* 5757/1997. Photo by Yoni Reif.

Shlomo Shloush, General Manager of the Kolelot haSephardim of Zefat and Meiron – is a teacher in the Bnei Akiva Ulpana in Meiron. His daughter Gila – married to Rabbi Achia Amitai of Kibbutz Sedei Eliyahu – is an educational consultant in Zvia Ulpana in Afula.

In the following pages, we will explore the religious and intellectual influences that helped shape Rabbi Halevy's worldview. We will consider major themes in his writings and will focus on his distinctive insights. With humility and reverence we will study his books and ponder his words. In so doing, we will all be participating as students in his yeshiva.

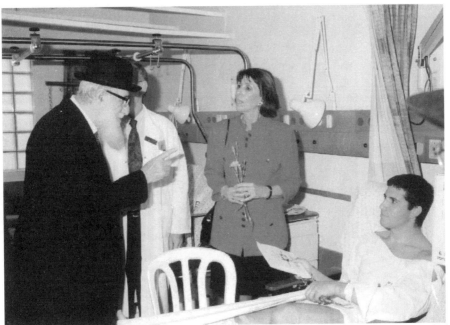

Rabbi Halevy visiting the sick at the Ichilov (today Sorasky) Medical Center of Tel Aviv c. 1990. Photo courtesy of the City of Tel Aviv, Department of Events.

Rabbi Halevy in his study, as a candidate for Chief Rabbi of Israel, January 1993. Courtesy of the Halevy family.

Rabbi Halevy with Prime Minister Yitzhak Shamir in Tel Aviv, 1989.
Photo courtesy of the city of Tel Aviv, Department of Events.

Rabbi Halevy with Prime Minister Rabin, May 1994.
Photo by Zvi Friedman.

Rabbi Halevy and President Yitzhak Navon, who grew up together in the same neighborhood in Jerusalem, 1990. Courtesy of the Halevy family.

Rabbi Halevy and Chairman of the Knesset, Professor Shevach Weiss, May 30, 1994. Photo courtesy of city of Tel Aviv, Department of Events.

Certificate given to the participants in the annual memorial study of *Mekor Hayyim*, sponsored by the religious education department of the Ministry of Education.

Title page of *Mekor Hayyim*.

Title page of *Asei Lekha Rav*.

Portrait of Rabbi Halevy in 1998, the year before he passed away.
Courtesy of the Halevy family.

Chapter Two

RELIGIOUS AND INTELLECTUAL FOUNDATIONS

Rabbi Halevy was perhaps the last great Torah luminary in the classic tradition of Sephardim of Judeo-Spanish background. After the expulsion of Jews from Spain in 1492, Judeo-Spanish communities developed and flourished in the territories of the Ottoman Empire, as well as in some European cities. The rabbis of intellectual centers, e.g., Istanbul, Salonika, Izmir, Rhodes, Jerusalem and Zefat, published thousands of volumes of rabbinic scholarship. They produced biblical and talmudic commentaries, responsa, halakhic commentaries, ethical works, studies in kabbalah, sermons, etc. Much of their literary work was geared for the intellectual elite, while some was aimed at the less-learned popular audience. Most publications were in Hebrew, but a significant number appeared in the Judeo-Spanish vernacular.

Rabbis of the Judeo-Spanish tradition were expected to be properly qualified halakhic authorities who could render authoritative legal rulings. They also were expected to be genuinely pious individuals, marked by humility and spirituality. They were highly regarded for their commitment to prayer, study of kabbalah, and concern for the everyday needs of their communities. They strove to be compassionate and caring religious leaders, not aloof scholars lost in their study halls.[1]

---

[1] See my books *Voices in Exile: A Study of Sephardic Intellectual History*, Ktav, Hoboken, 1991; *The Jews of Rhodes: The History of a Sephardic Community*, Sepher-Hermon Press, New York, 1978; *The Rhythms of Jewish Living: A Sephardic Approach*,

Rabbi Halevy's parents were Turkish Jews, deeply steeped in the Judeo-Spanish traditions. When they migrated to Israel, they settled in the Ohel Moshe neighborhood of Jerusalem, where almost all of their neighbors were also of Judeo-Spanish background. The young Haim David Halevy grew up in an environment where the Judeo-Spanish tradition was alive; where Sephardic values and customs were omnipresent; where outstanding rabbinic role models were present in the community.

Even during the period of his youth, Judeo-Spanish culture throughout the world had entered its twilight years. The early twentieth century witnessed large-scale migration of Sephardim to the United States, Israel, Europe, Africa and South America. Most of the children of these immigrants adopted the language of the lands in which they lived, leaving Judeo-Spanish as a secondary language. In most cases, the grandchildren of the immigrants had lost fluency in the language and were no longer living in primarily Sephardic settings. They married Jews from other backgrounds, and sometimes married non-Jews too.

In Turkey, the historic bastion of Judeo-Spanish civilization, Turkish nationalism led to the Turkification of all minorities, including Jews. During the Holocaust period, major centers of Judeo-Spanish life in Europe (e.g., Salonika, Rhodes, Monastir) were wiped out by the Nazis and their collaborators.

In the land of Israel, Sephardim of Judeo-Spanish background came into increasing contact with Jews of other origins. Hebrew became the language of communication. Intermarriage among groups increased. Rabbi Halevy himself married a wife of Moroccan background. She did not speak Judeo-Spanish, so the language was not transmitted to Rabbi Halevy's children as a living tongue used by the family.

Whereas Sephardim of Judeo-Spanish background had formed the elite rabbinic group during the period of the old *yishuv* (early Israeli settlement), their spiritual hegemony declined during the middle and latter twentieth century. For centuries, the Chief Rabbis of Israel were almost

Sepher-Hermon Press, New York, 1986; and *Foundations of Sephardic Spirituality: The Inner Life of the Ottoman Empire*, Jewish Lights, Woodstock, Vermont, 2006.

exclusively of Judeo-Spanish background. When Israel became a sovereign State in 1948, the Sephardic Chief Rabbi was Rabbi Benzion Uziel, a scion of the Judeo-Spanish rabbinic tradition. But Rabbi Uziel was the last of this tradition to serve as Chief Rabbi of Israel. His successors have been of Iraqi or Moroccan background.

Rabbi Halevy, then, was nurtured within a Sephardic milieu that no longer exists. He drew, consciously and subconsciously, on the rabbinic traditions of the Judeo-Spanish sages who preceded him. He was an organic part of a living tradition. Few, if any, rabbis of subsequent generations have been able to grow and study in a living community with Torah sages of Judeo-Spanish background. Access to this lost world is only available through research and an imaginative historical sense.

Memories of Childhood

Rabbi Halevy often referred to his childhood memories. They were not merely a source of nostalgia; they also helped shape his religious worldview.

He deeply appreciated the sacrifices his parents had made to insure that he receive a proper Torah education. His book, *Netzah Moshe*, was named after his parents: his mother's name, Victoria, was changed to its Hebrew equivalent, *Nitzhiah*, (*netzah* is the masculine form); and his father's name was Moshe. He was proud of the fact that his father had served as hazzan in the Taranto synagogue of the Ohel Moshe neighborhood.

His father's piety strongly influenced Rabbi Halevy. In the introduction to his index on the Zohar, Rabbi Halevy reminisced: "I mention here for good and blessing my rabbi and teacher, the crown of my head, my father and master R. Moshe Halevy, may the memory of the righteous be a blessing. (He died on 11 *Shevat* 5720.) With his great love for and devotion to the book of the Zohar, he implanted within me from the dawn of my youth a love for this holy book. I remember that he would wake up early in the morning and engage in it [the Zohar] with tremendous fervor until the time of the morning prayers."[2] Indeed, the Zohar was a vital component in the spiritual life of Rabbi Halevy, and he often quoted from it both in his halakhic and homiletical discussions.

In his writings, Rabbi Halevy mentioned several other things he had learned from his father. In listing the stops in the Torah portions according to the custom of Jerusalem, he noted that he had learned this information from his father who had served as a reader in Jerusalem for many years.[3]

Rabbi Halevy's father had also told him the custom in his hometown of Bursa, Turkey, relating to Shabbat practices. Synagogue services were held early on Shabbat morning. People would then go home for their morning meal. After this meal, they would return to the synagogue for Torah study. This would continue until the time for the afternoon prayers. This pattern was maintained in the Ohel Moshe neighborhood of Jerusalem, since most of the residents derived from Turkey and the Balkan countries.[4]

His father had participated in a funeral of a pious man, who had been given temporary burial in Jerusalem during Israel's War of Independence. After the war, his body was transferred for reburial in another cemetery. Rabbi Halevy's father testified that when the body was taken from the coffin to be buried, it appeared to have undergone no deterioration. The corpse looked exactly as the man did when he was alive. The men involved in the burial, including Rabbi Halevy's father, were astonished at what seemed to them a miracle. Rabbi Halevy cited this story to indicate the truth of a rabbinic teaching that the bodies of righteous people may be spared deterioration in the grave.[5]

---

[2] MZR, introduction, p. 15.

[3] MKH 3:124, p. 122.

[4] MH 3:18.

[5] ALR 1:51. See further discussion in the chapter on Metaphysical Issues.

The Sages of Ohel Moshe

Rabbi Halevy frequently cited lessons he had learned from the sages and scholars who lived in the Ohel Moshe neighborhood. The rabbinic presence was part of the texture of life, and was a constant influence on the residents. Yaakov Yehoshua (died 1982) reminisced about the rabbis of the neighborhood when he was growing up in Ohel Moshe. "We loved them. The fact that they were among us, in our neighborhood, gave a sense of security. We relied on their righteousness. We listened carefully to their prayer and we knew that it would not go unanswered. Not all the rabbis of the neighborhood were cut from the same material. Some engaged in communal work, others served as members of the Beth Din, as hazzanim, and as scholars in the *yeshivot*. Some were steeped in kabbalah and [extraordinary] piety."[6]

The main synagogue in Ohel Moshe was popularly known as "El Kal Grande," the great synagogue. Many of the community's leading figures prayed there. The Taranto synagogue, which Rabbi Halevy attended as a child, was smaller, and had no women's gallery. Women who attended services stood or sat outside the door of the synagogue or in the adjoining courtyard where they could view the service through the synagogue windows.

The Taranto synagogue was open all day and night. Members of the community came to the synagogue whenever they wished, and knew that they would find peace of mind and healing for the soul. Some individuals could be found in the synagogue chanting the book of Psalms. Others studied the Zohar. Yet others pored over pages of Talmud. Individuals were on hand to recite memorial prayers and blessings for anyone who so requested, for a small donation. Among the leading rabbinic figures associated with that synagogue were Rabbis Yaakov Franco, Bohor Padro, Shmuel Padro, Benzion Paredes, and Yaakov Alkalai. Rabbis were available in the synagogue for those who wished to

---

[6] Yaakov Yehoshua, *Shekhunot beYerushalayim haYeshanah*, Reuven Mass, Jerusalem, p. 116.

study Torah or to receive religious guidance. At night, a group of outstanding scholars gathered in the Taranto synagogue for Torah study. These included Rabbis Shalom Hedaya, Vidal Surnaga, Benzion Cuenca, Rafael Shako, Binyamin Levy, Yitzhak Barukh and others.[7]

Rabbi Halevy considered himself fortunate to have been raised in the midst of this vibrant religious civilization. Among his important early religious role models was Rabbi Benzion Cuenca (1867–1937).

Rabbi Cuenca was born and raised in Jerusalem. The Cuenca family traced its history to medieval Spain. After 1492, they found haven in Salonika where they remained for over three hundred years. Then family members came to settle in Jerusalem.

Rabbi Cuenca's uncle, Rabbi Hayyim Vidal Cuenca, was the leading kabbalist in Jerusalem, and had a major impact on the kabbalists of his – and subsequent – generations. He was known for his incredible devotion to Torah study, allowing only the briefest time for rest, eating, and caring for his physical needs.

Rabbi Benzion Cuenca was a child prodigy, demonstrating phenomenal mastery of Torah sources at an early age. He studied with great sages including Rabbi Eliyahu Hakohen and Rabbi Mordechai Yisrael Sharizli, masters of the Talmud and its commentaries; Rabbi Menahem Behar Yitzhak, known for his penetrating analysis of talmudic texts; and Rabbi Hayyim Vidal Angel, a profound scholar and kabbalist.

His father supported him so that he could devote himself exclusively to Torah study. After Rabbi Benzion Cuenca was married, his father bought him a home in the Ohel Moshe neighborhood, where he studied together with the leading Sephardic sages there. When his father died in 1891, Rabbi Cuenca had to engage in business himself – but was notoriously unsuccessful. In a short span, he had lost the entire estate that

---

[7] Ibid., pp. 120–121. For further description of the religious life in the Ohel Moshe neighborhood, see the pamphlet *Me'ah Shanah leShekhunat Ohel Moshe beYerushalayim*, published by the Sephardic Community of Jerusalem, Sivan, 5743 (1983). I thank Mr. Nissim Levy for sending me a copy of this pamphlet as well as the chapter by Yaakov Yehoshua.

his father had left to him. He later was more successful engaging in the sale of books of Torah scholarship.

In 1896, Rabbi Cuenca was appointed as head of the yeshiva Tiferet Yerushalayim, newly established by the Sephardic community of Jerusalem. He taught and inspired many students, among them Rabbi Benzion Meir Hai Uziel, who went on to become the Chief Rabbi of Israel.

Also in 1896, he began to publish a Torah journal *"HaMe'asef,"* which he continued to edit for nineteen years. The journal drew contributions from leading Torah scholars – Sephardic and Ashkenazic – and included a number of Rabbi Cuenca's own scholarly contributions.

In subsequent years, he traveled to various communities around the world to raise funds for institutions in Jerusalem and for his journal. He spent a year and a half in Alexandria as the associate of Rabbi Eliyahu Hazan.

In Jerusalem, Rabbi Cuenca was instrumental in the establishment of a home for the aged sponsored by the Sephardic community of Jerusalem. In 1923, he was appointed to serve on the Beth Din of the Sephardim of Jerusalem, and in 1929 he served for a period as the Chief Rabbi of Hebron.[8]

Rabbi Cuenca was widely respected for his vast Torah knowledge and his piety. He was also known for his quick wit, sense of humor and happy disposition.

Rabbi Halevy wrote: "I had the privilege in my childhood to live in the Ohel Moshe neighborhood of Jerusalem where the deceased [Rabbi Cuenca], of blessed memory, lived. [In that neighborhood] more than twelve outstanding Sephardic Torah sages lived. I was likewise privileged in those years to pray in the Taranto synagogue, where the deceased [Rabbi

---

[8] For information on Rabbi Cuenca's life, see Rabbi Ezra Basri's biographical sketch in *haMe'asef*, vol. 1, *Shevat* 5739, pp. 100f. The newspaper *Yediot Aharonot* ran an article about Rabbi Cuenca on February 23, 1979. These materials were sent to me by Mr. Nissim Levy.

Cuenca] prayed. Although I was only a boy, I was enriched [*hitbasamti*] by the radiant light of the face of that luminary [*gaon*]."[9]

He went on to relate that his father, who was hazzan in the Taranto synagogue, used to honor Rabbi Cuenca each year by inviting him to be hazzan for the *musaf* service on Yom Kippur. Rabbi Cuenca was pleased to accept. One year [1937], though, Rabbi Cuenca declined the invitation, claiming that he was not feeling well. The congregation was surprised to learn that Rabbi Cuenca would not be reading *musaf*. Rabbi Halevy's father was then asked to read the service. But when he reached the point of the *vidui* [confession] during the repetition of the *musaf*, Rabbi Cuenca went up to the reader's desk and asked if he could lead in the recitation of the *vidui*. He chanted the confession prayers in a voice filled with crying. The congregation trembled since they were not accustomed to hear Rabbi Cuenca crying. He was usually happy and cheerful; he did not even cry when reciting the elegies on the Fast of the Ninth of *Av*.

That night, after Yom Kippur had concluded, Rabbi Cuenca asked Rabbi Yaakov Barukh and Rabbi Eliyahu Pardes to come to his house after they had eaten their evening meal. When they arrived, Rabbi Cuenca wrote out his last will and testament, and asked his two colleagues to sign as witnesses. He informed them that he would die during the coming year. When they asked him how he could be sure of this, he told them that he had long known that the year he could not read *musaf* on Yom Kippur would be the year he would die. He fell ill shortly after the Sukkot festival. His situation deteriorated quickly, and his family members cried at his imminent death. Rabbi Cuenca told them not to cry yet, since he was going to live a bit longer. He gave them the exact date and time that he would die: and it was precisely as he had told them. Rabbi Halevy noted: "Then we knew that he was not only a giant in Torah, but also a *tzaddik gamur* [a perfectly righteous man], who knew how to direct the time of his death."

---

[9] ALR 6:43.

Halakhic Rulings Influenced by the Sages of Ohel Moshe

Rabbi Halevy often bolstered his halakhic rulings by referring to what he himself had witnessed as a child growing up among the sages of Ohel Moshe. Most of these rulings related to synagogue rituals.

He noted, for example, that the congregation in Ohel Moshe stood during the recitation of the Song of Moses during morning services, as well as when that portion of the Torah was read on Shabbat Beshallah and the seventh day of Passover.[10] He recommended this practice to other congregations.

Rabbi Halevy was asked: if the ark of the synagogue was not on the eastern wall, should the kohanim offer the priestly blessing in front of the ark, or should they stand in front of the eastern wall? After citing differing opinions on this matter, Rabbi Halevy wrote: "And I will add my own testimony. In the days of my youth, I prayed at the Taranto synagogue in the Ohel Moshe neighborhood. In this synagogue prayed rabbis, great in Torah and wisdom, and at their head the *gaon* Rabbi Benzion Cuenca, the memory of the righteous is a blessing. I remember that the kohanim always stood to bless the public in front of the ark, which was on the northern wall." At some later point, the custom changed and the kohanim went to the eastern wall for the blessing. Rabbi Halevy did not remember if this change happened during the lifetime of Rabbi Cuenca with his permission, or if it was instituted at a later date. Rabbi Halevy concluded that there were obviously good arguments for both positions, and that each congregation should follow its own custom.[11]

If no kohen were present, should a Levite or an Israelite be called to the Torah first? Rabbi Yosef Karo had ruled that, in the absence of a kohen, the Levite was not to be called first; rather, the honor should go to an Israelite. This would be the position normally followed by Sephardim. Rabbi Moshe Isserles, though, ruled that the Levite was to be called first. This would be the usual practice among Ashkenazim. Rabbi Halevy noted, however, that in this case even many Sephardic sages preferred the ruling

---

[10] ALR 7: short answers 4.
[11] ALR 8:18.

of Rabbi Isserles. "And so I saw in Sephardic synagogues in Jerusalem, in the presence of great sages, that a Levite was called first if no kohen were present. And this is our practice."[12]

Was it permissible for a boy under age thirteen to read the Torah during synagogue services? Rabbi Halevy ruled in the negative. "In the synagogue in which I prayed in my childhood, great, outstanding rabbis prayed. I knew how to read the Torah even before my bar mitzvah, but they did not allow me [to do so in the synagogue]. When I became bar mitzvah, I read regularly in their presence…."[13]

Rabbi Halevy also cited the following practices that he had witnessed during his childhood among the sages of Ohel Moshe. If the wrong Torah scroll was taken out of the ark by mistake, the hazzan should set it to the correct place and read from it. It should not be returned to the ark in order to retrieve the correctly set Torah scroll, even if that would save time and trouble.[14]

On each Shabbat, the haftarah for the coming Shabbat was auctioned off. A person who did not succeed in purchasing the right to read the haftarah could then try to find another synagogue where he could chant the haftarah in memory of a loved one.[15]

It was permissible for a synagogue to have a representation of the tablets of the Ten Commandments above the ark.[16] Men and women may attend Torah classes together; but the men should be seated in one room, the women in another room. The teacher should be in the area between the rooms, so as to be able to address each group simultaneously. Women were allowed to ask questions.[17] Weddings should not be performed at night.[18] Women may recite a blessing over the *lulav* on Sukkot.[19]

---

[12] MH 3, p. 107 note 8. *Shulhan Arukh, Orah Hayyim* 135:6.
[13] ALR 7:20.
[14] ALR 7:17.
[15] TH 2, *Devarim*, p. 65.
[16] ALR 4:44.
[17] ALR 4:56.
[18] ALR 6:72.

Aside from his childhood memories of the synagogue and sages of the Ohel Moshe neighborhood, Rabbi Halevy continued to maintain warm feelings for the yeshiva Porat Yosef of Jerusalem, where he had studied as a child and young man. In a dedication page to his first book, *Bein Yisrael laAmmim*, Rabbi Halevy thanked the administration of the yeshiva. He was grateful to have studied Torah from the sages of Porat Yosef, especially the head of the yeshiva, Rabbi Ezra Attiyah. Porat Yosef had educated many rabbis who gave noteworthy service to the Jewish communities in Israel and the Diaspora. Although the yeshiva building in the Old City of Jerusalem was destroyed in 1948 by Arab enemies, the yeshiva re-established itself in the new city of Jerusalem and continued to be the Torah center of the Sephardim of the world.

In one of his responsa, Rabbi Halevy wrote: "I remember when we were little students in the Talmud Torah of the Porat Yosef yeshiva, the spiritual overseer [*mashgiah ruhani*] would oversee us during prayers. He himself never prayed with us [but had prayed at an early *minyan*]. That way [he could devote full attention to us], and fear of him hung over us throughout the time of prayer." The spiritual overseer, since he himself was not engaged in prayer, could talk, walk around, instruct the students, and discipline them when necessary. Rabbi Halevy recommended this policy for all schools: the children should be guided by a spiritual mentor who had prayed earlier, and who could devote full attention to the students.[20]

Rabbi Halevy referred to a number of praiseworthy practices that he had learned at Porat Yosef. The teachers assigned the students to learn large sections of the Bible by heart.[21] When someone was ill, the rabbis and students of the yeshiva gathered in its large synagogue. They chanted Psalms as a way of beseeching the Almighty to bring a complete recovery

---

[19] MKH 1:5, p. 41; ALR 2:33. For other examples of Rabbi Halevy citing memories from his youth to clarify a custom or halakhic practice, see ALR 1:16; 1:33; 1:48; 2:26; 3:21; 3:28; 4:48; 5:27; 7:3.

[20] ALR 5: short answers 27.

[21] ALR 6:1.

to the stricken person. "And it is proper to follow this practice."[22] The teachers took students on field trips to the zoo, as a means of teaching them to recognize the wonders of God's creation.[23]

At Porat Yosef, Rabbi Halevy received a thorough grounding in Bible, Talmud, halakhic codes and commentaries. He studied the classic rabbinic works of Sephardic and Ashkenazic sages, medieval and modern. In his writings, he demonstrated an impressive mastery of these texts. He rarely based halakhic rulings on the opinions of little known halakhists or obscure books.

The Kabbalah

As noted earlier, Rabbi Halevy was introduced to kabbalistic texts at an early age. His father was devoted to the Zohar, and this love of the Zohar was transmitted to the son.

Rabbi Halevy prepared a volume to serve as an index to the topics and ideas included in the Zohar. He compiled this book as he was preparing to write the fifth volume of his code of Jewish law, *Mekor Hayyim*. Rabbi Halevy often referred to the Zohar in the first four volumes of *Mekor Hayyim*, but felt he wanted to study the Zohar in a more thorough and orderly way before undertaking volume five.

Professor Yosef Ahitov has pointed out that Rabbi Halevy viewed the Zohar as a classic rabbinic text that shed light on the inner meaning of the Torah and halakhah. Rabbi Halevy represented a "popular kabbalah," drawing on mystical texts to cast light on everyday issues and problems. He was not a kabbalist, in the sense of being a mystic primarily devoted to the mysteries of the kabbalah. Rather, he was a well-rounded Torah sage,

---

[22] ALR 5: short answers 81.

[23] ALR 1:69. See also ALR 4:21 and 6: short answers 13, where he notes that the practice at Porat Yosef was for those who responded to a *zimmun* to refrain from continuing their meal until after the first blessing (*hazan et hakol*). This followed the Rama rather than Rabbi Yosef Karo. See also MKH 2:80, p. 91.

who drew on the teachings of kabbalah as he drew on the writings of the Talmud, Midrash, and other authoritative rabbinic works.[24]

Professor Moshe Halamish noted that Rabbi Halevy interspersed quotations from halakhic and kabbalistic sources in a natural, organic way. These two bodies of knowledge were seen as being complementary and interrelated. In this respect, Rabbi Halevy followed the example of such sages as Rabbi Hayyim Yosef David Azulai, Rabbi Yosef Hayyim of Baghdad, and Rabbi Yaakov Sofer – authors whom he frequently cited.[25] Rabbi Halevy viewed the kabbalah as a means of giving spiritual insight to the troubled modern generations. For so many people, religion had become irrelevant. For others, it had been reduced to a mechanical system of behavior, lacking genuine religious inspiration. The kabbalah provided balm to the souls of those who lacked a deep understanding of Torah and *mitzvot*.

Rabbi Halevy's writings are filled with references to the Zohar, to the teachings of Rabbi Yitzhak Luria, and to the *hakhmei ha'emet* (the sages of the truth, i.e., kabbalah). He utilized kabbalistic sources to explicate biblical texts, to point out appropriate customs, and to explain deeper meanings of *mitzvot*. In halakhic matters, he ruled in accordance with kabbalistic sources, unless they were in clear conflict with established halakhic practice.[26]

For Rabbi Halevy, the kabbalah was a reminder that human reason could not always attain full truth on its own. There were mysteries beyond human ken. When biblical or rabbinic teachings seemed irrational, this did

---

[24] See his paper in the volume of essays about Rabbi Halevy, edited by Zvi Zohar and Avi Sagi.

[25] See his article in the volume edited by Zvi Zohar and Avi Sagi. See ALR 6:7, where Rabbi Halevy states that in every halakhic controversy among later sages, the halakhah follows the rulings of Rabbi H.Y.D. Azulai.

[26] See for example ALR 2:20; 4:38; 5:5; 5:45; 5: short answers 23; 6:61; 6:67; 6: short answers 88.

not mean they were incorrect. Rather, our limited minds simply were unable to grasp the deeper truths hidden within those teachings.[27]

In Pursuit of Human Knowledge

Rabbi Halevy respected the pursuit of knowledge and the achievements of the human intellect. In explaining the greatness of our forefather Abraham, he noted: "Abraham was born in a house of idolatry. By means of his human intelligence and his free will, he worked and struggled and found God." On the other hand, Moshe had not experienced this intellectual struggle to find God; rather, the Almighty appeared to him in the burning bush. "Therefore the world was created in the merit of Abraham, the highest and first of those who searched the way for faith in God. He spread [this faith] in the world through his own powers, based on conclusions he reached through his own free will; this is the crowning glory [gulat hakoteret] of humankind."[28]

In commenting on why the Torah began with the story of creation, Rabbi Halevy suggested that human beings could find the Almighty only after studying His creation. Rambam had pointed out that knowledge of God derived from contemplation of the universe. Thus, the Torah itself ascribed vital importance to human inquiry into the workings of God as manifested in nature.[29]

The study of "general wisdom," i.e., science, was an essential ingredient in one's religious development. Rabbi Halevy underscored the fact that judges appointed to the Sanhedrin were expected to be versed in general knowledge. "How wondrous is the wisdom of our holy Torah that required those sitting in judgment to know the principles of general branches of knowledge." In order for the judges not to be dependent entirely upon outside experts, it was necessary for them to be familiar with modern knowledge. This standard should apply equally to the rabbis of

---

[27] See for example ALR 5:60; MKH 1:2, p. 25; MKH leHatan veKhallah, chapter 10 on sod hataharah.

[28] TH 1, Bereishit, pp. 31–32.

[29] TH 1, Bereishit, p. 7.

each generation. Without awareness of current scientific knowledge, rabbis could easily err in halakhic decisions that depended on correct information.[30]

Rabbi Halevy remarked that Rambam, who was himself a prominent doctor, relied on contemporary medical and scientific knowledge, even when that information was at times in conflict with opinions of rabbis in the Talmud.[31] Indeed, the rabbis in the Talmud themselves admitted that non-Jewish scholars sometimes had more accurate scientific knowledge.[32] This was a tribute to our rabbis' commitment to truth.

In his writings, Rabbi Halevy referred to information he received in consultation with doctors, as well as to medical and psychological literature of which he was aware.[33] He tried to be informed on the current general knowledge that could have impact on halakhic rulings.

Rabbi Halevy was thoroughly trained in Torah and rabbinic literature; but he had minimal formal education in general studies. He studied some English, and took classes in pedagogy. He read newspapers, used encyclopedias, and consulted experts in various fields. He was not averse to quoting philosophers and scientists, even though he probably was only familiar with their works through secondary sources in Hebrew.

In his various writings, Rabbi Halevy referred to such intellectual figures as Socrates, Aristotle, Philo, Descartes, Hume, and Schopenhauer.[34] He quoted from the works of modern psychologists.[35] He cited Albert Einstein's statement that "if not for the fact that our ancestors transmitted to us faith in the existence of God, we would have had to discover it on

---

[30] DVM 1, p. 53.

[31] ALR 2:1, p. 11.

[32] ALR 5:49.

[33] See for example ALR 1:61; 2: essay on afterlife; 5:13; 5:37; 6: introduction; 6:44; 6:64; 8:64; MH 3:24.

[34] See for example ALR 4:6; 4:67; MH 2:50; TH 1, Bereishit, pp. 27–28; MKH *leHatan veKhallah*, chapter 10. NM, p. 21. See also TH 2, *Vayikra*, p. 123, where he refers to the American Civil War.

[35] ALR 2: essay on the afterlife; 3:36; TH 1, Bereishit, pp. 18–19.

our own."[36] He was interested in the findings of modern science, especially medicine; he was intrigued by philosophic ideas and the study of history.[37] Yet, he saw all these manifestations of human intellect as handmaidens to the study of Torah.

Rabbi Halevy also appreciated the contributions of academics to Torah studies. While he certainly was a traditionalist deeply steeped in the yeshiva methods of Torah study, he did not dismiss the value of academic study of rabbinic topics. He agreed to be guest speaker at a reception in honor of a book authored by Zvi Zohar, dealing with how some rabbinic authorities confronted issues of modernity.[38] Rabbi Halevy expressed appreciation of this important scholarly work, adding that it could only have been written by one trained in academia. The scholarly approach to the topic helped shed light on the teachings of the rabbis and the world in which they lived. These insights normally would not have been noticed in the standard yeshiva methods of study.[39]

Rabbi Halevy certainly believed that children should be given thorough Torah education; but he also recognized the importance of general studies. Through general education, children would learn skills necessary to gain employment when they grew older. They should also learn basic life skills, e.g., swimming, First Aid, CPR.[40]

Rabbi Halevy respected the achievements of modern science and scholarship, and valued the attainment of general knowledge. Yet, he stressed the primacy of Torah study. He feared that science had become, for many people, a new form of idolatry. By placing too much faith in science and rationalism they undermined true faith in God and Torah.

---

[36] TH 1, Bereishit, p. 12.

[37] See ALR 6:85 on his understanding of our sages' view of history. See also Zvi Zohar's article, "Sephardic Hakhamim, Modernity, and the Theology of Haim David Halevy," in W. Zenner and K. Avruch eds., *Critical Essays on Israeli Society, Religion and Government,* SUNY Press, Albany, 1997, pp. 115–136.

[38] Rabbi Halevy spoke at a reception in honor of the book *Masoret uTemurah,* in 1993.

[39] Extract from the tape of Rabbi Halevy's lecture.

[40] ALR 6:87; 8: short answers 54; MH 2:54. See also ALR 1:36; 4:31; 4:46.

They did not realize that life was not only physical – but also metaphysical.[41] In fact, like the ladder in Yaakov's dream, human life was tied both to heaven and earth. A person could fail by being too earthly; and could also fall short by becoming too spiritual. The Torah tradition taught the proper balance of spirituality and commitment to the realities of everyday life.[42]

In this chapter, we have explored some of the religious and intellectual foundations of Rabbi Halevy's worldview. We turn now to a discussion of the rabbinic personality who had the most influence on Rabbi Halevy as he began his rabbinic career: Rabbi Benzion Meir Hai Uziel.

---

[41] MKH 1:53, p. 210.
[42] TH 1, Bereishit, p. 81.

Chapter Three

The Influence of Rabbi Uziel

Rabbi Benzion Meir Hai Uziel (1880–1953) was one of the great rabbinic figures in Israel during the first half of the twentieth century. Scion of distinguished Sephardic rabbinical families, he was born and raised in Jerusalem. His father, Rabbi Yosef Raphael Uziel, was the head of the rabbinical court of the Sephardim of the city. His mother, Sarah, was born into the illustrious Hazan family. Both the Uziel and Hazan families had produced rabbinical scholars for generations. Benzion Uziel was trained from earliest childhood to become a rabbinical scholar.

When his father died in 1894, the young Benzion – as the firstborn child – had to take responsibility for earning money to support the family. He gave private Torah lessons and as he grew older, he held teaching positions in various Sephardic *yeshivot*.

In 1911, he was appointed Chief Rabbi of Tel Aviv-Jaffa. In 1921, he left to become Chief Rabbi of the Jewish community of Salonika. He returned to his position in Tel Aviv-Jaffa in 1923, ultimately becoming the Sephardic Chief Rabbi of Israel in 1939. He held that post until his death in 1953.

Rabbi Uziel was uniquely talented. His rabbinic scholarship was vast. He was a prolific author and gifted orator. His leadership was selfless, tireless, and compassionate. He was beloved by Sephardim and Ashkenazim alike, by Jews and non-Jews, by rich and poor. He was a living bridge among the diverse groups within Israel, and won the respect and admiration of a large cross-section of the society.[1]

Rabbi Halevy was deeply influenced by Rabbi Uziel, and viewed him as a model rabbinic sage and leader. Indeed, he thought that Rabbi Uziel was peerless; no one else had his unique combination of intellect, knowledge, communication skills, leadership talents, moral stature, commitment to his people, love and compassion.[2]

Rabbi Halevy served as Rabbi Uziel's private secretary for about two years. In this capacity, he worked with him on a daily basis, and saw first-hand how his mentor dealt with the various problems that confronted him. Through this personal contact, Rabbi Halevy recognized Rabbi Uziel as "a true nobleman, who conducted himself with gracious humility with all members of his household, including the household help…. His speech to all people, including members of his household, was pleasant and respectful; he never raised his voice…. He never refused to receive a person who knocked at his door at any time of the day or night, including during mealtime…. His first instruction to me when I began my service to him was not to leave anyone without an answer. He insisted on a personal response even to those who sent him cards with blessings for the New Year…. Even ordinary Jews who wanted to meet him for no substantial reason – he permitted them to enter."[3]

Rabbi Uziel worked in an efficient and focused manner. He scheduled his days so that he would have adequate time for studying Torah, answering questions in Jewish law, preparing articles and books for publication, attending various meetings, keeping his appointments with individuals who came to him with all types of questions and problems. He read the daily newspapers, kept informed of current political news,

---

[1] For a study on the life and work of Rabbi Uziel, see Marc D. Angel, *Loving Truth and Peace: The Grand Religious Worldview of Rabbi Benzion Uziel,* Jason Aronson, Northvale, NJ, 1999.

[2] Rabbi Halevy wrote a short biographical work on Rabbi Uziel, *Toledotav uMifalo haSifruti shel Maran haRav Benzion Meir Hai Uziel,* Imrei Fi Publishers, Jerusalem, 5739.

[3] Ibid., pp. 21–22.

maintained contact with government officials. He served as rabbinical judge and met all the multifaceted responsibilities of a Chief Rabbi.

Rabbi Halevy, in his inaugural address as Chief Rabbi of Rishon Letzion (28 Sivan, 5713/June 11, 1953), listed the outstanding qualities that should characterize a rabbi. As the prime example of rabbinic excellence, Rabbi Halevy referred to Rabbi Uziel in glowing terms. "As his student, I permit myself to describe him in a few words as a leader and great spiritual spokesman, excellent in all those precious and exalted qualities of soul that I have enumerated earlier, nobility of soul and purity of heart, aside from his greatness and genius (*gedulato vegaoni'uto*) in Torah, which is known and famous to all." Rabbi Halevy stated with satisfaction that he had learned much from Rabbi Uziel, and tried to develop in himself the virtues that Rabbi Uziel exemplified in his own personality. "I am confident that his noble image in all its glowing manifestations will accompany me in my new path of life, and will protect me from error and stumbling."[4]

The ongoing influence of Rabbi Uziel on Rabbi Halevy is evident in Rabbi Halevy's writings. It is fair to say that Rabbi Halevy was Rabbi Uziel's spiritual heir, drawing on the teachings of his mentor and fostering his grand religious worldview. Both Rabbi Uziel and Rabbi Halevy were products of the Sephardic tradition as manifested among the Judeo-Spanish speaking Sephardim of the Ottoman Empire. During the twentieth century, they were arguably the two greatest and most prominent exponents of that tradition.

Halakhic Lessons from Rabbi Uziel

Rabbi Halevy concurred with Rabbi Uziel's statement that a *posek*, halakhic decisor, "was not permitted to say to himself or to those who asked him questions: let me consult a book and give the halakhic ruling from that which is already available in the printed book. This is not the way of those who give legal decisions." Rather, the *posek* had to study the original

---

[4] BYL, p. 75.

sources, bring to bear his own expansive knowledge and reasoning powers. He had to consider the specific details of each case, keeping in mind that new circumstances arise in every generation that require fresh analysis. If one simply depended on opinions of predecessors, he was not fulfilling his duty properly.[5] Rabbi Halevy shared Rabbi Uziel's view that the rabbinic judicial process demanded thorough research, an open mind, creative thinking, and moral responsibility.[6]

In a number of his responsa, Rabbi Halevy referred to lessons he had learned from Rabbi Uziel. For example, Rabbi Uziel generally refused to answer halakhic questions sent to him by individuals, if those questions had communal ramifications. Rather, he would request that the questioner first consult his local rabbi. Then, if the rabbi felt it necessary, the rabbi could address the question to Rabbi Uziel. In explaining his policy to Rabbi Halevy, Rabbi Uziel stated that "it was obvious that there could be differences of opinion in deciding a halakhah, and there is a reasonable suspicion that the local rabbi had already issued his halakhic ruling. If [the questioner] were to receive an answer from me different from that of the local rabbi, this would cause much unpleasantness, and there is a possibility of a serious controversy."[7]

Rabbi Halevy had consulted Rabbi Uziel on the following question: when a congregation was composed of individuals from different backgrounds with different synagogue customs, which custom should be followed? If the congregation had a clear majority that wished to follow a particular tradition, then obviously the minority had to go along with the majority decision. However, if the congregation could not reach a consensus, Rabbi Uziel suggested – and Rabbi Halevy followed this opinion – that the congregation should be directed to accept the customs of Jerusalem. The Jerusalem tradition was to be considered as the standard.[8]

---

[5] Rabbi Benzion Uziel, *Mishpetei Uziel*, Tel Aviv, 5695, Introduction p. ix.
[6] ALR 6:21.
[7] ALR 1:25.
[8] ALR 7:5.

In a responsum dealing with workers' responsibilities towards their employers, Rabbi Halevy cited a lesson from Rabbi Uziel. As has been mentioned, Rabbi Uziel was orphaned at a young age. In order to earn money for the support of his mother and younger siblings, he tutored students in Torah studies. But this work took away time that he usually devoted to his own regimen of Torah study. To make up for this lost time, he would stay up late into the night studying Torah. He soon realized, though, that he did not have enough strength to give wholeheartedly to his students, since he was so tired from his nightly studies. Believing that it was not right to work for pay without giving full energy to one's work, Rabbi Uziel sought other ways of earning a living that would not conflict with his daily Torah study.[9] Rabbi Halevy applied this lesson to all workers, indicating that they were obligated to give full effort and energy to their work.

Rabbi Halevy also drew instruction from other practices of Rabbi Uziel. Rabbi Uziel, who was well known for his tremendous devotion to Torah study, would sometimes grow tired during the evening hours. When he felt too fatigued to continue effectively with his studies, he would sit in his armchair for a little while and listen to music. This relaxed him, and enabled him to continue with his Torah studies for several more hours into the night.[10]

Rabbi Uziel also had the practice of leaving non-Hebrew-language books, on secular topics, in the bathroom. Rabbi Halevy recommended this practice to all Torah students, as a way of avoiding thinking of Torah or reading Hebrew while in the bathroom.[11]

From time to time, Rabbi Halevy cited specific halakhic opinions of Rabbi Uziel. For example, he related an incident that occurred to Rabbi Uziel when he had been serving as Chief Rabbi of Salonika. The electric power went out on a particular Shabbat, and the question arose whether it

---

[9] MH 2:80; see also Rabbi Halevy's biographical booklet on Rabbi Uziel, op. cit., p. 24.

[10] ALR 7:31.

[11] ALR 5:27.

was permissible to flip a light-switch to the off position. Thus, when the power was restored, the lights would not go on. Rabbi Uziel apparently had no halakhic objection to this, and Rabbi Halevy concurred.[12]

Rabbi Halevy cited and agreed with Rabbi Uziel's opinion (universally held among *poskim*) that printed or photo-offset texts were not valid for Torah scrolls, *tefillin*, or *mezuzot*. These texts must be written by hand by a qualified scribe.[13] Rabbi Halevy endorsed Rabbi Uziel's opinion permitting the establishment of courts of appeal within the rabbinic court system.[14] He also referred favorably to Rabbi Uziel's lenient ruling allowing the use of grafted *etrogim*, grown in Israel, on the Sukkot festival.[15]

One of the halakhic issues that had to be confronted when the State of Israel was established related to the practice of polygamy. Jews of Ashkenazic background had been forbidden to practice polygamy going back to the decree promulgated by Rabbeinu Gershom (960–1028). Did this decree also apply to Jews of Sephardic and Middle Eastern backgrounds? To be sure, polygamy was generally not practiced among Sephardim, and a clause in the marriage contract specifically forbade a husband to take another wife without his wife's permission. Yet, some Middle Eastern communities which followed the Sephardic halakhic tradition did allow a man to take an additional wife under certain circumstances. Bigamy, for example, was allowed for the sake of a levirate marriage, i.e., if a man died childless, his brother was required to marry the widow (*yibbum*) or free her by means of a ceremony known as *halitzah*. If the brother were already married, though, marriage to his widowed sister-in-law would necessarily entail bigamy. Within the Ashkenazic world,

---

[12] ALR 5:8.

[13] ALR 5:24.

[14] MH 2:76.

[15] MH 3:23. For other references to Rabbi Uziel, see introduction to MKH 1, p. 14 on the importance of studying Rambam; ALR 1:43, on an interpretation of Rabbi Uziel relating to the laws of *mikveh*; and TH 2, *Devarim*, pp. 8–9, where Rabbi Halevy testified that Rabbi Uziel was the author of the prayer for the government of Israel that is in general use throughout the Jewish world. See also DVM 1, p. 180 and p. 188; DVM 2, p. 56.

halitzah became the only acceptable means of dealing with the situation. Yet, within the Sephardic world, many sages believed that *yibbum* must take precedence to *halitzah*, thereby allowing a man to take an additional wife.

In 1950, Rabbi Uziel and the Ashkenazic Chief Rabbi Yitzhak Isaac Herzog issued a number of ordinances relating to marriage practices. For the sake of the unity of the Jewish people in Israel, they wanted all Jews – Sephardic or Ashkenazic – to be bound by the same rules of marriage and divorce. The Chief Rabbis ordained that no man was allowed to marry an additional wife, without first obtaining written permission from both Chief Rabbis – a very unlikely eventuality. They also issued a ruling that *yibbum* was not to be practiced in Israel, even if the parties consented. Rather, *halitzah* was to be the required procedure to end the halakhic bond between a childless widow and her brother-in-law.[16]

In dealing with the issue of polygamy, Rabbi Halevy argued that the Sephardic world had universally accepted monogamy as the norm, and effectively had adopted the ruling of Rabbeinu Gershom.[17] Thus, Rabbi Halevy thought that Rabbi Uziel had acted wisely in cooperating with Rabbi Herzog in banning the practice of a man taking an additional wife. He also approved of Rabbi Uziel's agreement with Rabbi Herzog that no man could divorce his wife against her will, effectively adopting this ruling of Rabbeinu Gershom for all Jews – Ashkenazim and Sephardim alike.

While Rabbi Halevy's concurrence with Rabbi Uziel on these issues hardly seems controversial, this point of view was rejected by Rabbi Ovadya Yosef, the most influential Sephardic halakhic authority of the latter twentieth and early twenty-first centuries. He had served as Sephardic Chief Rabbi of Tel Aviv and went on to become Sephardic Chief Rabbi of Israel. Subsequently, he was the spiritual head of the Shas party which became quite influential in the Israeli political system.

Rabbi Yosef argued emphatically that the Sephardic communities never had accepted the decrees of Rabbeinu Gershom. Thus, a Sephardic

---

[16] The ordinances are found in Yitzhak Isaac Halevy Herzog, *Tehukah leYisrael al pi haTorah*, Vol. 3, Mossad haRav Kook, Jerusalem, 5749, pp. 168–9.
[17] ALR 2:59.

man could marry an additional wife when the situation warranted it, i.e., no children were born to his wife during the first ten years of marriage, or he had to marry the brother's widow in case of levirate marriage. Moreover, a man could divorce his wife even against her will, under certain circumstances. And finally, Rabbi Yosef argued that *yibbum* had priority to *halitzah*.[18] Rabbi Yosef believed that Rabbi Uziel had erred in agreeing to issue those ordinances in cooperation with Rabbi Herzog. He felt that Rabbi Uziel was too conciliatory to Rabbi Herzog, thereby undermining the classic halakhic positions of Sephardic sages.

Rabbi Halevy took issue with Rabbi Yosef, and sided clearly with Rabbi Uziel in the matter of prohibiting bigamy and in the matter of prohibiting divorces against the will of the wife. Yet, when it came to the question of whether *yibbum* had precedence to *halitzah*, Rabbi Halevy found himself in a bit of a bind. On the one hand, he believed that *yibbum* was very important, and had profound significance especially according to the kabbalah. He certainly was sympathetic to the position of Rabbi Yosef on this issue. Yet, he apparently did not wish to take a public stand against Rabbi Uziel.

Dr. Elimelech Westreich has noted that Rabbi Halevy chose not to involve himself too much in the rabbinic court that dealt with these issues. He neither wanted to enter into open controversy with Rabbi Ovadya Yosef, nor did he feel he could defend Rabbi Uziel on the question of giving precedence to *yibbum*.[19] But in his writings, Rabbi Halevy made his opinions known, without specifically indicating the positions of either Rabbi Uziel or Rabbi Yosef. On these issues, he preferred to sidestep public controversy and was content to state his views and then let history take its course.

In several of his responsa, Rabbi Halevy did take issue with halakhic positions taken by Rabbi Uziel. Yet, these differences of opinion

---

[18] Rabbi Ovadya Yosef, *Yabia Omer*, vol. 5, Jerusalem, 5746, *Even haEzer* no. 1.

[19] See Elimelech Westreich's article, *"Shifut uMishpat beMishnat haRav Haim David Halevy: Bein haRav Uziel leVein haRav Ovadya Yosef,"* in a volume of essays about Rabbi Halevy edited by Zvi Zohar and Avi Sagi.

were presented in a mild and respectful way; Rabbi Halevy avoided outright attacks on opinions of Rabbi Uziel. For example, Rabbi Uziel had ruled that women may vote and be elected to office.[20] Rabbi Halevy, discussing the issue of women's right to vote and be elected, noted the permissive ruling of Rabbi Uziel. But he added: "However, there is room for discussion concerning what he wrote in regard to the right [of women] to be elected."[21] In other words, Rabbi Halevy was not comfortable with the notion of women being elected to public office, even though Rabbi Uziel had permitted this. Rabbi Halevy voiced his disagreement with this opinion simply by saying that there was room for further discussion on the topic.

In another responsum, Rabbi Halevy referred to Rabbi Uziel's opinion justifying a relatively new practice of not reciting supplicatory prayers on days when a bar mitzvah was being celebrated in the synagogue. Since the bar mitzvah was a festive occasion when the thirteen-year-old boy was accepting upon himself the obligations of the commandments, Rabbi Uziel felt that supplicatory prayers could be suspended. Rabbi Halevy stated that Rabbi Uziel's arguments in favor of the new practice were not compelling. There were very strong arguments in favor of reciting the supplicatory prayers. Rabbi Halevy decided that, since there were good points on both sides of the question, he would not give a definitive ruling. Rather, he left it up to each congregation to decide for itself.[22] Thus, while not agreeing with Rabbi Uziel's decision, Rabbi Halevy did not actually issue a ruling categorically opposed to Rabbi Uziel.

Rabbi Halevy dealt with the question of shaving during the intermediate days of Passover and Sukkot. The Talmud ruled against shaving on these days, and this became the normative halakhah for many

---

[20] Rabbi Benzion Uziel, *Mishpetei Uziel*, Jerusalem, 5700, *Hoshen Mishpat* no. 6. See also, Zvi Zohar, "Traditional Flexibility and Modern Strictness: A Comparative Analysis of the Halakhic Positions of Rabbi Kook and Rabbi Uziel on Women's Suffrage," in Harvey Goldberg, ed., *Sephardi and Middle Eastern Jewries: History and Culture,* Bloomington, Indiana University Press, 1996, pp. 119–133.
[21] ALR 4:56.
[22] ALR 6:12.

centuries. Yet, in modern times, some have felt that the old rule no longer applied. Today, men were accustomed to shaving every day – unlike the practice in olden times. If they did not shave during the intermediate days of the festival, they appeared sloppy and unkempt – something the Talmud was trying to prevent. Rabbi Halevy cited the opinion of Rabbi Uziel insisting that one must not shave during the intermediate days of the festivals. He believed that the act of shaving diminished the holiness and honor of the holidays. While Rabbi Halevy was not convinced by Rabbi Uziel's line of reasoning, he chose not to make a definitive decision on this matter. Since there were convincing opinions on both sides of the issue, he decided not to discuss this halakhah in public, i.e., not to forbid shaving on these days, but not to openly permit it either. He left it to each individual to decide for himself.[23] Here too, then, he disagreed with Rabbi Uziel without actually ruling against him.

Approach to Halakhah

In 1921, Judge Benjamin Nathan Cardozo – later to become the first Sephardic Jew to serve on the United States Supreme Court – published a series of lectures he had delivered at Yale University. In describing the nature of the judicial process, Cardozo delineated various features that went into the decision-making process of every judge. One of these features was the particular worldview that the judge brought to the cases before him.

Cardozo wrote: "There is in each of us a stream of tendency, whether you choose to call it philosophy or not, which gives coherence and direction to thought and action. Judges cannot escape that current any more than other mortals. All their lives, forces which they do not recognize and cannot name, have been tugging at them – inherited instincts, traditional beliefs, acquired convictions; and the resultant is an

---

[23] ALR 1:39; for another example of Rabbi Halevy disagreeing with Rabbi Uziel, see MH 2:39, concerning whether the requirement to eat extra on the eve of Yom Kippur applies also to women. Rabbi Halevy published Rabbi Uziel's notes on the tractate *Berakhot* under the title *Gilyonei Uziel*, at the end of ALR 7, pp. 1–44.

outlook on life, a conception of social needs…which, when reasons are nicely balanced, must determine where choice shall fall.… We may try to see things as objectively as we please. None the less, we can never see them with any eyes except our own."[24]

Cardozo's comments are equally appropriate when applied to rabbinic judges, halakhic decisors. True, each *posek* is governed by the authoritative legal texts; but so are judges in any legal system governed by earlier legal texts and precedents. The fact is, as Cardozo stated so well, every person – including judges – has a stream of tendency of thought, a core philosophy based on a range of influences, so that no two people see things in exactly the same way. This fact explains why different judges reach different conclusions and why different *poskim* rule differently, even though they base their decisions on the same authoritative texts.[25]

Earlier in this book, we have considered some of the main influences in the development of Rabbi Halevy's "stream of tendency": his family background and childhood upbringing; the Sephardic religious traditions; his rabbis and teachers; the kabbalah. It surely is clear that Rabbi Uziel was an important influence on him.

Yet, it is also true that Rabbi Halevy was predisposed to the teachings of Rabbi Uziel because he saw in Rabbi Uziel a kindred spirit. Rabbi Uziel's religious worldview – the stream of tendency of his thought – was very much in tune with Rabbi Halevy's own way of thinking. Rabbi Uziel was a major influence on Rabbi Halevy precisely because Rabbi Halevy chose Rabbi Uziel to be so. In Rabbi Halevy's writings about Rabbi Uziel, he emphasized those aspects in the thought of his mentor with which he himself identified. In a real sense, Rabbi Halevy's description of

---

[24] Benjamin Nathan Cardozo, *The Nature of the Judicial Process,* Yale University Press, New Haven, 1921, pp. 12–13.

[25] For an example of this, see my articles "A Study of the Halakhic Approaches of Two Modern *Posekim,*" *Tradition,* 23:3 (Spring, 1988), pp. 41–52; and "A Discussion of the Nature of Jewishness in the Teachings of Rabbi Kook and Rabbi Uziel, in *Seeking Good, Speaking Peace: Collected Essays of Rabbi Marc D. Angel,* ed. Hayyim Angel, Ktav, Hoboken, 1994, pp. 112–123.

Rabbi Uziel's approach to halakhah is also a mirror to Rabbi Halevy's own approach to halakhah.

In the early 1980s, Rabbi Halevy delivered a lecture on the halakhic approach of Rabbi Uziel, opening with a discussion of the talmudic controversies between the schools of Shammai and Hillel (*Eruvin* 13b).[26] The Talmud relates that the two schools argued for several years, each claiming that the halakhah should be decided according to its rulings. At last, a heavenly voice was heard, saying that both schools represented the word of the living God; and that the halakhah was to be decided according to the school of Hillel. Why was the school of Hillel preferred? Because they were pleasant and long-suffering. They not only studied the opinions of the school of Shammai, but even gave precedence to the words of that school over their own. This spirit of humility and compassion on the part of the school of Hillel ultimately won the sanction of the heavenly voice.

Rabbi Halevy raised the question: shouldn't issues of halakhah be decided on the basis of who has the strongest arguments and proofs? Why did the Talmud assert that the law followed the opinion of the school of Hillel due to its fine moral qualities? What do kindness, patience and humility have to do with determining halakhic truth?

Rabbi Halevy noted that there is a category of *halakhot* that is subject to controversy, with each side able to cite equally good arguments. Both sides can be "true," in the sense that they are halakhically justifiable. Yet, even if both sides espouse true points of view, a decision needs to be made to guide normative behavior. Thus, the schools of Shammai and Hillel each had truth on their side; but since a normative decision had to be made, it was made on the basis of moral character. The law came down on the side of the school of Hillel because its followers were sympathetic human beings, recognizing human frailty and the difficult challenges of life. They were sensitive to the human predicament and tended to be lenient in their rulings.

---

26 ALR 5:48.

Certainly, there are traditional rules governing the determination of halakhah. Nevertheless, the moral qualities and tendencies of a *posek* play a role in his decision-making.

Rabbi Uziel was an extraordinary *posek* because he was very much in the tradition of the school of Hillel. His awesome mastery of halakhic literature was matched by his moral qualities and his keen sensitivity to human needs. He was humble and patient, imbued with a deep and abiding love for the Jewish people. Respect for others was a hallmark of his personality and his approach to deciding halakhic questions.

Rabbi Halevy wrote an extended essay on the love of Israel as a factor in the halakhic decision-making of Rabbi Uziel.[27] He stated: "...Anyone who knew at first-hand our teacher, Rabbi Uziel of blessed memory, knows that his personality was stamped with the love of kindness and mercy to all people, and certainly to Jews, who are called children of God. It is not plausible that the heart that beat with pure love did not wield its influence on his general and halakhic thinking. I am a witness that all his public service was deeply influenced by that love of Israel which infused him.... How would it be possible that his halakhic thinking not be influenced in this direction?[28]

Rabbi Halevy then went on to a discussion of the controversies between the schools of Shammai and Hillel, and the conclusion that the halakhah follows the school of Hillel. This demonstrates that moral qualities and ethical sensitivities are given great weight in the halakhic process. It is not just a matter of adducing sources and offering finely reasoned arguments. No, halakhic decision-making is impacted by the tendency of thought of the *posek*. Thus, Rabbi Uziel's love of Israel did inevitably factor into his halakhic decision-making.

Rabbi Halevy offered a number of examples to prove his point, three of which are presented here. For many generations, halakhic sages

---

[27] ALR 8:97; I translated this article into English, "The Love of Israel as a Factor in Halakhic Decision-making in the works of Rabbi Benzion Uziel," *Tradition* 24:3 (Spring, 1989), pp. 1–20.
[28] Ibid., p. 1.

debated over the question of whether a grafted *etrog* was permissible for use on Sukkot. During the early twentieth century, the question arose in regard to grafted *etrogim* grown in Israel. In his responsum dealing with this question, Rabbi Uziel cited the opinions on both sides of the question. He concluded that those who buy Israeli *etrogim* may rely on the permissive view. But then he went further: "…Because of the love of the land and the mitzvah of settling the Land of Israel, it is a mitzvah to seek out *etrogim* grown in Israel. This is in order to aid those who exert effort to establish the land among the Jewish people. Anyone who prefers *etrogim* grown in the Diaspora sins against his people and his land, since he weakens the position of his brethren who dwell in the land of Israel and who wish to support themselves by their labor."[29]

Although there is no compelling halakhic reason to permit grafted *etrogim* – and a good case to forbid them – Rabbi Uziel's love of Israel surely played a dominant role in his ruling. His emotional plea on behalf of settling the land of Israel and supporting its laborers is powerful.

A question arose relating to cattle suffering from a stomach illness that endangered their lives. To cure them, an implement was inserted through the skin into the stomach. Excess air was thus released from the stomach, and the animal returned to health. In a short while, the puncture mark in the stomach healed. The question was whether an animal, thus punctured in the stomach, was thereby no longer to be considered kosher due to this blemish in a major body organ. If it was not kosher, then it was forbidden to drink its milk while it was alive or eat its meat when slaughtered. After a careful halakhic analysis of the issue, Rabbi Uziel stated that such animals should not be declared to be unfit for consumption. "If we do prohibit them, we will preclude the possibility of Jewish involvement in the milk industry, and we will remove an important economic enterprise which supports purveyors of drink and food to the entire public…. So we will rely on the opinion of those who declare the animal to be *kasher*."[30] Rabbi Uziel would certainly not issue a ruling

---

[29] *Mishpetei Uziel*, 5695, *Orah Hayyim* no. 24.
[30] *Mishpetei Uziel*, 5710, *Yoreh Deah* no. 3.

against halakhah merely in order to achieve a social or economic goal. Yet, since he did find proper halakhic arguments for permitting these animals, his concern for the well-being of the people of Israel moved him to choose to follow the lenient opinion within halakhah. The stream of tendency of his thought led him to find ways to advance the Jewish settlement of the land of Israel.

Even before the State of Israel was established in 1948, Rabbi Uziel was dealing with questions relating to governing a Jewish state according to halakhah. He wanted to demonstrate that the halakhah was capable of serving the needs of a modern, progressive nation. "The new government rule in our land awakens a number of problems which have political and civil importance. One of the questions relates to testimony. Is it possible to validate the testimony of a non-Jew according to the Torah? Or at least are the rabbis empowered to make a regulation allowing non-Jewish testimony, when the public accepts this concept? This question is of great significance and relevance at the time when we are building our national home. One of the greatest yearnings of the people of Israel is the re-establishment of Jewish justice according to the laws of the Torah. And one of the most important goals of the redemption is to establish our system of justice as it was in ancient times. Therefore, when justice returns to our power, and Jewish judges sit on the chairs of judgment, and the Torah rules in all matters among people – will we then be able to accept the testimony of a non-Jew and pass judgment based on it? It is impossible to answer this question negatively, because it would not be civil justice to disqualify as witnesses those who live among us and deal with us honestly and fairly. Weren't we ourselves embittered when the lands of our exile invalidated us as witnesses? If in the entire enlightened world the law has been accepted to receive the testimony of every person without consideration of religion or race, how then may we make such a separation?"[31]

---

[31] *Mishpetei Uziel,* 5700, *Hoshen Mishpat* no. 17.

In this responsum, Rabbi Uziel voiced indignation at the past discrimination against Jews in non-Jewish lands. His empathy for the plight of Jews was transferred also to non-Jews who would be living under Jewish hegemony. The halakhah *must* have a morally acceptable way of including non-Jewish citizens in a Jewish state. Rabbi Uziel did find halakhic sanction for allowing non-Jewish witnesses, but it cannot be doubted that his innate sense of justice was an important factor in his decision-making process. Before he even began his research into the topic he had an inkling of what the correct answer should be.

In identifying Rabbi Uziel as a paragon of the school of Hillel, Rabbi Halevy obviously reflected his admiration – and emulation – of his mentor's approach to halakhah. It can equally be stated of Rabbi Halevy that he was a paragon of the school of Hillel, and that his moral character and ethical sensitivity played a significant role in his halakhic decision-making.

In his biographical booklet on Rabbi Uziel, Rabbi Halevy cited a number of Rabbi Uziel's responsa.[32] Rabbi Halevy was impressed with Rabbi Uziel's love of Israel, defense of its honor, commitment to its holy institutions and traditions. He admired how Rabbi Uziel dealt with difficult modern questions relating to new technology, autopsies in medical schools under Jewish auspices, conversion to Judaism, and other topics.

In his writings about Rabbi Uziel, Rabbi Halevy described the greatness of his Torah master as expressions of love and respect. While he did not always agree with Rabbi Uziel's decisions, and while he developed his own distinctive style and halakhic approach, he nevertheless was always a devoted and admiring student. He drew strength from Rabbi Uziel's "stream of tendency," his philosophy and religious worldview. As Rabbi Uziel's spiritual heir, Rabbi Halevy shared his teacher's commitment to thorough halakhic analysis that was imbued with the patience, humility and compassion characteristic of followers of the school of Hillel.

---

[32] Op. Cit., pp. 27–37.

Chapter Four

RABBINIC RESPONSIBILITY AND AUTHORITY

For some years, Rabbi Halevy conducted a popular radio program, "*Asei Lekha Rav*" (make for yourself a rabbi). People asked him questions about what the Jewish tradition had to say on a wide range of topics. In 5736 (1976), Rabbi Halevy published volume one in a series of books based on his radio program. Also entitled *Asei Lekha Rav,* the series came to include nine volumes, with hundreds of Rabbi Halevy's answers to questions in halakhah, Jewish thought, ethical issues, political and economic matters, etc. (He subsequently published three more volumes of responsa under the title *Mayyim Hayyim.*)

In the very first responsum in volume one of *Asei Lekha Rav,* Rabbi Halevy noted that a rabbi was not simply a decisor of rabbinic law, informing people concerning what was forbidden and what was permitted, what was impure and what was pure. "Rather he was also – and perhaps mainly – an advisor to everyone in his community for all questions, small and large."[1]

The rabbi was supposed to be a source of genuine Torah knowledge and guidance, to whom people could turn for advice on all aspects of their lives. The *Asei Lekha Rav* series, both on radio and in book form, was designed to address questions on the minds of the general public. It demonstrated that the Torah's teachings related to the multifarious areas of life; every question had an answer within halakhah.

---

[1] ALR 1:1.

Moreover, it served to educate the public on the need to consult a rabbi on the various questions that arose in the course of life.[2]

In Rabbi Halevy's view, the rabbi-layman relationship was an essential feature of healthy Jewish life. The rabbi was expected to be a Torah scholar, a master of Jewish religious tradition, a wise and compassionate guide, a sensitive leader. His authority came not from his title or official position: it derived from the trust invested in him by his community. He had to win the public's confidence so that they would want to turn to him for instruction. On the other hand, the layman was expected to be respectful and loyal to his rabbi.[3] Both rabbi and layman shared (or should be sharing) the same goal of serving the Almighty in righteousness.

The ideal model for a rabbi was Moshe Rabbeinu, Moses our teacher.[4] While no one could expect to attain the spiritual heights of Moshe, yet each could strive to emulate his qualities of humility, commitment to justice, and compassion. Along with Torah knowledge, a rabbinic leader needed wisdom, humility, fear of God, aversion to materialism, love of truth, love of his fellow human beings. The rabbi must have a good reputation as an ethical and trustworthy person.

Rabbi Halevy wrote: "A good leader, who is righteous and pure, is not satisfied merely to fulfill his duty with devotion and trustworthiness. Rather, he also knows how to stand in prayer before the Lord of the universe at times of trouble, and to seek [His] mercy on His people. He should reach the level of self-sacrifice of Moshe Rabbeinu, who because of [this quality] merited the appellation 'faithful shepherd'."[5]

To be a faithful shepherd entailed a total commitment to the well-being and spiritual development of the community. In the modern era,

---

[2] ALR 1: introduction.

[3] See MH 1:71, where Rabbi Halevy noted that a layman should follow the halakhic rulings of his rabbi. If on some issues a layman had good reason to rely on other rabbinic authorities who ruled differently from his rabbi, then he should do so only privately, so as not to cause controversy in the community.

[4] Rabbi Halevy discussed Moshe as the prototypical rabbinic leader in ALR 6:84.

[5] TH 1, Bereishit, p. 39.

when so many Jews had drifted away from traditional religious belief and observance, the rabbi had to find ways of bringing them closer to Torah. Through patience, love and kindness, he had to project the message of Torah even to those who seemed not to be receptive to it. While Rabbi Halevy appreciated the challenges faced by rabbis in the land of Israel, he also was quite sympathetic to the problems confronting the rabbis in the Diaspora. In responding to a question from a Diaspora rabbi, Rabbi Halevy wrote: "Reading your letter brought me pain. I remembered the Jewish communities that I visited on my travels in America and their critical [spiritual] situation, and the conclusion I reached that there is no place for a Jew in the world except in Israel alone. Meanwhile, one must do all he can to guard the ember of Israel in the Diaspora lest it go out, Heaven forbid. Fortunate are you, rabbis of the Diaspora, that this merit has fallen to you to stand in the breach, and to stop in some measure the [spiritual] decline."[6]

Persuasion, Not Coercion

How was the rabbi to exert authority over the public? Rabbi Halevy's answer was clear and unequivocal: through persuasion and compassion, not through coercion. He took issue with those modern philosophers who thought of a leader as a superman, a person who stood above the people as an all-powerful authority. The Torah view rejected this approach, but insisted that a leader excel in the qualities of humility, compassion, love and ethical concern for those whom he led.[7]

In the State of Israel, the religious community led by its rabbis was anxious that Israeli society be governed by the laws of the Torah. Rabbi Halevy, of course, shared this desire. Yet, Rabbi Halevy did not believe that the religious point of view would ultimately prevail due to the work of religious parties. Although one could not completely discount the importance of religious political parties, yet "this is not the way of the

---

[6] ALR 2:25. For other responsa relating to the duties and comportment of a rabbi, see ALR 4:49; MH 1:31; MH 3:55.
[7] BYL, p. 74.

Torah, and not in this way will we succeed."[8] Genuine victory for religion will only come by means of education, by teaching and demonstrating that the ideals and practices of traditional Judaism represent the best fulfillment of human life for the Jewish people. The appropriate approach for rabbinic leadership is the way of quiet, kind persuasion.

Rabbi Halevy stated: "We will not achieve our goal by these means [of political power]. All of our efforts to increase the presence of religious Jewry in the Knesset elected by the nation, can only be – in the best of circumstances – only a means to achieve the goal. Let us assume that some day we will succeed to increase our representatives in a notable measure, until it would be difficult to establish a government without our participation in it. Will the establishment of the State in the spirit of religion then be assured? Surely not. Even to coalition agreements there is a certain boundary. We will never be able to force our ideas and beliefs on the entire nation by means of legislation."[9] The challenge to religious leadership was to convince the general public of the profundity of Torah values and traditions, to instill in their hearts a desire to follow the ways of Torah. Coercion did not win hearts; only enlightened and compassionate education could win hearts. The religious community must devote its main efforts to educating the youth, but must also reach out to adults. Through a comprehensive program of religious instruction, and by setting a moral example, rabbis and their followers could influence the larger society in positive ways.

To succeed at influencing the public to follow the paths of Torah, the religious community had to think beyond its own parochial needs. It had to be concerned with those issues that engaged the society as a whole.[10]

Rabbi Halevy's attitude is well reflected in a number of responsa he wrote in 1987–88 to his colleague Rabbi Moshe Malka, Chief Rabbi of Petah Tikvah. The proprietor of a movie-house in that city decided to keep

---

[8] BYL, p. 82.
[9] BYL, p. 85.
[10] BYL, p. 89.

his business open on Friday nights, in violation of the Jewish Shabbat. Members of the religious community, outraged at this flagrant disregard of the sanctity of Shabbat, organized demonstrations at the theater every Friday night. Protestors marched up and down the street, calling on people not to attend the movies, and urging the management to respect the Shabbat. After thirty-three weeks of these demonstrations, the movie-house still remained open and patrons still attended the movies. Rabbi Malka felt uneasy about continuing the demonstrations and offered halakhic reasons why, in fact, the demonstrations should be stopped. First, the demonstrators had already done their duty of chastising violators of Torah law, and had received much abuse from the violators. Second, the Torah commandment to chastise transgressors referred to those who were essentially religious, but simply violated a particular Torah commandment. Those people might very well be receptive to the chastisement, and would repent from their misdeeds. But in the case at hand, the people attending the movies on Friday night were not religiously observant; they publicly scorned Torah law in their violation of Shabbat. Finally, Rabbi Malka argued that the commandment to chastise transgressors referred to individuals, not to groups of people. In the latter case, one effort at chastisement was sufficient to fulfill the obligation.

Rabbi Halevy agreed with Rabbi Malka, but indicated that the real issue here was not about the interpretation of the commandment to chastise transgressors. Rather, this was a battle about establishing the religious dimension of Israeli society, at least in public places. It was part of a broader conflict: the religious wanted Israeli society to observe the halakhah, at least in public; the secular wanted Israeli society to be governed by freedom of choice, where each individual could observe as much or as little religion as desired. In fact, asserted Rabbi Halevy, those religious Jews who demonstrated against the movie-house were not doing so from their wish to observe the commandment of chastising transgressors. No, they were demonstrating to insist that Israeli society be ruled by halakhic norms.

Rabbi Halevy feared that confrontations between the religious and secular elements only served to deepen the rift between them. The religious community needed to take into consideration the negative backlash created by the demonstrations. Did these confrontations ultimately do more harm than good to the cause of religious life? "I have not given up hope, Heaven forbid, but I believe with full heart that through the ways of pleasantness with appropriate explanations on the part of people of Torah and spirituality (excluding politicians and public functionaries), we will perhaps far better be able to reach proper goals."[11] He reminded Rabbi Malka of a statement of Maimonides (Rambam, *Hil. Melakhim* 11:4), that one of the tasks of the Messiah will be to compel people to follow the laws of the Torah. The implication is that until that time, we will not be able to win the entire people of Israel to repentance. In other words, the obligation upon us is to set realistic goals, and to do our best to win as many hearts and minds to Torah by means of moral example: persuasion, not coercion.

The Rabbi as *Posek*

Rabbi Halevy devoted much research and writing relating to the role of the rabbinic judge, the *posek*. All rabbis are called upon to give halakhic rulings and must be prepared to answer correctly. Although certain rabbis attain higher levels of halakhic authority due to their greater learning, wisdom, and stature as *poskim*, each rabbi must assume the responsibilities of a *posek*

---

[11] ALR 8:32. Rabbi Malka had also raised other reasons for halting the demonstrations: they actually caused more violation of Shabbat. Police and media people came to the demonstrations. Those who supported the movie-house's rights, even if they would not have normally attended on Friday nights, came as a sign of support. And the religious Jews themselves, by demonstrating on Friday nights, deprived themselves and their families of the tranquility of Shabbat. Rabbi Halevy felt that all these points were irrelevant if the demonstrations were in the category of *"eit la'asot laShem."* But since he agreed with Rabbi Malka's assessment that the demonstrations were not achieving anything constructive, they should be stopped on that basis alone.

for his community. In terms of his role as halakhic authority, the rabbi's task is akin to that of a rabbinic judge.

Rabbi Halevy noted that even the best book of laws cannot produce justice, unless judges are learned, upright, and trustworthy. The success of a legal system is dependent on the competence and integrity of its judges.[12]

The overarching role of rabbis is to bring people closer to the ways of Torah. To achieve maximum effectiveness as a *posek*, the rabbi should enjoy the affection and respect of the public. His decisions should be authoritative, not authoritarian.

In rendering a halakhic decision, the rabbi purports to express God's will as manifested in halakhah. This, obviously, is a serious enterprise. The Talmud (*Sanhedrin* 6b) reminds the rabbinic judge that he is responsible to God for his decisions; if he errs, he will have to answer for his mistakes. Because of the awesome responsibility involved in rendering halakhic decisions, a person might say: why do I need this burden? To allay such fears, the Talmud teaches that *ein ledayyan ela mah she'einav ro'ot*, a judge can only reach decisions based on his best understanding. He is not held responsible for errors if he has truly done his best to arrive at a correct ruling.[13]

A proper *posek* must be thoroughly steeped in halakhic literature and must have the confidence to issue decisions. An unqualified person who renders halakhic rulings is arrogant and irresponsible. Through ignorance and pretentiousness, he misleads the public by giving unreliable halakhic guidance. On the other hand, a qualified person who fears to issue decisions is doing a disservice to the community. He does not fulfill his obligation to God and to the Jewish people.

In a discussion of the statement *ein ledayyan ela mah she'einav ro'ot*, Rabbi Halevy pointed out that this concept had various applications.[14] First, it served to encourage the qualified rabbinic judge to render

---

[12] DVM 1, first page of the introduction.
[13] See Rambam, *Hil. Sanhedrin* 23:9.
[14] ALR 3:50.

decisions; he was only required to do his best, and should not be afraid to pass judgment for fear of erring. Moreover, it demanded that the judge be completely satisfied that he had reached the correct decision. If he was not fully convinced by the evidence – even if the evidence appeared to be correct formally – he should not issue a decision contrary to his own understanding. The judge must be alert to the body language of witnesses, defendants and plaintiffs; he must rely on his knowledge of human nature to determine whether they were testifying truthfully. In giving a halakhic ruling, the rabbinic judge must draw on "what his eyes see," i.e., his understanding of all the factors of the case, the evidence as well as his own insights. Rabbi Halevy underscored this point in another responsum: "Jewish judges who judge according to the laws of the Torah are commanded to judge according to the truth that is clarified for them, and not on the basis of testimonies and evidence that were presented to them in and of themselves. A judge may rely on his understanding and even on his own estimation when the matter is exceedingly clear [to him]."[15]

Rabbi Halevy noted that the concept of *ein ledayyan* teaches that a rabbinic decisor must not rely blindly on rulings issued by other courts or sages in similar cases. Rather, he must analyze each case according to his own best judgment. "Not only does a judge have the right to rule against his rabbis; he also has an obligation to do so [if he believes their decision to be incorrect and he has strong proofs to support his own position]. If the decision of those greater than he does not seem right to him and he is not comfortable following it, and yet he follows that decision [in deference to their authority], then it is almost certain that he has rendered a false judgment."[16] Certainly, the rabbinic judge or *posek* should analyze the opinions of the greater authorities, and should not dismiss them casually. Yet, if after serious study and analysis he still concludes that his own position is preferable to theirs, he must rule according to his own understanding.[17]

---

[15] ALR 3:47; see also ALR 3:45; MH 3:47.
[16] ALR 2:61.
[17] See ALR 7:44; MH 2:76.

The halakhic system has an inherent tension. *Poskim* strive to reach the true answer to each halakhic problem presented to them. But they know that other halakhic decisors may reach different conclusions than theirs. The halakhic process is characterized by faithfulness to authoritative sources, but also by a creative sensitivity as to how to apply the traditional sources to each situation. Rabbi Halevy asserted powerfully: "And he is very mistaken who thinks that the halakhah is frozen and that one should not veer from it to the right nor to the left. On the contrary, there is no flexibility like the flexibility of halakhah. Only due to the merit of the flexibility of the halakhah has the people of Israel been able – through the power of numerous and useful creative interpretations which were innovated by the sages of Israel in each generation – to walk in the way of Torah observance for thousands of years. And if the fortitude of the sages of our generation will serve them to innovate interpretations of halakhah [getting at the] truth of Torah, with total faithfulness to the bodies of written and transmitted halakhah…, then halakhah will continue to be the way of the people of Israel to the end of all generations."[18] Rabbi Halevy believed that the Oral Law was alive and eternally relevant because the rabbis of each generation were able to apply its teachings to new situations. For this process to be authentic, though, the rabbis had to be learned, pious, and blessed with understanding and discernment.[19]

A rabbinic authority, therefore, was charged with taking responsibility for rendering halakhic decisions. He was not to repress his own judgment out of deference to others, even if they were greater sages and even if they were his own teachers. Each decisor brought his knowledge, insights and sensitivities to the issues he confronted, as well as his powers of reasoning and creative thinking.

Rabbi Halevy's discussion of the role of the rabbinical judge/*posek*, reflected his deep belief that rabbis needed to be excellent Torah scholars; and that they had to have the moral courage to issue rulings according to the best of their knowledge. Halakhic decision-making, while obviously

---

[18] ALR 7:54.
[19] ALR 9:30–33.

tied to the authoritative halakhic texts and traditions, was a creative process.

Rabbi Halevy felt that too many people, including religiously observant individuals, thought of halakhah as a stultified system that resisted innovations. This view was not only factually incorrect, but was also dangerous. It fed the popular misconceptions about the Jewish religion as an antiquated, irrelevant, and authoritarian system that had little of value to contribute to a modern, progressive society. Thus, it was a particular responsibility of rabbis to present the halakhah as the dynamic, creative system that it actually was. As teachers and as *poskim*, rabbis needed to demonstrate to the public that halakhah was a living system, organically linked to life. The rabbi's authority as a *posek* came with the responsibility of educating the public as to the nature of the halakhic process.

Rabbi Halevy as a Rabbinic Model

Rabbi Halevy was himself a prime model of the ideal *posek* and explicator of the Torah tradition. In his responsa, he answered a wide array of questions, demonstrating a remarkable knowledge of rabbinic sources – halakhic, aggadic, kabbalistic. His responsa are prototypes of clarity, fine reasoning, clear thinking and genuine concern for those who asked the questions. He was respectful of the great halakhic authorities, but he was an independent thinker who did not shy away from breaking new halakhic ground when necessary.

Since Rabbi Halevy wanted to influence the Jewish people to a greater observance and love of Torah, his halakhic writings were a natural means of communication. Aside from his twelve books of responsa, he also published a five-volume code of Jewish law, *Mekor Hayyim*. What distinguished Rabbi Halevy from his predecessors was the philosophical underpinning of his opus. "Halakhah is the body of the Torah. It enables a person to discern between right and wrong. It is the wisdom of life. It is the armament of a person in the battle of life. Complementarily, the aggadah is poetry and song. From it, a person draws strength and fortitude, to know how to make proper use of the strength of halakhah. That is to say: a person attains wholeness in service to God by combining halakhah and aggadah."[20]

In his introduction to *Mekor Hayyim*, Rabbi Halevy informed his readers that he had spent much time pondering the religious decline of the Jewish people during the modern period. Various thinkers had offered different explanations for the phenomenon. Rabbi Halevy thought that Rabbi Avraham Yitzhak Kook had identified the true nature of the problem.

Rabbi Kook had argued that the spiritual decline of the Jewish people was the result of a separation between halakhah and aggadah. The halakhah was treated as an independent body of religious law; it was studied, codified, observed without clear reference to the aggadah. The aggadah (essentially that body of Jewish thought and literature that dealt with emotions, imagination, spirituality) was neglected; or was seen as a separate field of study.

Rabbi Halevy agreed with Rabbi Kook that both halakhah and aggadah had to be integrated. Both spheres of thought shared the same roots in Torah. In Rabbi Halevy's view, Jews drifted from halakhah because it had become a cold, legalistic system. They did not understand the reasons for the laws, and did not see the spiritual value of observing halakhah. If they had studied halakhah and aggadah in tandem they would have had a correct understanding of the grandeur and power of the Jewish religious way of life.

In the *Mekor Hayyim*, Rabbi Halevy set for himself the goal of combining halakhah and aggadah (including kabbalah). Before presenting each section of laws, he first cited the biblical verses, talmudic interpretations, kabbalistic teachings and other rabbinic insights relating to those particular laws. The student, thus, can gain an appreciation of the roots of the laws in biblical and rabbinic tradition, can ponder their meanings, and understand their role in the development of religious life.

---

[20] MKH 1, preliminary introduction, p. 1.

God Himself had chosen to present the Torah to the people of Israel in an appealing form – with stories, explanations, emotional passages. It was not a sterilized list of laws. "From all this it appears clearly that this was God's will, that the Torah and *mitzvot* be given to us not in a frozen framework of dry law, but with a pleasant spirit, with persuasion and explanation, and if you wish to say, with reasons and arguments, or nearly this [way]."[21]

The underlying goal of *Asei Lekha Rav* and *Mekor Hayyim* was to make halakhah intelligible and meaningful to the public. Rabbi Halevy believed that the more people understood, the more they would want to live their lives in accord with Torah teachings. A rabbi's responsibility was to teach and explain, as well as to issue halakhic rulings; if he accomplished this with competence, love and honesty, he would thereby fulfill his role as teacher and representative of Torah.

---

[21] MKH 1, introduction, p. 18.

Chapter Five

DEALING WITH CONFLICTING SOURCES

To understand Rabbi Halevy's religious outlook, it is important to consider his general approach to conflicting sources in aggadah, broadly defined as rabbinic statements in the non-legal realm. He was deeply steeped in rabbinic and kabbalistic sources, and stressed the validity and authority of those teachings.[1]

At the same time, he recognized that many rabbinic teachings were individual opinions rather than received traditions, and that rabbis throughout the ages have debated central matters of faith.[2] He observed that the system of aggadah is not nearly as refined or developed as that of halakhah.[3] Additionally, the rabbis often cloaked deep truths in deceptively simple or allegorical language. As a result, their statements are not readily understood and are subject to different interpretations. Particularly with kabbalistic sources, Rabbi Halevy noted that although the deeper mystical truths may elude us, they still have the power to bring us closer to God.[4]

---

[1] See further discussion in the chapter on his Religious and Intellectual Foundations.

[2] See ALR 5:49. In MH 1:40, Rabbi Halevy cited a different midrashic opinion from that normally taught in Jewish schools. He quoted it primarily to teach that there exists another opinion besides the Midrash cited by Rashi.

[3] MH 1:50.

[4] See, for example, ALR 7:30, where Rabbi Halevy emphasized that he did not understand the deeper mystical secrets of what he was discussing, but he did his best to understand their surface meanings. Cf. MKH 1:49, pp. 189–191, where Rabbi Halevy gave an overview of Jewish mysticism, explaining why so few

In light of these factors, Rabbi Halevy generally adopted the following approach: if a questioner appeared to doubt the authority of a traditional teaching, Rabbi Halevy instinctively defended the veracity and authenticity of rabbinic tradition. But if the questioner did not doubt rabbinic tradition, Rabbi Halevy allowed himself freedom to evaluate rabbinic sources with a more critical eye. Moreover, he selectively quoted different sides of rabbinic debates, or framed discussions in several ways, in order to suit his broader educational goals of religious guidance and inspiration of the public.

The Metaphysical Power of Cursing

One questioner explained that he had been cursing an acquaintance who had wronged him. The questioner's friend had warned him that cursing is halakhically forbidden, not to mention that it was a primitive and ineffective superstition. Rabbi Halevy adduced biblical and rabbinic sources, all of which affirmed the metaphysical powers of cursing. He then cited Rambam's ruling, that cursing is prohibited because it promotes the trait of anger.[5] Medieval commentaries such as *Sefer haHinukh* (mitzvah 231) understood Rambam to mean that cursing lacked metaphysical power, and was merely a bad character trait. Rabbi Halevy doubted that Rambam would reject so many explicit talmudic statements affirming the power of cursing. He therefore reinterpreted Rambam's statements to be consistent with the Talmud.[6]

---

people are capable of true mastery of that system. See also his introduction to MZR (p. 17): he composed the index to the Zohar in order to expose those less familiar with kabbalah to essential mystical ideas.

[5] *Sefer haMitzvot, lo ta'aseh* no. 317.

[6] ALR 3:54. In MKH 5:264, p. 237, Rabbi Halevy ruled that one may not curse himself, or others – since that curse will revert to him. He placed these laws in the chapter discussing the prohibition of putting oneself in danger.

The Belief in *Gilgul*

Rabbi Halevy responded to one who challenged his certainty regarding *gilgul* (reincarnation).[7] The questioner cited medieval rabbis who denied the existence of *gilgul*; he criticized Rabbi Halevy for having presented it as a universally accepted Jewish belief.[8] Rabbi Halevy expressed astonishment at the questioner: "I never would have imagined that you would have sharply attacked such an ancient belief rooted in the Zohar and kabbalistic teachings. Because of my love for you, and my knowledge that you are indeed a truly God-fearing person, and because it certainly was a grave error to express this – I take upon myself the great burden to prove to you the root of belief in *gilgul*, and to convince you as much as I am able."[9]

Rabbi Halevy conceded that some medieval thinkers in fact did deny *gilgul*. He asserted, though, that the dissenting position was well in the minority, and that much of the non-Jewish world joined most Jewish thinkers in affirming *gilgul*. In order to persuade the questioner, Rabbi Halevy cited the opinions of several non-Jewish thinkers before moving to traditional Jewish sources. Because of the widespread consensus on this belief, Rabbi Halevy had felt justified in treating *gilgul* as a commonly held position in his original responsum. He had ignored the dissenting opinions because they would only detract from the faith he was trying to promote.

Rabbi Halevy upheld the mainstream talmudic and kabbalistic views regarding both cursing and *gilgul*. In the case of cursing, he reacted to the questioner's suggestion that a rabbinic teaching was primitive and superstitious; consequently, Rabbi Halevy stressed the truth of the rabbinic teaching, even arguing that Rambam shared the rabbinic belief in the efficacy of curses. In the instance of *gilgul*, however, Rabbi Halevy did not attempt to deny or play down intra-rabbinic dissent. Instead, he attempted to demonstrate that the overwhelming majority of Jewish thinkers accepted the belief. In both cases, Rabbi Halevy's selective quotation of

---

[7] ALR 4:67.
[8] ALR 3:35.
[9] ALR 4:67, p. 333.

sources was appropriate for promoting what he regarded as important beliefs.

Similarly, Rabbi Halevy employed selective quotation in halakhic rulings in order to preempt dissenting opinions that he considered unacceptable. For example, Rabbi Halevy published a correspondence with Rabbi Shlomo Tal, then head of the Makhon Gold Seminary for Women.[10] Rabbi Halevy had ruled that married tourists visiting Israel for the religious festivals and who intended to return to the Diaspora after the holidays, must observe two days of Yom Tov while in Israel. Unmarried visitors from the Diaspora may observe only one day of Yom Tov. He stated unequivocally, "nobody ever has challenged this ruling."[11]

Rabbi Tal cited several *poskim* who ruled that visitors to Israel may observe one day of Yom Tov while in Israel. He therefore questioned Rabbi Halevy's assertion that *nobody* had challenged the decision. Rabbi Halevy responded that he was fully aware of the dissenting opinions, but believed them to be fundamentally mistaken halakhically. He chose to allude to them in his footnotes (rather than quoting them outright), since he did not want his readers to cite that minority opinion to justify acting leniently. Similar to his aforementioned discussions of cursing and *gilgul*, Rabbi Halevy's response here again illustrates a desire to play down dissent when there was a clear educational purpose in doing so.

Animal Sacrifice in the Messianic Age

Rabbi Halevy addressed a question challenging the appropriateness of animal sacrifice in the messianic era, since the practice seemed to the questioner to be a primitive ritual of antiquity. Rabbi Halevy censured the questioner's attitude, pointing out that the Torah is eternal and that none of its laws are primitive: "I will permit myself to express severe astonishment towards you, insofar as you are a believing Jew. How could it have entered your heart, that a specific detail of the Torah could have been relevant in an earlier period, but not in a later period? Is it possible for one

---

[10] MKH *Livnot Yisrael* 25, pp. 98–102.
[11] MKH 4:198, pp. 164–165.

who believes that God gave the Torah to His nation Israel to say this? Is your perception of God as one who 'sees until the last generation'? Think carefully about what you are saying and it will become obvious how great your error is."[12]

Rabbi Halevy noted that we pray for the return of animal sacrifice in the *musaf* prayer: "May it be Your will that You should bring us joyously to our land, and there we will bring offerings before You – the *temidim* according to their order, and *musafim* according to the law." To doubt their return in the future was to be deceitful in prayer.[13] Rabbi Halevy proceeded to give an exposition on the significance of animal sacrifice. In addressing one who doubted a traditional belief, Rabbi Halevy sided strongly and unambiguously with tradition, affirming the return of animal sacrifice.

But in a later discussion, when he was not responding to one expressing such doubts, Rabbi Halevy suggested that animal sacrifice generally would be eliminated in the messianic age, in favor of meal offerings. Since people will not sin in the messianic age, animal sacrifice will become obsolete.[14] He adopted this position, despite the fact that the Torah prescribed many voluntary animal offerings, and festival offerings as well! Animal sacrifice was by no means limited to sin and guilt offerings. Rabbi Halevy recognized the originality of his interpretation, noting that "I am aware that no earlier interpreter explained [the matter] this way, nor did our Sages, but this is what my heart tells me."[15]

When someone asked a follow up question on the latter responsum, though, Rabbi Halevy returned to a more conventional

---

[12] ALR 1:16, p. 53.

[13] ALR 1:16; cf. DM, pp. 118–122; MKH 3:131, pp. 170–173.

[14] ALR 9:36. Cf. ALR 8:45, where Rabbi Halevy contended that in the period of the final redemption, Yom Kippur will become a purely joyous celebration, since there will be no more sin.

[15] ALR 9:36, p. 121. In a footnote there, Rabbi Halevy noted with satisfaction that Ahiyah Amitai subsequently had showed him that Rabbi Avraham Yitzhak Kook had adopted a similar position regarding animal sacrifice in the future.

approach.[16] Elsewhere, Rabbi Halevy quoted Midrashim saying that in messianic days, we will have only (animal) thanksgiving offerings, since there will be no need for sin offerings.[17]

What *was* Rabbi Halevy's final position on animal sacrifice in the messianic age? It is difficult to determine his definitive stance in light of conflicting statements in his writings. Clear, however, is his methodological distinction between addressing people who expressed doubt,[18] and his abstract discussions.[19]

Regardless of Rabbi Halevy's philosophical position on sacrifices in messianic times, he insisted that they should not be instituted before that time. When asked if the Passover sacrifice could be reinstated today even without a Temple in Jerusalem, Rabbi Halevy quoted Rabbi Yehiel of Paris and *Hatam Sofer*, who maintained that it would be acceptable to bring the Passover sacrifice even without the Temple. But he then cited Rabbi Hayyim Yosef David Azulai's criticism of that position: since all contemporary Jews have the status of being ritually impure, they are unfit to bring sacrifices. Moreover, the exact site of the altar in the ancient Temple is not known. Apart from these technical halakhic objections, kabbalistic sources indicated that it would be inappropriate to bring sacrifices without some revelation of the *Shekhinah* (God's Presence).[20] In his responsum, Rabbi Halevy addressed current political realities and kept animal sacrifice in the realm of the theoretical until the full messianic redemption.

Do Accidents Happen?

Rabbi Halevy offered theological explanations of recent historical events, including the Holocaust and the founding of the State of Israel. He

---

[16] MH 1:2.

[17] MKH 1:46, p. 168.

[18] ALR 1:16; MH 1:2.

[19] ALR 9:36; MKH 1:46.

[20] MH 2:1; cf. MKH 3:131, pp. 170–173; ALR 1:16.

admitted that we could never ascertain how God's plans operated; but it was religiously appropriate to learn from historical events.

When encouraging Diaspora Jewry to make aliyah, Rabbi Halevy emphasized that the Holocaust may have come as a result of punishment for sins.[21] Likewise, he suggested that sin may have been responsible for the tragedy of the Yom Kippur War: "We should begin with the basic assumption that there is no suffering without sin (*Shabbat* 55a)."[22]

But in other responsa, Rabbi Halevy took a different approach. When a bus of schoolchildren from Petah Tikvah fatally crashed, some rabbis had proclaimed that this tragedy was a punishment for violations of the laws of *mezuzah*, or Shabbat. Rabbi Halevy sharply rejected this view, maintaining that when there are rational explanations of tragedies, they can be deemed as accidents rather than as Divine punishments.[23] In a follow-up responsum, Rabbi Halevy censured those rabbis who maintained that the Petah Tikvah bus crash was the result of sins. They had adduced various rabbinic teachings and then extrapolated theological conclusions to interpret the bus accident. Rabbi Halevy accused them of intellectual arrogance: "How obvious is their error! We are not permitted to add anything to the words of our talmudic Sages. All of their words are divinely inspired; they said what they said, and no more."[24]

Rabbi Halevy distinguished between the fate of the nation of Israel and that of individuals. In the former, Divine Providence for the nation affected everyone, whether or not they had contributed to the collective fate of the people. But suffering individuals may attribute their afflictions

---

[21] DM, pp. 12–14; ALR 4:6. In ALR 2:19, Rabbi Halevy stressed that national punishment comes through God's hiding His presence (*hester panim*) and letting nature take its course.

[22] ALR 1:7–12, p. 35.

[23] ALR 7:69. In a related responsum (ALR 7: short answers 78), Rabbi Halevy made the same point regarding soldiers killed in battle. Cf. MKH 4:232, pp. 347–351, where Rabbi Halevy argued that the Purim story also did not happen because of any sin – there existed a rational explanation for Haman's persecutions. See further discussion in the chapter on Questions of Faith.

[24] ALR 8:93, p. 295.

to natural causes. The view that all tragedies are preordained punishments is that of Arab fatalism, "but this is not the thought of our holy Torah."[25]

However, Rabbi Halevy conceded that there was indeed another rabbinic opinion that *did* approach the view he was trying to reject. Rashi (*Devarim* 22:8) accepted the more fatalistic interpretation of an individual's destiny. Rabbi Halevy cited Rashi's opinion, only to remark that "this position is not universally accepted."[26] He went on to cite several other sources that rejected that line of thinking.

Rabbi Halevy was aware of both sides of the talmudic debate regarding accidents (Shabbat 55a). He selectively quoted opinions, depending on his agenda for each case. To promote aliyah and faith after the Holocaust or the Yom Kippur War, it was appropriate to suggest Divine causation. To avoid the desecration of God's Name, though, Rabbi Halevy cited the other talmudic opinion that recognized accidents separate from the category of punishment. In effect, he distinguished between the fate of the community and the fate of individuals. Significantly, however, he consistently maintained that we could not truly know how God operated in history. His radically different starting points reveal educational agendas beyond simple source analysis or categorically held philosophical positions.

Using Current Scientific Information

Rabbi Halevy was asked if we should make a blessing on solar eclipses today, since we now consider them to be natural phenomena.[27] The Sages

---

[25] ALR 7:69, p. 285. In ALR 8:93, Rabbi Halevy illustrated how ludicrous it is to claim that we understand God's ways: around the same time as the Petah Tikvah bus disaster, another bus remarkably was spared certain doom. Many newspapers referred to this salvation as "miraculous." But Rabbi Halevy noted that the saved bus was driving on Shabbat, whereas the Petah Tikvah bus was filled with schoolchildren, driving during the week, carrying their *tefillin* with them to celebrate a bar mitzvah of one of their friends. "This should open our eyes to realize clearly, that the ways of Providence are beyond human comprehension" (p. 295).

[26] ALR 7:69, p. 287.

[27] ALR 5:7.

of the Talmud did not institute such a blessing because they considered the solar eclipse a sign of Divine wrath (*Sukkah* 29a). In this instance, Rabbi Halevy did not defend the talmudic belief; he agreed that eclipses were natural phenomena and should elicit a blessing. He recommended that instead of making a full blessing with God's Name, one should say the beginning of "*Vayvarekh David*," biblical verses containing the essentials of the blessing formula.[28] Thus, while conceding that the ancient rabbis had incomplete scientific data, he still was not willing to coin a blessing that the Talmud had not ordained. By advocating a recitation similar to a blessing, he was able to remain faithful to the Talmud as well as to defer to current scientific knowledge.[29]

Rabbi Halevy, however, did not always fully accept current scientific knowledge. In MKH 3:161:p. 291, he uncritically cited Rambam's ruling, that killing bugs created by spontaneous generation is not a punishable offense on Shabbat (generally, one may not take the life of any living creature on Shabbat).[30] When someone challenged this ruling given that we now know that there is no spontaneous generation (and therefore killing these bugs should be prohibited the same as killing any other animal), Rabbi Halevy responded only that this is a difficult issue and that he had no clear answer.[31] From his response, it is evident that Rabbi

---

[28] "Then David blessed the Lord in the sight of all the congregation and said, 'Blessed be You, Lord God of our father Israel for ever and ever. Yours, O Lord, are the greatness, power, glory, victory and majesty, all that is in the heavens and on earth'" (*I Divrei haYamim* 29:10–11). By reading these verses, one is studying Bible (and therefore not taking the Name of God in vain), but also achieves the general formulation of a blessing over a natural wonder.

[29] See also DVM 1, p. 53; ALR 2:1, where Rabbi Halevy emphasized the importance of rabbis following current scientific information. See also ALR 1:61; 5:13; 5:37; 6:44; 8:64; MH 3:24. See further discussion in the chapter on his Religious and Intellectual Foundations.

[30] *Hil. Shabbat* 11:2.

[31] ALR 7:short answers 17; MKH 3:173, p. 372. See further discussion in the chapter on Old Texts, New Realities.

Halevy grappled with his faithfulness to classical texts and modernity, and did not always adopt consistent positions.[32]

The overarching purpose of Rabbi Halevy's writings was to teach Torah, to win people's hearts, and to sanctify God's Name. Depending on the religious agenda of each questioner, he selectively cited sources and opinions that would best further these goals. Fully aware of the diversity of opinion in rabbinic debates, Rabbi Halevy drew on those arguments that were most effective in answering each particular question. In this manner, Rabbi Halevy balanced faithfulness to traditional texts with an ability to handle rabbinic dissent – utilizing the different opinions and noting our inability to know precisely how God works – to bring people closer to God.[33]

---

[32] See also MKH 5:264, p. 235, where Rabbi Halevy uncritically quoted the talmudic ruling that one may not eat fish and meat together, since that combination could cause *tzara'at*. See MH 3:24, for an elaborate discussion of the interrelationship of traditional teachings and contemporary scientific knowledge.

[33] For applications of these principles, see especially the chapters on Jewish Education, Metaphysical Issues, and *At'halta deGe'ulah*.

Chapter Six

OLD TEXTS, NEW REALITIES

One of the most difficult areas of halakhic decision-making relates to questions concerning new situations, where the classic halakhic texts do not provide clear and unequivocal guidance. This challenge faced *poskim* of every generation; they had to relate earlier halakhic sources to the realities of their times.

The modern era has witnessed phenomenal sociological, political and technological changes. Previous generations of sages did not deal with and could not have foreseen various situations that have arisen in our times. To what extent do pre-modern halakhic sources bind the *posek* and to what extent is he obliged to break new halakhic ground based on the changed reality? Since the rabbinic decisor must make rulings based on "what his own eyes see," he cannot ignore the current situation; and yet, neither can he ignore the classic halakhic sources. A consideration of Rabbi Halevy's responsa will help us to understand how he evaluated traditional halakhic texts in light of modern realities.

Rabbi Halevy dealt with a number of questions that reflected a dissonance between certain halakhic texts and contemporary behavior patterns. For example, the *Shulhan Arukh* ruled that men were not permitted to look into mirrors, since this behavior was characteristic of women.[1] Rabbi Halevy noted that a number of later *poskim* had already set this ruling aside, since it had in fact become common for men also to use

---

[1] *Yoreh Deah* 156:2.

mirrors. It was no longer to be considered a purely female activity and so was not forbidden to men. Another halakhic opinion was that men may not use fragrances, since perfumes were used exclusively by women. To this, Rabbi Halevy remarked that it had become common for men to use colognes. Indeed, it was a popular custom in some synagogues to sprinkle fragrances on male worshippers when celebrating with a bar mitzvah or a bridegroom. Thus, the view prohibiting fragrances for men was no longer applicable in the current context.[2]

Rabbi Halevy was asked whether non-Jewish music may be incorporated into the synagogue service. While some halakhic authorities had prohibited this practice, Rabbi Halevy noted that many Middle Eastern hazzanim have borrowed melodies from Arabic songs "and no one protests or raises an objection; so let the Jews be [with this practice]."[3] On another issue, the question was raised whether supplicatory prayers were to be recited during synagogue services if mourners were present. Rabbi Halevy stated that this was a matter of custom "and our eyes see now that in most synagogues, they do not recite supplicatory prayers when a mourner is in attendance, and there is no need to object to this practice."[4]

In the above cases, Rabbi Halevy's rulings were based on his observation of general practice. Although halakhic sources were available that would lead to prohibitive rulings, Rabbi Halevy felt that these sources were offset by permissive arguments, especially in light of actual contemporary practice.

Rabbi Halevy was asked a question by a person who had found a sum of money while riding in a taxi.[5] Since he had found the money in the

---

2 ALR 8:50. Rabbi Halevy did not extend this line of reasoning to men dying their hair. This was forbidden since it was a practice exclusively for women. But he permitted a young unmarried man who had turned gray prematurely to color his hair, in order to enable him to find an appropriate bride. Dying his hair would have the effect of making him appear to be his own actual age. See ALR 2:50.
3 ALR 3:5.
4 ALR 7:12.
5 ALR 2:66.

back seat, and therefore could assume it did not belong to the driver, was he entitled to keep it? Rabbi Halevy pointed out that the halakhah assumed that a person who lost money gave up hope of ever recovering it. Money did not normally have a distinguishing mark, so there was no proof as to its real owner. Thus, the finder was allowed to acquire the money, since it was essentially ownerless, i.e., the one who lost it had given up hope of retrieving it and had no way to prove it was his anyway.

But, stated Rabbi Halevy, contemporary conditions have changed. We now have a system of lost-and-found. Anyone who found something of value, including money, was expected to bring it to the police, giving the exact circumstances in which he found it. Then, a person who lost something can go to the police and make a claim by indicating the exact details of the lost article or money, the date and time of the loss, the place he lost it, etc. Thus, a person who had lost a large sum of money in a taxi would not immediately give up hope of recovering it. He would report his loss to the lost-and-found department of the police and hope that an honest person might turn it in. If no one claimed the money after a certain period of time, only then would the police give it to the one who had found it. Rabbi Halevy ruled, then, that if one had found a small amount of money in a taxi, he could keep it. It was reasonable to assume that the owner had given up hope of ever getting it back. But if he had found a sum that an owner might still have hopes of recovering, then he was obligated to turn it in to the nearest police station and fulfill the commandment of returning lost objects. Changed circumstances, then, affected the halakhic ruling.

The Changing Status of Women

One of the significant areas of sociological change during the past several generations has related to the role of women in society. Rabbi Halevy was certainly unhappy about various aspects of this social revolution. He stressed that women's true honor was in the home; that "mixed" events, where men and women sat together, were generally forbidden by halakhah;

that the virtues of modesty and quiet piety were the proper characteristics that women should cultivate.[6]

Yet, he also realized that the changed role of women in society had halakhic ramifications. For example, the *Shulhan Arukh* ruled that it was forbidden for a man to walk behind a woman. If a man happened to find himself in such a situation, he was to rush to the side of the road so as to escape walking behind a woman.[7] Rabbi Halevy asserted that this law was intended for those times when women generally stayed home and were not often found walking in public. But in our times, the public thoroughfares were frequented by many women. If a man would run away every time he found a woman in front of him people would think he was a fool. In his seeming piety, he would actually be causing religion to be subjected to ridicule. Therefore, Rabbi Halevy stated that a man who found himself walking behind a woman should simply try to keep his eyes from looking at her. He should not follow the *Shulhan Arukh*'s ruling to rush to the side of the road.[8]

Rabbi Halevy was asked about the halakhic permissibility of a husband staying with his wife during labor and childbirth.[9] While expressing opposition to this practice, Rabbi Halevy also took into consideration the modern situation. A number of studies had been published indicating that a husband's presence during childbirth was very helpful to his wife. Since hospitals could not assign a nurse to stay with each woman throughout her time of labor, the husband's presence would relieve her of loneliness, fear and suffering. The notion had arisen that it would be best for a woman if her husband were to stay with her during her labor and when she gave birth. "As far as these women are concerned, the presence of the husband has become almost a necessity, and it seems to me to approach *pikuah nefesh* (a life-threatening situation)." Rabbi Halevy

---

[6] See for example, ALR 3:40; 4:56; 5:97; 6:71; 7: short answers 61; MH 1:70; 2:71; 2:72; 3:5.

[7] *Even haEzer* 21:61.

[8] MH 2:45.

[9] ALR 4:58.

permitted a husband to remain with his wife during labor and childbirth if she insisted on his presence. He should do his best to maintain the rules of modesty.[10]

On another topic, Rabbi Halevy discussed the question of whether women were permitted to study the Oral Law.[11] The Mishnah in *Sotah* (20a) quotes Rabbi Eliezer's strong opposition to fathers teaching Torah to their daughters. Rambam (*Hil. Talmud Torah* 1:13) codified this idea by stating that our sages have commanded us not to teach our daughters the Oral Torah, claiming that most women's minds are not inclined to be educated in such a manner; due to their poor understanding they would not comprehend the real meaning of what was being conveyed to them. However, women could be instructed in the Written Torah and those laws that they needed to know for their own religious observance, e.g., Shabbat, *kashrut*, *mikveh*, etc.

These classic texts are fairly clear that women may not be taught the Oral Torah. Following these texts, a leading twentieth-century *posek*, Rabbi Moshe Feinstein, ruled that girls should not be taught Mishnah. He did allow, though, that girls could study Pirkei Avot, which is devoted to ethical conduct and proper behavior.[12]

Rabbi Halevy carefully analyzed the issue of women studying the Oral Torah. He noted that a number of women throughout the generations had, in fact, excelled in such study. While it could be posited that these women studied on their own and were not taught by their fathers, yet this supposition itself begs the question. Why was the halakhah recorded as a prohibition for fathers to teach the Oral Torah to their daughters, rather than as a blanket prohibition for women to study it? Rabbi Halevy observed that Rambam had stated that the prohibition

---

[10] See Rabbi Moshe Feinstein, *Iggrot Moshe, Yoreh Deah* 2:75. Rabbi Feinstein prohibited a husband's presence at childbirth. Rabbi Halevy, though, permitted it in those cases where a woman strongly felt that she needed her husband to be with her.

[11] ALR 2:52.

[12] *Iggrot Moshe, Yoreh Deah* 3:87.

stemmed from the fact that the "majority" of women were not disposed to such education; but this assumed that some women (i.e., those not part of the majority) were capable of serious Torah study.

Rabbi Halevy then asserted that if a particular woman were known to be intellectually capable of studying the Oral Torah, then she was obviously not part of the "majority" mentioned by Rambam. It would be permitted to teach such a woman the Oral Torah.

Carrying this reasoning further, Rabbi Halevy wrote that a father should not teach his very young daughters the Oral Torah, since he did not yet know their intellectual aptitude. But once they grew older and demonstrated the desire and capacity to study the Oral Torah, then it was permissible to teach them. He added the observation that many women today received advanced education in various fields. If they can excel academically in so many other areas, why should it be assumed that they cannot do well in studying Talmud?

Rabbi Halevy suggested that in earlier times, girls received no formal education at all; thus, to teach them Talmud certainly would have been beyond their ken. After all, they lacked the rudimentary intellectual training required for proper analysis of Talmud. But today, women received serious education. Why should they be able to study so many subjects, but be restricted from studying Talmud? Rabbi Halevy concluded that it was permissible to teach Talmud to female students in high school – since by then they will have attained a good general education and will have demonstrated a serious interest in and capacity for Talmud study.

Rabbi Halevy stressed that his "innovation" was rooted in the halakhah itself, and was not at all a deviation from halakhah.[13] What he did was to offer a reasonable interpretation of the classic texts. He did not, after all, suggest that all women may study the Oral Torah, but only those who had demonstrated that they were not part of the "majority" of women referred to by Rambam.

---

13 MH 2:89.

While one might appreciate Rabbi Halevy's apologia, it still seems fair to say that he did in fact issue a new ruling based on new circumstances. To be sure, his ruling was grounded in an interpretation of the words of Rambam. But his very interpretation was based on his awareness that a change had occurred in the education of women. Whereas in olden times, most Jewish women received little or no formal education, today almost all of them do. This changed reality motivated Rabbi Halevy to seek his "innovation," finding a way within halakhah to allow women to study Oral Torah. Other rabbinic decisors did not feel the motivation to seek an "innovation" on this topic; rather, they have clung faithfully to the plain understanding of the halakhic texts that forbade teaching Oral Torah to women.

Rabbi Halevy received a question from a religious woman who had wanted to run for office in a local Israeli election on the slate of a religious party. Members of another religious party raised objections, claiming that it was not appropriate for a woman to serve as a representative of a religious party. In light of the objections and in order to avoid controversy, she withdrew her candidacy. But she was unhappy about this and turned to Rabbi Halevy for guidance. She asked him for *da'at halakhah* – the authoritative halakhic understanding – on whether women could hold positions of communal leadership.

Rabbi Halevy began his response by stating that he never would be so presumptuous as to claim that he was giving *the da'at halakhah* on any public issue. Since halakhah had room for various legitimate points of view, it would be arrogant for any rabbi to claim that he had the unequivocal truth on any controversial matter. "Rather, each *posek* may express his opinion according to halakhah as it appears to him, as long as he substantiates his words with convincing proofs; and let each person choose [which *posek* to follow]."[14]

After examining halakhic sources relating to women holding positions of leadership, Rabbi Halevy concluded that women may indeed

---

[14] MH 1:70.

vote and be elected to office. If the public elected women to office, this was a clear demonstration that they had agreed to accept women's leadership.

But when it came to women being elected to serve on religious councils, Rabbi Halevy offered a sociological – not strictly halakhic – objection. Traditionally, the religious councils had been run entirely by men, including those who would feel uncomfortable having to deliberate with women. If women were to enter the religious councils, then a number of men would withdraw from running or serving. This would cause a serious disruption in the work of religious councils. So even though women had the halakhic right to be elected to such councils, Rabbi Halevy suggested that they avoid pressing this right. Their victory would be costly, in that the councils would very likely disintegrate and lose their power. Rabbi Halevy thought that women would be better served in choosing more important areas for advancing their rights. "It would be appropriate for them rather to invest energy in their struggle for partnership in the economic life of our society, which consistently discriminates against women." Since the Chief Rabbinate of Israel had expressed the opinion that women should not serve on religious councils, Rabbi Halevy thought that religiously sensitive women should heed this directive.

For Rabbi Halevy, then, having a halakhic justification for something did not necessarily mean it must be implemented. While one might agree or disagree with his conclusion regarding women serving on religious councils, his methodology is cogent. A halakhist had to consider not merely the narrow legal arguments of a case, but also the sociological framework in which the halakhic decision was to be applied.

Rabbi Halevy answered other questions relating to the changing status of women in society. He ruled that one should make the *shehehiyanu* blessing on the occasion of the birth of a daughter, since this was a special occasion of great happiness.[15] Although earlier *poskim* generally did not record this view, this may have been because in past times the birth of a

---

[15] MH 3:8.

boy was preferred; the birth of a girl was seen, at least in some sense, as a disappointment – so no blessing of thanksgiving was offered. Today, the situation has changed, so that the birth of a girl is greeted with happiness and enthusiasm.

A question was asked whether a married woman, who did not normally keep her head covered, should be trusted fully in matters of *kashrut*.[16] Rabbi Halevy, who strongly urged married women to keep their hair covered, noted that in our times many women did not understand the importance of hair covering; yet they were quite careful in matters of *kashrut*. Therefore, they should be trusted in *kashrut*, unless there were specific indications casting doubt on their trustworthiness in matters of *kashrut*. Their lack of hair covering did not, in itself, undermine their credibility as religious women.

Rabbi Halevy was asked about the permissibility of women's prayer groups.[17] He was not favorably disposed, arguing that "our religiously proper mothers would never have considered such a thing." He viewed women's prayer groups as being unfaithful to the holy traditions of Israel. When asked whether women may participate in the recitation of the seven wedding blessings, Rabbi Halevy responded that this constituted a breach of modesty and should not be condoned.[18] In these cases, then, he felt that traditional halakhic norms should not be set aside due to changes in the sociological factors relating to the status of women in society.

As a general rule, Rabbi Halevy was not afraid to break new halakhic ground when changed circumstances required a re-evaluation of earlier halakhic texts. But he was reluctant to grant halakhic permission to activities that compromised the halakhic norms of public modesty. Rabbi

---

[16] ALR 4:49.

[17] MH 3:5.

[18] ALR 5:97. See also ALR 7: short answers 60. For other responsa relating to the role of women in halakhah, see ALR 1:63; 3:24; 5:32, 33; MH 1:10; 1:28; 1:69. See MKH *Livnot Yisrael*, p. 44, where he expressed general displeasure about the innovation of bat mitzvah ceremonies (he wasn't happy with many bar mitzvah ceremonies either); he saw nothing wrong, though, in a family celebration in honor of a bat mitzvah.

Halevy, like every *posek*, had to balance competing claims of tradition and modernity, ancient texts and new realities.

The Halakhic Status of Non-Observant Jews

The Talmud (*Hullin* 5a) stated that "one who desecrates Shabbat in public is as an idol worshipper." A number of *halakhot* flowed from this notion. A *mehallel Shabbat*, one who willfully transgressed Shabbat laws, was considered to be a *rasha* (a wicked person) and therefore was disqualified as a witness. Some *poskim* have ruled that he may not be counted in a *minyan* nor be called to read from the Torah. Some even thought that wine touched by such an individual became ritually impure and may not be drunk, just as if it had been touched by an idolater.

The strictures against a Shabbat desecrator reflect the great sanctity of Shabbat. One who brazenly scorned this sanctity was obviously a religiously wicked person. He was openly separating himself from the religion of Israel and therefore deserved to be sanctioned as a scoffer of Torah, akin to an idolater.

During the nineteenth century, though, large numbers of Jews began to abandon traditional halakhah. Influenced by the movements of enlightenment and emancipation, they sought to become more "modern." Yet, many still considered themselves to be loyal members of the Jewish people. They did not see their violation of Shabbat laws as a rejection of their Jewishness, nor did they view themselves as in any way akin to idolaters.

Rabbi David Zvi Hoffmann, a leading nineteenth century German rabbinic authority, was asked whether a *mehallel Shabbat* may be counted in a *minyan*. After listing sources that would forbid this, he added: "In our time it is customary to be lenient in this, even in Hungary and certainly in Germany."[19] He quoted the opinion of the *Binyan Zion haHadashot* (no. 23), that "Shabbat desecrators in our time are considered somewhat like a *tinok shenishbah* [a child captured and raised among non-Jews, who does not

---

[19] *Melammed leHo'il*, no. 29.

know the laws of Torah and hence cannot be held fully responsible for transgressions], since, due to our many sins, the majority of Jews in our country are Shabbat desecrators and it is not their intention to deny the basic tenets of our faith."

Rabbi Hoffmann and other *poskim* of his era recognized that the early halakhic texts simply did not correspond to the contemporary situation. They had to make halakhic rulings based on what their own eyes saw – not merely on what the classic texts stated.

Rabbi Halevy, too, had to confront questions relating to non-observant Jews. He was asked, for example, about a small synagogue that had a *minyan* only if Shabbat desecrators were counted in.[20] Should the synagogue continue to operate on this basis or should it close due to a lack of a halakhically proper *minyan*? While fully aware of the problem of counting Shabbat desecrators into a *minyan*, Rabbi Halevy asserted: "It is incumbent upon us to find a way of being lenient." He did not want a synagogue to shut down due to this halakhic technicality, so he offered the following analysis: "A *mehallel Shabbat* in public who is disqualified from being counted into a *minyan* of ten – this refers to those early days when they understood and valued the seriousness of the prohibitions [of Shabbat]; and, moreover, nearly everyone was scrupulous in observing Shabbat according to the law, so that one who 'breached the fence' was disqualified. But this is not true in our time. Our eyes see a multitude of Shabbat desecrators, and the overwhelming majority do not understand and do not realize the seriousness of the prohibitions. Behold: they come to the synagogue and pray and read in the Torah…and afterwards they desecrate the Shabbat! Perhaps such as these are as a *tinok shenishbah*."

In another responsum, he dealt with the question of whether a bar mitzvah boy and members of his family may be called to the Torah on Shabbat, if they had come to synagogue in a car.[21] Rabbi Halevy quoted his own halakhic codification, *Mekor Hayyim* (3:122:20), where he wrote that even though it was technically forbidden to call a Shabbat desecrator to the

---

[20] ALR 5:1.
[21] ALR 3:16.

Torah, yet "if there is a fear that this will cause ill feelings, then such people should be called to the Torah as extras since in our generation, an orphan generation, it is proper to be lenient in such circumstances. It is our obligation to bring them closer and not to push them further away, and God in His goodness will have mercy on us."

In dealing with the question of whether wine touched by a Shabbat desecrator became forbidden (as in the case if an idolater touched wine), Rabbi Halevy indicated that recent generations of rabbis have tried to rule leniently. Thus, if the Shabbat violator touched an open bottle of wine, the wine was not deemed to be prohibited. But if actual contact with the wine itself took place, then the wine may be given to Jews who are themselves desecrators of Shabbat.[22]

Rabbi Halevy thought, like Rabbi David Zvi Hoffmann before him, that the early halakhic texts referred to individuals for whom desecration of Shabbat in fact represented a repudiation of Judaism in general. Today, most Shabbat desecrators were not willful sinners, just careless, ignorant or misled individuals.[23]

Scientific and Technological Advances

A *posek* needed to be familiar with current scientific and technological knowledge when that information was directly related to questions of halakhah. Sometimes, earlier halakhic practice was based on scientific notions now proven to be incorrect.

A question was asked to Rabbi Halevy: our sages had prescribed specific blessings for remarkable events in nature; why did they not establish a blessing for eclipses?[24] Rabbi Halevy explained that blessings had been established for those natural phenomena that reminded us specifically of God's acts of creation. In antiquity, it was believed that eclipses were signals of God's wrath and were not part of the original natural system at the time of creation. God utilized eclipses as warnings to

---

[22] ALR 5:20.
[23] ALR 8:32–35.
[24] ALR 5:7.

the people on an ad hoc basis. Therefore, the rabbis did not institute a blessing over eclipses.

But now, of course, we have better scientific information. We know that eclipses are natural phenomena built into the laws of nature. They are as much part of the acts of creation as thunder and lightning and other phenomena over which blessings are recited.

Rabbi Halevy's line of thought led to the conclusion that indeed a blessing should be recited upon witnessing an eclipse. He was reluctant to go that far, since he did not feel it was proper for any individual to establish a new blessing not already sanctioned by our Sages. So he faced a dilemma. On the one hand, the ancient Sages had not instituted a blessing over an eclipse; but on the other hand, they had based their exclusion on incorrect scientific data.

Rabbi Halevy reached a middle position. Yes, a blessing should be recited; but, no, it could not be in the form of the standard blessings established by our sages. He suggested that one recite the verses of *Vayvarekh David* (*Divrei haYamim* 29:10–11) followed by the words *oseh ma'asei bereishit* (who performs acts of creation). This formula, in effect, had the qualities of a standard blessing – God's name and kingship; but it was not the formal blessing the sages had prescribed for those who witnessed natural phenomena. While not establishing a new blessing, Rabbi Halevy suggested a suitable way of blessing God for a natural phenomenon that our ancient sages did not fully understand.

New scientific knowledge also played an important role in Rabbi Halevy's ruling that cigarette smoking was forbidden by Torah law.[25] His basic argument was that smoking had been proven to be dangerous to one's health. The Torah commanded that we protect our lives and avoid unnecessary risks to our health. Why, then, was cigarette smoking not forbidden by the rabbis of previous generations? And why did a number of Torah scholars continue to smoke cigarettes?

---

[25] ALR 2:1.

Rabbi Halevy answered: in earlier generations, the rabbis were not aware of the health dangers of smoking. But with the advance of research, we now knew much more about the hazards of smoking. Contemporaries who smoked were guilty of ignoring the scientific evidence linking cigarette smoking to a variety of diseases and health problems.

Rabbi Moshe Feinstein, an older contemporary of Rabbi Halevy, attempted to justify cigarette smoking by arguing that "the Lord protects the simple." Certainly, one should take into consideration the health risks. Yet Torah luminaries of the past and present generations have themselves smoked cigarettes; they would not have done so if halakhah had forbidden smoking.[26]

Rabbi Halevy rejected this reasoning. Halakhah was not to be determined on the basis of actions of people who were unaware of the dangers of smoking, or who ignored current medical evidence. It was inappropriate to give halakhic sanction to a dangerous activity. Rabbi Halevy argued that new information in scientific and medical research must be incorporated into halakhic decision-making.[27]

On another topic, Rabbi Halevy ruled on the status of raw unsalted meat that had not been washed or soaked for three consecutive days. According to the established halakhah, such meat can no longer be salted to be *kasher* for eating. Rather, it must be roasted in order to remove the blood from within it. The halakhah assumed that if raw meat were soaked or washed during the three-day interval, it remained fresh; the blood within it did not congeal and can therefore be removed by salting. However, after the lapse of three days without washing or soaking, it was assumed that the meat will have dried out, and the blood within it will have congealed; it could no longer be kashered by salting.

In modern times, we have use of freezers. If raw unsalted meat were placed into a freezer and remained there three days or longer, could it

---

[26] *Iggrot Moshe, Yoreh Deah* 2:49; see also *Iggrot Moshe, Hoshen Mishpat* 2:76.

[27] For other of Rabbi Halevy's responsa relating to smoking, see ALR 3:18; 3:25; 6:58; the end pages of volume six; and 9:29. See also ALR 5:47, where he discusses health and halakhic issues relating to vegetarianism.

be salted after being defrosted; or could it only be roasted to purge it of its blood? According to the formal halakhic procedure, any unsalted meat that went three days without soaking or washing must be roasted. Salting was not adequate. Yet, the new technology, i.e., freezers, created a situation where the meat stayed "fresh" for longer than three days.

Rabbi Halevy ruled that unsalted meat that had been placed into a freezer may be defrosted and salted even after three days. "Our eyes see that its blood does not congeal inside it." It was pointless to insist on the previous halakhic practice, since the earlier halakhic codifiers did not have freezers as an option. Now that freezers did maintain the freshness of meat for three days and beyond, meat taken from the freezer and defrosted could then be kashered by salting and did not require roasting.[28]

Rabbi Halevy recorded the halakhah that one was not allowed to do laundry on Friday since this would interrupt preparations for Shabbat. This ruling made sense in the days before automatic washing machines, when doing laundry was a labor-intensive and time-consuming task. But now that we had washing machines, did the prohibition of doing laundry on Friday still apply? Rabbi Halevy gave a guarded answer: "To those who have automatic washing machines so that doing laundry does not trouble their preparations for Shabbat, it seems to me that they may do laundry even on Friday; although it is not appropriate to do so in the first place (*lekhat'hilah*)."[29] Intellectually, he believed that the activity was now permitted; but emotionally, he was not comfortable giving blanket permission to set aside the original halakhic practice.

Rabbi Halevy was asked a question relating to the destruction of non-fruit-bearing trees. Rambam seemed to rule that it was permissible to destroy such trees, even when there was no urgent need to do so. Apparently, he assumed that these trees had no value. Yet, modern research has shown that trees, even non-fruit-bearing ones, are important

---

[28] MKH 5:261, pp. 214–215. See also MH 1:49; 2:48.
[29] MKH 3:108, p. 40.

to the environment. Should the halakhah, as recorded by Rambam, be reformulated?[30]

Rabbi Halevy began his discussion by stressing the immutability of halakhah. If scientific information appeared to conflict with a particular halakhah, then the *posek* should try to resolve the seeming conflict. "And if we cannot find an explanation, we will decide that our intelligence is too weak to understand." He went on to demonstrate that Rambam did not, in fact, permit the wanton destruction of any trees, and that his halakhic ruling was consonant with current ecological knowledge.

The above responsum points to a struggle within Rabbi Halevy about the relationship between halakhah and new scientific knowledge. On the one hand, as we have seen, he was quite ready to incorporate scientific findings in his halakhic decisions. He restated certain *halakhot* to be in conformity with the best available knowledge. On the other hand, he was reluctant to admit openly that modern scientific evidence might offset earlier halakhic rulings. In the case of the non-fruit-bearing trees, he found a way of reconciling Rambam's position with current ecological insights. That was a way of sidestepping a potential dilemma.

In another case, though, he did not reconcile the discrepancy between a halakhic text and scientific knowledge.[31] He ruled that it was permissible to kill lice on Shabbat, based on the Talmud's mistaken notion that lice reproduced by spontaneous generation. Even though he knew that modern science had disproved the ancient rabbinic notion, he still adhered to the rabbinic ruling. Although he was troubled by the problem,[32] he remained faithful to the traditional ruling.

Rabbi Halevy was willing and able to apply new scientific knowledge to the halakhah, when he felt that halakhic practice depended on correct scientific information, e.g., prohibiting smoking, allowing salting of meat that had been in the freezer three days or longer. At the same time, he was reluctant to deviate from authoritative halakhic texts

---

30 ALR 2:65.

31 MKH 3:161, p. 291.

32 As is evidenced in ALR 7: short answers 17.

when the halakhah could be reconciled with new scientific information or when a traditional prohibition caused little inconvenience.[33]

The State of Israel

With the rise of the State of Israel in 1948, nearly nineteen hundred years of Jewish statelessness came to an end. During that long period of exile, Jews never lost hope for their return to the land of Israel and to the holy city of Jerusalem.[34]

The rise of the Jewish State was, of course, a major landmark in Jewish history. The transition from centuries of exile to a period of Jewish statehood entailed drastic demographic and psychological changes for the Jewish people. As the State of Israel grew in numbers and strength, and especially after the Six Day War of June 1967, the Jews of the world gradually gained confidence in its permanence.

The halakhah had to take into consideration the new reality of a sovereign Jewish state.[35] One issue related to the liturgy of the Fast of the Ninth of *Av*. The afternoon service of that solemn day of national mourning included the *nahem* prayer, which referred to Jerusalem as "the destroyed, humiliated and desolate city without her children."

Rabbi Halevy felt that, in light of the reunification of Jerusalem in the Six Day War, this passage should no longer be recited. The words were simply not true. Jerusalem was not desolate, humiliated, nor empty of her children. Jerusalem was a thriving city under Jewish rule, with hundreds of thousands of Jews living and visiting there. In Rabbi Halevy's view, the recitation of the traditional *nahem* prayer would constitute lying before God, denying the new vibrancy evident in Jerusalem.

---

[33] For other responsa dealing with halakhah and changing realities, see ALR 6: short answers 71; 7:42; MH 3:17; 3:45. For his loyalty to rabbinic teachings even in the face of scientific knowledge, see also MKH 3:173, p. 372; MH 3:24.

[34] Rabbi Halevy's approach to Israel and Zionism will be discussed at length in the chapter on *At'halta deGe'ulah*. The examples cited here relate specifically to the issue of how halakhah confronts a new reality.

[35] The chapter on Governing the Jewish State will deal with Rabbi Halevy's views on how halakhah can operate in a modern, democratic Jewish state.

He recommended the emendation of the text to refer to Jerusalem as the city that *was* destroyed, humiliated and desolate without her children.[36] As a further acknowledgement of the changed realities, Rabbi Halevy suggested that the number of elegies chanted on the Fast of the Ninth of *Av* should be reduced. This was in recognition of the fact that we were now living at a time when the flowering of our redemption had begun.[37]

Rabbi Halevy had received a letter from an individual who justified Jewish families living in the Diaspora, because religious education for youth was not adequate in Israel. In proof of his contention, he cited a medieval responsum, *Terumat haDeshen* 2:88, in which that author wrote that he had heard that conditions in the holy land were difficult for religious Jews.

Rabbi Halevy stated that the words of *Terumat haDeshen* may have been true when they were written – in the middle ages; but they were certainly not true any longer. Rabbi Halevy was astonished with those who cited a medieval responsum to bolster their rationalization for living in the Diaspora. It was patently clear that the land of Israel in our times had become a bastion of Torah study, where religious families thrive. There was no place in the world where Torah can be taught, studied and observed better than in Israel. The facts of modern Israeli life proved the irrelevancy of the medieval responsum to current realities.[38]

The issue of evaluating the relevance of ancient sources was key to a difference of opinion between Rabbi Halevy and Rabbi Shlomo Goren. In 1985, Israel released 1150 Arab terrorists from prison in exchange for several captured Israeli soldiers. Rabbi Goren argued that this action by the State of Israel violated halakhah; therefore, the decision lacked religious sanction and was incorrect. Rabbi Goren cited halakhic sources

---

[36] ALR 1:14; see also his defense of his position, ALR 2:36–39 and 7: short answers 35. For other responsa dealing with changes in traditional texts due to changed historical circumstances, see ALR 1:18; 8:14; MH 1:9; MKH 1:62, p. 288.

[37] ALR 4:34.

[38] ALR 1:18.

that taught that it was forbidden for Jews to redeem captives above the "market price." This rule was made to protect the Jewish people. If bandits knew that Jews would pay exorbitant prices to redeem their captives, this would provide an incentive to engage in the kidnapping of Jews. If, on the other hand, little profit were to be gained from taking Jewish captives, the bandits would leave Jews alone. Rabbi Goren felt that by releasing so many Arab prisoners for so few Israeli soldiers, the Israeli government had transgressed the halakhah governing the redemption of captives. This behavior, he believed, would encourage Arab enemies to capture Israeli soldiers in the thought that they could extract very high payment from Israel.

In reacting to Rabbi Goren's opinion, Rabbi Halevy began with a premise: halakhah did not have clear and indisputable answers to a variety of new questions that had arisen in our times. Rabbi Halevy asked: where in halakhic literature can one find a situation identical to ours today? Did the Talmud, Codes and responsa deal with the governance of a modern Jewish state and its confrontations with warring and terrorizing enemies? No! "At this time we need halakhic innovation, in the spirit of earlier *halakhot* and in consonance with them; we need a new halakhic decision."[39]

In the case of redemption of captives, Rabbi Halevy cited halakhic sources that allowed for paying above "market price" for captives in certain circumstances, e.g., for children or for rabbinic sages. Moreover, the talmudic sources dealt with cases involving the capture of individual Jews by bandits, not with battles between enemy countries and a Jewish state. A state had different considerations in protecting its soldiers than a community did in ransoming kidnapped individuals. The situations were not analogous.

Rabbi Halevy argued that the State of Israel was justified in ransoming the few Israeli soldiers even at an exorbitant price. This policy was ultimately a positive influence on the morale of Israeli soldiers. They now realized that the government would do anything possible to redeem

---

[39] ALR 7:53.

them if they were captured. Because of this confidence in the government's overwhelming concern for them they would fight with greater courage and daring.

Rabbi Halevy, then, pointed out the inadequacy of halakhic precedents to deal with the actual situation facing the modern State of Israel, when it came to dealing with ransoming soldiers. Rabbi Goren's citation of the earlier sources was not compelling; those sources spoke to a different social and political reality than exists today. It was necessary for *poskim* to break new halakhic ground in those cases where binding halakhic precedents were inadequate or lacking.

On a different issue, in ruling that it was forbidden for women to hitchhike in Israel, because of the specific dangers they faced, Rabbi Halevy suggested why this ruling had not been made by earlier authorities.[40] "In my humble opinion, if this phenomenon [women hitchhiking] had been existent in the days of the Jewish sages of the talmudic period, or even during the period of the great *poskim* or later authorities, we would have found in the *Shulhan Arukh* this halakhic ruling [forbidding] hitchhiking for women. For our earlier rabbis lived and worked in the midst of [actual] life, and the Torah was for them a real living Torah."

For Rabbi Halevy, modern day *poskim* also needed to live and work in the midst of the real world. They had to understand the halakhic texts and contexts. In his own writings, Rabbi Halevy sought to demonstrate that the Torah was indeed a living Torah.

---

[40] ALR 6:71.

Chapter Seven

Jewish Education

One of Rabbi Halevy's foremost concerns was education of youth in the ways of Torah. He emphatically believed that schools had the religious obligation to teach students honestly and correctly, and to inculcate proper religious behavior. At the same time, he emphasized that parents (especially the father) bore the primary obligation of education; schools were created to assist parents. Rabbi Halevy supported secular study, and advocated teaching Torah, including the Oral Law, to girls as well as boys. Rabbi Halevy struck a fine balance between reaching out to people from less observant homes while still preserving the integrity of the religious community. He addressed some delicate educational issues, such as opening the mail of a student suspected of misconduct, reading the diary of a student, and administering corporal punishment in class.

Schools Must Teach Everything Properly

Rabbi Halevy was emphatic and consistent that schools should always teach halakhah fully and correctly, since the imprint made during childhood education was powerful.

He received a question from a school that accepted many students from less observant homes. The teachers wanted to know if they may omit teaching certain *halakhot* that they knew would not be observed by the majority of students. They invoked the rabbinic principle, "it is better that they act in error, than to violate the law willingly." Rabbi Halevy explained that this rule applies only to those who publicly violated a halakhah, and who likely would continue to violate it even if they were instructed properly. When educating children, though, it is the responsibility of every school to teach Judaism correctly and fully. The students need to have a clear and thorough knowledge of halakhah, whether or not they come from observant homes.[1]

A school should not allow prayers requiring a *minyan* in younger classes where no *minyan* was present. It is inappropriate to do anything in school not in accordance with halakhah, even for educational purposes. Rabbi Halevy recommended bringing a *minyan* of post-bar mitzvah students or adults to the class so that younger children could learn to pray properly with a *minyan*.[2]

One educator reported that due to students' talking during the repetition of the *amidah* in morning prayers, he decided that the *amidah* should be read once aloud with *kedushah*.[3] The repetition would thus be omitted. Rabbi Halevy disagreed with this decision. The halakhah does not permit routinely skipping the repetition of the *amidah* in the morning services. It is allowed, though not preferred, to omit the repetition during the afternoon prayer. Rabbi Halevy ruled that the school policy should be for students to recite morning *amidah* properly with repetition. "It is your obligation to educate the students to pay attention to the blessings of the hazzan and to respond 'amen' as per the law; if you do not educate them now to fulfill the halakhah according to its letter and spirit, when will they learn, and who will teach them?"[4] As to the students talking during the repetition, a famous rabbi should be invited to address students on the importance of not talking during prayers.

Similarly, a school should not allow its students to go to recess after lunch before reciting the Grace After Meals. Students may forget the rule of saying the Grace immediately following their meal.[5]

---

[1] ALR 1:75.

[2] ALR 3:7; cf. ALR 6:38.

[3] ALR 4:13.

[4] ALR 4:13, p. 139.

[5] ALR 6: short answers 12; ALR 8:12.

In another instance, a school wanted to teach young children to count the *omer* with a blessing. Yet, the blessing is recited only when counting the *omer* at night. Was it acceptable to let the students recite that blessing in the morning, for the purposes of education? Rabbi Halevy ruled negatively. Since the impressions from childhood education are lasting, students might grow up thinking that it was appropriate to count the *omer* with a blessing in the morning. Rabbi Halevy noted further that the primary obligation of Jewish education falls on the father, not the school. Therefore, *he* should take his children to evening services all year long, and during the *omer* period they would be able to count with a blessing.[6]

Parents' Obligation to Educate Their Children

Although schools bear responsibility to educate children, in fact parents have the foremost obligation in the educational process. Rabbi Halevy assiduously followed this principle in ruling on some difficult issues of educational policy.

A woman reported that her husband did not make an effort to provide religious education to their children.[7] Did this responsibility now devolve on her? Rabbi Halevy criticized the husband's negligence – he should do more. "First, it is my intention to inform your husband of his primary obligation as a father (with the hope that you will show him my response to you). Granted the importance of worrying about supporting a family, [but] this is [an] insufficient [excuse]… What is the point of providing [physical] sustenance for the children, if accompanied by educational negligence?"[8] Although the Talmud (*Nazir* 29a) indicated that a mother is not technically obligated to provide religious instruction to her children, Rashi included both parents in the obligation. Rabbi Halevy pointed out that many *poskim* have ruled that in cases where the father was not alive, the mother became obligated. In the case at hand, the husband

---

[6] ALR 6:38.
[7] ALR 1:41.
[8] ALR 1:41, p. 125.

was effectively non-existent. Even if the mother were technically exempt from this commandment, it obviously was a meritorious deed that she should perform. "There is no doubt that a great mitzvah has fallen into your hands. You should do everything in your power to raise your children in the path of God... May God give you strength and health, and may you receive complete reward from the Lord of Hosts."[9]

It is worthwhile to contrast the tone of this responsum with Rabbi Halevy's ruling in *Mekor Hayyim Livnot Yisrael*.[10] There, he took for granted that women are obligated to partake in the religious education of their children. Although he quoted the dissenting position, he concluded that most *poskim* have ruled that women, as well as men, are obligated to educate their children. He referred to the aforementioned responsum (ALR 1:41), that if the father was negligent in his responsibilities, then the mother became obligated.[11] In that responsum, however, he deliberately placed more weight on those opinions that did *not* require the woman to educate her children, since Rabbi Halevy wanted the father to become more involved. While citing the same opinions in both cases, Rabbi Halevy presented the sources in his responsum in a manner that would be best for that family's situation.[12]

---

[9] ALR 1:41, p. 127.

[10] MKH *Livnot Yisrael* 7, p. 45.

[11] Likewise, in MZR (p. 99), Rabbi Halevy quoted Zohar Hadash (*Bereshit* 7b), that a woman has a special obligation to provide religious education for her children. In MKH 5:250, p. 132, however, he says only "there are some *aharonim* (later decisors) who maintain that the obligation of religious education devolves onto the mother as well." Perhaps he adopted a stronger formulation in MKH *Livnot Yisrael*, since he was addressing a predominantly female audience. See also MKH 5:250, p. 132 (laws of educating children): "There are some later authorities who believed that the mitzvah of education also devolves on the mother." This formulation is considerably less emphatic than the instances where Rabbi Halevy directly addressed female audiences.

[12] It also is noteworthy that Rabbi Halevy introduced MKH *Livnot Yisrael* (p. 8) by expressing deep gratitude to his recently deceased mother Victoria, who had played a vital role in his own religious upbringing.

A religious man had three observant sons, and one who no longer was observant.[13] He wanted to write the non-observant son out of his will. Rabbi Halevy cited the *Shulhan Arukh* (*Hoshen Mishpat* 282), that even if a son wrongs his father directly, he still should inherit with the other children. Rabbi Halevy realized that merely citing the halakhah would be insufficient to persuade the father in this emotionally charged case. "The halakhah is clear, and I did not need to go to such great lengths, except to quiet your heart."[14] Rabbi Halevy proceeded to offer further reasons why the father should follow the halakhah, rather than writing his non-observant son out of his will: 1) the non-observant son may yet repent one day, but most likely would not do so if he were cut out of the will; 2) that son, if disinherited, will deeply resent his siblings, causing permanent rifts in the family. Although Rabbi Halevy was saddened that the fourth son was non-observant, he tried to preserve family unity and to keep the door to repentance open. Rabbi Halevy concluded, "Follow the Torah commandment upon you, and do not penalize this son at all even though he is not conducting himself properly. Since he received his primary education in your God-fearing household, there is yet hope that he will change his mind and return to the path of God.... God does not withhold good from those who walk in purity."[15]

During a lengthy teachers' strike in Israel, many rabbis had ruled that teachers were not allowed to disrupt their teaching of Torah to children. Rabbi Halevy considered the issue from a different perspective.[16] His starting point was: "is it possible that our holy Torah, whose ways are the ways of pleasantness, would prohibit a person from fighting for his daily bread?"[17] Rabbi Halevy noted that the primary obligation for religious instruction devolves on the parents of the child, not the school (*Kiddushin*

---

[13] ALR 1:64.

[14] ALR 1:64, p. 199.

[15] ALR 1:64, p. 201.

[16] ALR 3:23; 5:23.

[17] ALR 5:23, p. 168.

29a).[18] He contended that all workers, including teachers, have the right to strike for better compensation.[19] The parents themselves must then fulfill their own primary obligation to teach their children Torah. It was unfair to accuse teachers of the sin of *bittul Torah* when the parents in fact bore the full responsibility for this sin.

Rabbi Halevy noted, however, that the striking Torah teachers may not prevent other willing teachers from entering the school. In this regard, the unique problem of *bittul Torah* created halakhic distinctions between a strike of Torah teachers and all other labor strikes. In a later responsum, he added that unless striking teachers had stipulated that they would not return to class unless they were paid for the lost time, they were not entitled to compensation for the period of the strike.[20]

Studying Secular Subjects

Rabbi Halevy, who quoted secular scholars and thinkers on occasion in his writings, recognized the value of secular study.[21] A student asked if he may study on Shabbat for an upcoming secular examination. Rabbi Halevy wrote that Rambam prohibited such study on Shabbat, whereas Ramban and Rashba permitted it. In the *Shulhan Arukh*, Rabbi Yosef Karo first cited Rambam's opinion, and only then referred to the permissive opinion with the preface "some say." From this formulation, Rabbi Halevy concluded that, in general, one should not engage in secular study on Shabbat.[22] However, with the pressure of a forthcoming test, a student may be overly worried, and not enjoy Shabbat properly. Presumably, the *Shulhan Arukh* included the permissive ruling in order to allow leeway in

---

[18] This talmudic passage was codified into law by Rambam (*Hil. Talmud Torah* 1:1), and the *Shulhan Arukh* (*Yoreh Deah* 245:1).

[19] See also ALR 2:64.

[20] ALR 5:23.

[21] See further discussion in the chapter on Rabbi Halevy's Religious and Intellectual Foundations.

[22] Cf. Rabbi Halevy's similar ruling in MKH 3:166, p. 306.

such pressured situations. Therefore, Rabbi Halevy permitted the student to study for the examination on Shabbat.[23]

In a later responsum, Rabbi Halevy followed up on this decision with an explanation of why studying for a test was not considered preparation from Shabbat to a weekday, something generally prohibited. The forbidden variety of preparation was when one derived no benefit on Shabbat itself (e.g., setting a table for a meal on Saturday night). In the instance of studying, however, the knowledge gained on Shabbat was beneficial.[24]

Elsewhere, he addressed a High School student who did not wish to study for his comprehensive examinations *(bagruyot)* at all, since he believed this preparation would distract him from Torah study.[25] Rabbi Halevy began by praising the student: "I am exceedingly pleased by the nature of your question, which attests to the love of Torah in your heart. May God bless you, and may you merit becoming a great sage and a God-fearing Jew who will be a source of pride to your family and all of Israel!"[26]

Rabbi Halevy then advised the student that since he had already reached this level of education, he should complete his degree by studying for the final examinations. Rabbi Halevy added that there is great value in secular study, both for the education itself and for earning a living later on. He suggested that if the student genuinely was bothered by losing this time from Torah study, he should make a careful accounting of the time spent preparing for the exams, and make up this time with additional Torah study after the examinations.

Torah Education for Girls and Women

In his ruling prohibiting the teaching of Oral Law to girls, Rambam had stated that a majority of them were incapable of understanding the concepts involved (*Hil. Talmud Torah* 1:13). Rabbi Halevy noted, though,

---

[23] ALR 1:36.
[24] ALR 4:31.
[25] ALR 4:46.
[26] ALR 4:46, p. 259.

that the success of women in so many academic fields militated against Rambam's ruling. Already in the 18th century, Rabbi Hayyim Yosef David Azulai listed historical instances of women who gave halakhic rulings. Rabbi Halevy demonstrated that within Rambam's own wording, one could find permissibility for women to study Talmud. A woman who demonstrated a willingness and capacity to study the Oral Law was not part of the "incapable majority" described by Rambam. Rabbi Halevy concluded that very young girls should not study Talmud. Once they reached High School and showed motivation, they could be taught Talmud.[27] In this responsum, Rabbi Halevy did not attempt to show that Rambam's ruling was no longer applicable. He worked within the existing textual framework to reach a novel conclusion.

Rabbi Halevy's commitment to that earlier source became more pronounced in a later discussion, where he responded to members of a religious kibbutz that had begun teaching Talmud to girls.[28] The leaders of the kibbutz had complained that in light of the change in women's status, why had rabbis not addressed the issue of females studying Talmud. Rabbi Halevy responded that 1) he *did* address the matter in ALR 2:52; and 2) his response had *nothing* to do with the current change in the social status of women. He had quoted Rabbi Azulai, who lived in the 18th century, to support his permissive ruling. "From here, we see that rabbis in all generations, including before there were changes in the social status of women, never rebuked women who studied Torah."[29] Rabbi Halevy criticized the kibbutz leaders for suggesting that *halakhot* may be eliminated on the basis of social change.

In the final analysis, Rabbi Halevy reached the same decision as the kibbutz leaders, permitting and encouraging women to study the Oral Law – but they arrived at their conclusions from different starting points. Rabbi Halevy represented faithfulness to the precedents of the past; the kibbutz had hoped to bypass the system as a result of a new social reality. At the

---

[27] ALR 2:52. See further discussion in the chapter on Old Texts, New Realities.
[28] MH 2:89.
[29] MH 2:89, p. 310.

end of his responsum, Rabbi Halevy exhorted the members of the kibbutz: "Our rabbis were great of spirit and deep of mind; would that we could even understand their words.... They were not only great in Torah and wisdom, but also in their holiness. Therefore, it is appropriate for a person to relate to their words with all respect due to them."[30]

Rabbi Halevy demonstrated the same consistent balance between faithfulness to Rambam's ruling and finding permissibility for women to study the Oral Law in *Mekor Hayyim Livnot Yisrael*.[31] In discussing the halakhic exemption for women to study Torah, Rabbi Halevy quoted Rambam's ruling in full, that a father should not teach his daughters the Oral Law. But in the footnote, he cited his responsum (which was subsequently published in the aforementioned ALR 2:52) that explained the permissibility of women studying Oral Law within Rambam's formulation. By citing Rambam's ruling in the body of the text, and his own responsum in a footnote, Rabbi Halevy presented a fine balance for his educational program: anyone motivated enough to read his lengthy footnote was indeed qualified to study the Oral Law! One just reading his book with the rulings in the body of the text probably would not have sufficient motivation to study halakhah from its roots, including its talmudic underpinnings.

A couple asked Rabbi Halevy if they needed to make significant financial sacrifices to keep their daughter in a religious High School. Rabbi Halevy responded that the greatest honor for parents is to support their children in Torah study. This applies to girls as well as boys, even though girls do not have the same technical obligation to study Torah as boys.[32]

Rabbi Halevy was asked whether a school could stop having afternoon prayers for girls in order to enable all the teachers to attend the boys' *minyan*. Rabbi Halevy responded that a school always must teach

---

[30] MH 2:89, p. 312.

[31] MKH *Livnot Yisrael* 50, pp. 205–208.

[32] ALR 1:74. See MKH *Livnot Yisrael* 2, p. 21; 7, pp. 44–45; 11, pp. 57–58; 25, pp. 97–102 for further discussion and rulings on the obligations and exemptions women have in Torah study.

what is correct. Since women also are obligated to pray *minhah*,[33] the teachers must give equal attention to the prayers of their female students.[34]

Rabbi Halevy did not permit mixed education, where boys and girls sat together in the same classes. He even forbade teaching in a co-educational religious school. It was better to teach in a purely secular school, where it was clear that the teacher did not support the religious values of the institution.[35] In an adult education setting, however, Rabbi Halevy ruled that men and women may attend the same classes if men were in one room, women in an adjacent room, and the teacher stood in the middle. Women also could participate in the group discussions.[36]

Separatism vs. Inclusiveness

A non-religious man sought a religiously observant woman in marriage.[37] He promised that he would become observant for the sake of the marriage. Rabbi Halevy noted that as long as the man had not adopted a Torah way of life, he had the status of a sinner. Although he promised to be observant, the woman should not be so confident that he would succeed. On the contrary, he might influence her to become less observant. Non-observance often prevailed because it was less demanding. Enormous tensions could plague the marriage. If the husband wanted to go out on a Friday night, the wife either would feel pressured to join him, or to remain alone while he went out. Rabbi Halevy therefore discouraged the marriage. He tried to protect the woman's religious observance, and pointed out how vastly different levels of religious commitment could be detrimental to a marriage.

---

[33] In MKH *Livnot Yisrael* (4, pp. 26–27, n. 7), Rabbi Halevy concluded that all authorities require women to say *shaharit* and *minhah*, and many require *arvit* as well. Therefore, he ruled that women must say the first two prayers each day, and if they pray *arvit*, they deserve further blessing.

[34] ALR 6: short answers 9.

[35] ALR 2:60.

[36] ALR 4:56.

[37] ALR 1:62.

A school's policy of requiring all parents to affirm that they were Shabbat-observant offended one parent. Rabbi Halevy, though, was sympathetic to this policy, even though it would exclude taking children from less observant homes. Religious students might go to the homes of less observant students and be influenced negatively. Moreover, the likelihood of the school influencing children from the less observant families was mitigated by the fact that their parents did not model the same observance at home. He concluded that it was preferable to send children to a school with an all-observant population.[38]

In another responsum, Rabbi Halevy ruled that a synagogue should conduct a bar mitzvah ceremony for a family known to violate Shabbat. However, food brought by car to the synagogue on Shabbat may not be eaten, since Jews may not derive benefit from another's Shabbat violation.[39] In this decision, Rabbi Halevy again balanced outreach to the not fully observant, with the necessity of remaining faithful to halakhah.[40]

Parents are obligated to seek the best possible religious education for their children. Therefore, if a distant school provides a better religious education than the local school, parents have the right to send their children there, rather than feeling an obligation to support the local school.[41] But one praying in a local *minyan* with less observant Jews should remain there if they would not have a *minyan* without him.[42]

These responsa are particularly telling as to Rabbi Halevy's educational philosophy. While he emphasized that one always should encourage the possibility of repentance, he realistically considered the religious hazards in these instances to be greater than the potential benefits. It was preferable to protect one's religious identity rather than attempting to bring others closer.

---

[38] ALR 6:60.

[39] ALR 3:16.

[40] For further discussion, see the chapter on Respect for Others.

[41] ALR 4:52.

[42] ALR 5:1–2.

Difficult Questions in Educational Policy

An educator in a girl's High School expressed concern that a student may have been involved in a correspondence with a boy. The school's policy forbade such correspondence. The question was: may a school official open the student's mail to ascertain the facts of the case? Rabbi Halevy noted that Rabbeinu Gershom (11th century) instituted the prohibition of opening the mail of another. The only possibility justifying opening another person's mail was to prevent something sinful. Thus, it would be permissible to open the student's mail. That having been said, Rabbi Halevy strongly discouraged the opening of her letters. Rather, the girl's teachers should have a private discussion with her. If she did not appear forthright, then only her primary educator may open her mail, and may not discuss the matter with anyone else.[43]

In a related responsum, Rabbi Halevy ruled that teachers must not read a student's diary, unless it could be verified that the child was violating religious conduct. The teacher also must make sure that this reading was done exclusively to correct the problem.[44]

Is lying permissible in an educational setting? For example, a father noticed that his children tended not to be punctual. He decided to switch the clocks ahead in his house, so that the children would think it was later than it really was. Rabbi Halevy responded that willful deception is a serious prohibition. Although the primary categories of forbidden deception were for personal benefit – either in business, or to project a better self-image – Rambam prohibited all deception, even for a good purpose.[45] Rambam even prohibited sleight of hand tricks under this category.[46] In the end, Rabbi Halevy ruled that one may use deception only

---

[43] ALR 1:42.

[44] ALR 6: short answers 91.

[45] *Hil. De'ot* 2:6.

[46] It is noteworthy that in his responsum permitting children's magic shows (ALR 2:44), Rabbi Halevy did not stress this problem of willful deception (see discussion in the chapter on Metaphysical Issues). Here, Rabbi Halevy appealed

to prevent someone from violating halakhah; therefore, it would be permitted to change the clocks in the house to encourage the children to come to synagogue services on time.

Similarly, a teacher deceitfully told his students that they would have daily tests for two weeks, simply to frighten his students to see how they acted under pressure. Rabbi Halevy ruled in one word – prohibited. Even with the best educational intentions it is forbidden to be deceitful in education.[47] Likewise, students are not allowed to cheat on examinations, and Rabbi Halevy adduced many reasons to support his point.[48]

May a teacher physically strike a student who was misbehaving? Rabbi Halevy quoted Rambam and Meiri, who allowed hitting a child lightly in order to promote education. One who struck a child with cruelty, however, should be punished in court and then excommunicated. Rabbi Halevy cited the original talmudic source (*Bava Batra* 21a), which permitted a light slap if a child were overly lazy. But there was no reference to hitting a child for misbehavior. Rabbi Halevy concluded that it was forbidden to strike a misbehaving child. One who disrupted class on an ongoing basis should be expelled rather than struck, since the primary obligation to educate fell on the parents.[49] In a follow up responsum, Rabbi Halevy defended his distinction between laziness and misbehavior. A light slap for laziness will make a child pay more attention; this rationale did not apply to disruptive behavior.[50] Although traditional sources permitted striking a student under certain circumstances, Rabbi Halevy interpreted the sources so as to curtail the practice.

A student asked if he had the right to report students or teachers who were acting against halakhah. Rabbi Halevy sternly discouraged this type of reporting, since one's motivations needed to be unusually pure. He

---

to Rambam's strict ruling, since he was trying to discourage the father from deceiving his own children.

[47] ALR 4:62.

[48] ALR 8:59.

[49] ALR 1:76.

[50] ALR 5:28.

quoted the Talmud (*Pesahim* 113b) that one seeing another person violate halakhah must not report it, since one witness cannot do anything other than damage someone's reputation. Yet, he may be wary of the sinner. Meiri limited this rule to apply specifically to court testimony. However, he may inform a teacher, or warn others who might trust the sinner. The *Hafetz Hayyim* in turn restricted Meiri's permissive ruling to cases where five conditions were met: 1) the person reporting the sin must have witnessed the sin firsthand; 2) the sin must a be well-known prohibition, allowing the offender no excuse to say that he was unaware; 3) when reporting, no exaggeration is allowed; 4) this could be done only with the intent to keep people distant from the sinner until he repented; 5) one may not report the sinner, and then act flatteringly to him. Rabbi Halevy concluded that since it was so rare for one to meet all of these criteria, it was preferable to try to speak to the person privately, without publicizing the matter.[51]

On a related subject, Rabbi Halevy was asked whether students may conduct group discussions about teachers' personalities.[52] Rabbi Halevy lamented that this question even was asked: "I will note with sorrow, that the mere fact that someone can even suggest this, is sufficient to demonstrate the extent our generation is afflicted by a lack of appreciation of the grave prohibition of *lashon hara*."[53] Those who criticized the teachers were guilty of *lashon hara*, and those who defended the teachers still were guilty of secondary *lashon hara*, since they were defending them in the presence of those known to dislike them. Of course, one may debate *ideas* with teachers, or else truth cannot be clarified,[54] but character evaluation is expressly prohibited. Rabbi Halevy concluded that if one

---

[51] ALR 1:71.
[52] ALR 1:72.
[53] ALR 1:72, p. 222.
[54] Cf. ALR 7:44.

needed actual *protection* from a teacher, then one may complain to the administration.[55]

Given the significance of religious education, there is little wonder that Rabbi Halevy devoted so much attention to these matters. He was indeed an educator's educator, providing guidance to individuals and schools in order to promote a society that imparts proper Torah education to all its constituents.

---

[55] Rabbi Halevy discussed other educational issues in ALR 1:58; 1:77; 2:69; 3:27; 3:52; 4:50; 5: short answers 3; 5: short answers 27; 6:85; 6:87; 6: short answers 88; 8:54; 8:58; 9:20; MH 1:50; 2:53; 3:18.

Chapter Eight

The Role of *Minhag*

Over the centuries, Jewish communities have adopted religious practices that were not specifically mandated by halakhah. These customs were enhancements or safeguards of legal requirements. Sometimes they were initiated by the rabbis, and sometimes they developed through the enthusiasm of the general Jewish public. These practices generally constitute the category of *minhag*, custom.

Once a custom had been accepted by a community, it gained the status of an obligation. Members of the community were expected to maintain the custom, almost as though it had the authority of the halakhah itself. Whereas the halakhah could be viewed as a set of requirements imposed from Heaven, *minhag* could be described as rules imposed by pious Jews to bring themselves closer to Heaven.

Rabbi Halevy wrote at length on the topic of *minhag*. He stated: "I am very fearful and wary about annulling customs, even if they are as strange as can be. I do not agree to the annulment of any custom unless it completely violates the halakhah, and there is no way to find any halakhic justification for it."[1] He assumed that customs, sanctified by the devotion of generations of Jews, had been established wisely. Even if we no longer knew the reasons for the institution of these customs, yet we must defer to the wisdom of those who originally established them – who must have had good reasons.[2]

---

[1] ALR 6:21. See also ALR 3:21 for a fuller discussion of the topic of *minhag*.
[2] ALR 6:26.

A bridegroom, whose father had died some time ago, was asked by his mother to go to his father's grave on the day of the wedding to invite him to the celebration. The bridegroom was not comfortable with this request, but the mother was insistent. This was the custom: an orphaned bride or bridegroom was to go to the deceased parent's (or parents') grave and extend an invitation to the wedding.

Rabbi Halevy began his answer to the bridegroom with a general principle: "All the customs of the communities and groupings of the Jewish people – they all have foundations; but they [the foundations] have been forgotten [in some cases]. Therefore, as long as they [the customs] do not oppose an express halakhah, it is appropriate to maintain these customs."[3] Rabbi Halevy went on to suggest reasons for the custom of inviting deceased parents to weddings, largely based on kabbalistic considerations.[4]

Rabbi Halevy was asked about a custom of the Jews of Salonika, who did not eat potatoes, garlic or onions on Passover. Although this was a strange custom that might easily be set aside, Rabbi Halevy urged the Jews of Salonikan background to maintain the custom. "Therefore, I do not suggest that you annul your old custom, with all its strangeness, particularly since it relates only to seven days of the year [in Israel]. From this [example] is a great instruction relating to every *minhag* for which we do not know its reason – not to annul it at all."[5]

Some Moroccan Jews had the custom of eating a small meal on Friday afternoon prior to the onset of Shabbat. This meal was called *se'udat bo'i kallah*, the meal of welcoming the Shabbat bride. Yet, this custom would seem to be in violation of the halakhah that forbade eating before the onset of Shabbat so that one would have a good appetite for the Shabbat evening meal.

Rabbi Halevy found halakhic precedent for tasting food prior to the onset of Shabbat, where it was customary to fast every Friday. In order

---

[3] ALR 1:50.
[4] See further discussion in the chapter on Metaphysical Issues.
[5] ALR 8:36.

not to enter Shabbat while overly hungry, fasters would taste a little food before Shabbat began. This did not hurt their appetite for the evening Shabbat meal. Rabbi Halevy theorized that the original custom in Morocco must have been for people to fast on Friday and then taste a bit of food late Friday afternoon before Shabbat. The custom of fasting must have stopped at some point, but the custom of tasting food continued anyway. Admitting that this was simply his theory, he suggested that there may have been another reason which had been forgotten over the years. Since Rabbi Halevy strongly believed in maintaining customs where they did not openly violate halakhah, he suggested that the Moroccan Jews continue their practice of having the *se'udat bo'i kallah*, making sure not to eat so much that they would lose their appetites for the Friday night Shabbat meal. Since the great sages of Morocco obviously had permitted this custom, and may have observed it themselves, it would be inappropriate to annul it.[6]

I had asked Rabbi Halevy a question relating to a custom of Congregation Shearith Israel of New York City. Like several other Spanish and Portuguese congregations of the Western Sephardic tradition, our congregation maintains a "perpetual list of *hashkabot*." Congregants may leave bequests to the congregation, requesting that their names be added to this list. A memorial prayer is recited for all those listed in the book of perpetual *hashkabot* on Yom Kippur, on the first day of each Rosh Hodesh (except *Tishrei*), and on the Shabbat afternoon after the anniversary of the person's death. Since the list at Shearith Israel goes back to 1718, it has grown quite long; it now takes thirty to forty minutes to read off all the names.

I asked Rabbi Halevy if it would be permissible to change the custom so that the list would not need to be read each Rosh Hodesh, so as not to be such a burden on the hazzanim of the congregation. (The congregations in Amsterdam and London, who also have perpetual lists of

---

[6] ALR 3:14.

hashkabot, did make alterations in their custom as their lists grew to be unwieldy.)

Rabbi Halevy underscored his strong opposition to annulling customs. He offered halakhic sources that may have tended to justify the custom of reading memorial prayers on Rosh Hodesh. He then made a practical suggestion that the list be divided into four or five sections, each of which could be read by a hazzan or congregant. In this way, the custom could be maintained, and the hazzanim would be spared the necessity of reading the entire list of names. Instead of taking thirty to forty minutes, the process would now be reduced to ten minutes or less.[7]

Rabbi Halevy prided himself on not agreeing to the annulment of a *minhag*, unless it clearly violated a halakhah, or unless the annulment would add to the honor of the Torah.[8] Once a custom was established, he was reluctant to undermine it, even if some halakhic arguments could be brought against the custom. For example, he stated that old Torah scrolls – which had deteriorated beyond repair – should be put aside respectfully in a storage area. The halakhah, though, stated that such Torah scrolls were to be buried. Yet, Rabbi Halevy preferred to rely on a well-established custom of storing such scrolls in a *genizah*, a storage area where worn out sacred texts were placed. Where there was no appropriate storage area, then burial of the scrolls in earthenware vessels was the correct procedure.[9]

Rabbi Ovadya Yosef had ruled that in lighting the Shabbat eve candles, women should first recite the blessing and then light the candles. This conformed to the normal halakhic practice, where the blessing preceded the actual performance of the mitzvah. Rabbi Halevy, though, ruled that women should continue to follow the long-standing practice of lighting the candles first, and then reciting the blessing afterwards. (After lighting the candles, women covered their eyes or put their hands in front

---

[7] ALR 9:24.

[8] ALR 6:39.

[9] ALR 6:65. In MKH 3:119, pp. 96–97, he lists the halakhah to bury worn out Torah scrolls, not mentioning the option of *genizah*.

of the candles to avoid deriving benefit from them. Once the blessing was recited – after the lighting – they could then open their eyes or move their hands so as to see the light of the candles.) Rabbi Halevy certainly recognized the validity of Rabbi Yosef's point; yet, he believed it was difficult to change an ingrained practice. Women would not want to deviate from the pattern they have followed and that they had learned from their own mothers and grandmothers. Moreover, Rabbi Halevy thought there could be negative practical ramifications from asking women to change their customary practice.[10]

A question arose about the recitation of supplicatory prayers in synagogue when a mourner was present. Supplicatory prayers were not to be recited in the home of a mourner, yet that rule did not necessarily apply in the synagogue. The original practice seems to have been that supplicatory prayers were indeed recited in the synagogue, even if a mourner were present. Yet, a number of congregations omitted these prayers in the synagogue in consideration of the presence of the mourner. The question arose: what was the correct practice? Rabbi Halevy said that each community should follow its own customs. Although halakhic reasoning would seem to favor the recitation of supplicatory prayers in the synagogue, Rabbi Halevy felt there was no reason to quibble with those communities that omitted these prayers in the presence of a mourner. Indeed, if a congregation did not have a fixed custom in this matter, it was free to choose not to have supplicatory prayers recited when a mourner attended services in the synagogue.[11]

Rabbi Halevy dealt with several questions involving a perceived conflict between the wishes of a parent and the fulfillment of a traditional practice. In one case, a son had become a follower of a Hassidic sect, and had grown a beard as was the practice among men in that community. The

---

[10] MKH 3:110, p. 54, note 42. See also, Rabbi Ovadya Yosef, *Yabia Omer* 2:16. See also MKH *Livnot Yisrael* 9:10.

[11] ALR 7:12. For other cases where Rabbi Halevy allowed current practice to prevail, rather than to insist on following other halakhic considerations, see ALR 3:5; 6: short answers 36.

parents, who were traditional-minded if not scrupulously observant Jews, were disturbed by their son's behavior. The young man's family told him that he could be religious without needing to follow the practices of the Hassidic sect; they claimed that there was no obligation in Judaism to grow a beard. The son, though, was keen to maintain the practices he had learned as part of the sect.

Rabbi Halevy upheld the son's right to keep his beard and to follow other Hassidic practices. He raised a halakhic objection only to the young man's abandoning the prayer liturgy of his own native community in order to adopt the liturgy of the sect. But other than that, the son's behavior was not in violation of halakhah. The tradition of men growing their beards had a long and honored history among the Jewish people, and it was appropriate for the son to grow his beard. A child was not obligated to follow the wishes of parents, except in matters of direct service to the parents themselves. In areas that were of personal importance to the child, the parents had no right to impose their wills. He advised that the parents and family of the young man conduct themselves with love and respect towards him; and that the young man behave with love and respect towards them.[12]

In another case, a son thought that his father was following a halakhically improper practice. When the father recited kiddush, he expected his family – who were fulfilling the mitzvah of kiddush through his recitation – to respond at the appropriate places with the words *barukh hu uvarukh shemo* and 'amen'. This was the widespread custom among Jews from Turkey and other Sephardic communities. Yet, many halakhic authorities had ruled that one should not respond *barukh hu uvarukh shemo* since this would constitute an interruption. Rabbi Hayyim Yosef David Azulai had noted that it was preferable not to make this response, but that one should not stop those who had the custom to so respond. Rabbi Halevy agreed with Rabbi Azulai's approach. The halakhah recommended no response, but a custom called for a response. The son should explain to

---

[12] ALR 9:16.

his father, in a respectful way, that it was preferred not to have family members respond *barukh hu uvarukh shemo*. If the father agreed to this, that would be best. If not, the son should drop the issue and honor his father.[13] After all, the father was following a time-honored custom that had been observed in communities where great sages flourished. If the sages had allowed the custom to take root, then obviously they had good reasons for not stopping it.

When Customs Could Be Dropped

Although Rabbi Halevy strongly favored maintaining customs, there were certain cases in which he thought customs could be dropped. He received a question from a congregation whose members had originally come from Aden. Their longstanding custom was to auction off the honor of being called to the Torah. They did this each Shabbat, without giving precedence to a bridegroom, a bar mitzvah boy or anyone else who may have been celebrating a special occasion. Any person who wished to be called to the Torah had to buy the honor during the auction. A suggestion was now raised that the congregation should change this practice, and offer to call to the Torah a bridegroom or bar mitzvah boy without their having to buy the honor at the auction. Rabbi Halevy favored this suggestion, but only on the condition that the entire congregation approved of the change. If this issue became a matter of controversy, it was preferable to maintain the custom as of old.[14] Apparently, Rabbi Halevy thought that the practice of these Jews from Aden was based on a communal agreement; it was not truly in the category of an officially established custom. Since the original practice had been established through the consensus of the community, it could also be altered with the community's agreement.

Rabbi Halevy was asked if it was permissible to annul the custom of calling all the men of the congregation to the Torah on the festival of Simhat Torah. The custom led to much chatter and levity in the synagogue. Instead of being a way of honoring the Torah, the custom

---

[13] MH 1:6.
[14] MH 2:88.

actually seemed to lead to a deterioration in the honor due to the synagogue and to the Torah.

After a lengthy discussion on the importance of *minhag* in general and on the background of this particular *minhag*, Rabbi Halevy noted that it was permissible to annul a custom that engendered conversation and lightheartedness in the synagogue. Yet, the annulment of the custom could only be instituted if all the members of the congregation agreed to it. Controversy was to be avoided.

Rabbi Halevy offered an alternative suggestion based on what was done in the Ohel Moshe neighborhood in Jerusalem where he grew up. The men of the congregation were called to the Torah during the entire month of *Tishrei*. On Rosh Hashanah and Yom Kippur, the rabbis and scholars were called to the Torah. On the Shabbat between Rosh Hashanah and Yom Kippur, *aliyot* were given to members who devoted time to Torah study. On Sukkot and the intermediate Shabbat, *aliyot* were given to those who regularly attended morning and evening prayer services. On Simhat Torah, the remainder of the congregation – as well as children – were called to the Torah. This custom had the advantage of avoiding an overly long Torah reading on Simhat Torah.[15] On a related issue, Rabbi Halevy stated that the rabbis of each generation could make ordinances for improving the religious behavior of the community. Thus, it was permissible to make rules limiting the number of people who could be called to the Torah on Shabbat, even in places where it was customary to call many congregants beyond the mandatory seven.[16]

Rabbi Halevy called for the elimination of the custom of some communities to slaughter chickens on behalf of every family member on the eve of Yom Kippur. Known as *kapparot*, these chickens were then eaten or given to the poor. The ceremony was a symbolic way of showing repentance: instead of us being slaughtered for our sins, the chickens were slaughtered in our place. This custom has a long history, and has been maintained by some rabbis and condemned by others. Rabbi Halevy

---

[15] ALR 3:21.
[16] ALR 7:18.

thought the custom was problematic for various reasons and that it should be stopped entirely. If one felt the need to have a ceremony for *kapparot*, he should do it with money rather than chickens.[17] Yet, in *Mekor Hayyim* (4:216:2), Rabbi Halevy suggested that people should avoid performing this custom, but that if they wished to follow the custom of their ancestors they should do so. Thus, Rabbi Halevy took a middle position. He stated unequivocally that he was opposed to the custom and that it should be dropped. On the other hand, he knew that some people were emotionally attached to the custom of *kapparot*, and would not be ready to give it up. So he did not wish to forcibly stop them from following the custom of their ancestors.

Rabbi Halevy adamantly opposed a practice called to his attention by a certain congregation. Their custom was for all the women to enter the synagogue during the priestly blessing during the closing service of Yom Kippur. They would stand together with the men, and the head of the family would place his hand on the heads of his children, male and female, during the blessing. Rabbi Halevy was outraged by this custom and stated that "it was a holy obligation to stand in the breach and to annul this custom, and to issue a strong prohibition that no woman should enter the [men's section of the] synagogue during public prayer services, and certainly [not] on Yom Kippur during the closing service."[18]

A certain congregation had the custom of having the bar mitzvah boy give an address during the Torah reading. Rabbi Halevy called for a stop to this custom, since it violated the halakhic prohibition of interrupting the Torah reading.[19]

---

[17] ALR 3:20; MH 3:22. See *Shulhan Arukh, Orah Hayyim* 605.

[18] ALR 5: short answers 117. For other responsa relating to changes in custom, see ALR 4:33; 4:44; 6:21; 6: short answers 37; 7:9. Rabbi Halevy was adamantly opposed to the mixing of men and women in religious or social contexts, unless conforming strictly to the laws of modesty. For some responsa relating to this topic, see ALR 2:60; 3:15; 3:40; 4:56; 5:36; 5:40; 6: short answers 87; 7:22; 8: short answers 48; 9:25; MH 2:71–72.

[19] ALR 8:30.

Different Customs Among Different Groups

Jews from throughout the world have settled in the modern State of Israel. They have brought their own local customs and traditions. On the one hand, there was the natural tendency for each group to strive to maintain its own distinctive customs. On the other hand, there was a pervasive sociological pressure to blend in with other groups and to meld into a more unified system of religious practice.

In fact, Israeli society was increasingly integrated, so that Jews of various backgrounds found themselves praying together in synagogues, schools, the army and other communal settings. Whose customs should prevail? Was it desirable or possible to establish a unified form of prayer and synagogue ritual, so that all Jews would leave their old customs behind and adopt a new Israeli set of customs?

Rabbi Halevy did not foresee a unified form of prayer for all the Jews of Israel, at least not for the coming few generations. Each family was to follow the customs of its father/husband, so that the particular traditions of each community will be maintained. In cases where a mixed group had a controversy as to which custom to follow, it should work out an appropriate solution by consulting its rabbi.[20] Normally, the majority of the congregation should prevail; but if controversy persisted, compromises should be made to satisfy the concerns of the minority.[21] If no satisfactory agreement could be reached, Rabbi Halevy offered the advice of his mentor Rabbi Uziel that the congregation should adopt the custom of Jerusalem.[22]

A member of one group (e.g., Sephardic, Ashkenazic, Yemenite) who prayed in a synagogue or school that followed a different liturgical tradition – such an individual should outwardly conform to the practices

---

[20] ALR 6:91.
[21] ALR 4:15.
[22] ALR 5: short answers 88.

of the prevailing custom. But he should recite the silent prayers in his own tradition, since this in no way disturbed the other worshippers.[23]

Rabbi Halevy dealt with a number of questions relating to differences in custom between Sephardim and Ashkenazim.[24] In cases where the wife and husband were of different traditions, one being Sephardic and one being Ashkenazic, the general rule was for the wife to follow the husband's customs. Yet, this rule did not apply to those practices that did not disturb matrimonial harmony, i.e., the wife could continue to pray the silent prayers according to the traditions in which she was raised. Likewise, a husband could not compel his wife to violate those practices which were in the category of actual halakhah rather than *minhag*. For example, if the wife were Sephardic and the husband Ashkenazic, she should continue to eat only *halak* meat. Since Sephardic rules in regard to the inspection of slaughtered animals were more stringent than the Ashkenazic rules, she should follow the practices of the Sephardim. For her, this was not a matter of custom, but a question of law. Likewise, if a wife were raised in a family that waited six hours between eating meat and dairy, the husband could not compel her to wait a lesser time according to his family tradition.[25]

Sephardim living in settings where Ashkenazic customs prevailed sometimes felt the need or desire to conform to the Ashkenazic modes. For the most part, Rabbi Halevy did not approve of this. He felt Sephardim should maintain their *minhagim*, just as Ashkenazim should maintain theirs.

Ashkenazim had the custom of fasting on the day of their wedding. A Sephardic student in an Ashkenazic yeshiva was told by his classmates that he should fast on his wedding day. Rabbi Halevy instructed

---

[23] ALR 1:66–67; MH 2:13. See also ALR 6:22.

[24] ALR 7: short answers 73. For questions specifically relating to Sephardic practices, see ALR 7:5; 8:46; MH 2:10.

[25] ALR 6:37; 8:20. If she wanted to adopt the practices of her husband's tradition, she should consult her rabbi. In matters relating to the laws of *niddah*, the wife should follow her own family traditions, not those of her husband's family. See ALR 4:59.

the student to ask his parents what their own custom was, since some Sephardic communities also had the practice of fasting on the wedding day. If they informed him that it was not their custom, then he should not fast at all on his wedding day, and should not follow the advice of his Ashkenazic friends.[26]

An Ashkenazic custom was to bring the bride and groom into a private room (*yihud*), following the wedding ceremony. Rabbi Halevy noted that the Sephardic community did not have this custom and should not introduce it.[27]

The Ashkenazic practice was to allow the recitation of the seven wedding blessings (during the week following the wedding) after meals that were eaten in the presence of the bride and groom. The original Sephardic practice was to recite these blessings only at meals eaten in the home of the bride and groom. Rabbi Halevy realized that many Sephardim had adopted the Ashkenazic practice, and that the seven wedding blessings were recited after meals held in the homes of friends and relatives of the bride and groom. He felt that the Sephardic practice, as codified by Rabbi Yosef Karo in the *Shulhan Arukh* (*Even haEzer* 62:10), referred to the sociological conditions prevailing in those days, but that the situation today was quite different. It was simply too expensive and too labor-intensive to try to organize seven days of wedding meals at the home of the newlyweds. It was more practical to share the honors and expenses of these meals among a larger group of relatives and friends. Sephardim had gradually come to accept the prevailing Ashkenazic practice. Those Sephardim whose families had continued to follow the practice enunciated by the *Shulhan Arukh* could continue to follow it. But those who had adopted the Ashkenazic practice, or whose families had not clung to the Sephardic custom unwaveringly – they could continue to observe the Ashkenazic practice.[28]

---

[26] ALR 7:58.

[27] ALR 6: short answers 80; MKH 5:237, pp. 30–32; MKH *Livnot Yisrael* 37:12.

[28] ALR 5:38–39.

Ashkenazim had the custom of not shaving or having haircuts during the three weeks between the fasts of 17 *Tammuz* and 9 *Av*. The Sephardic practice was to refrain from these activities only during the week in which the fast of the 9th of *Av* occurred. Rabbi Halevy realized that a number of young Sephardim, living in an Ashkenazic-dominated milieu, unthinkingly had adopted the Ashkenazic stringencies. When they were later informed of the Sephardic custom, they were allowed to adopt it; they had only been following the Ashkenazic practice because they had not been properly informed of the Sephardic custom.[29]

A widespread practice in the Ashkenazic yeshiva world was for the rabbis and students to wear their *tzitzit* (ritual fringes) outside of their shirts, so that they hung down the side of the pants. The longstanding Sephardic practice has been to wear the *tzitzit* under one's shirt, without letting them hang down on the outside of one's clothes. While Rabbi Halevy thought Sephardic students should follow the Sephardic custom, he also was sensitive to the pressures faced by Sephardic students in Ashkenazic *yeshivot*. If such students felt they wanted to wear the *tzitzit* outside, as did the Ashkenazic students, there was no prohibition for them to do so — as long as they thought that by doing so they were enhancing their religious life.[30]

On Passover, Ashkenazim have the custom for a child to "steal" the *afikoman* and hide it. The adults then searched for it. A prize was usually given to the child at the end of this game. This custom was a means of keeping children awake and interested in the proceedings of the seder. Sephardim do not follow this custom, but place the *afikoman* in a sack or towel and pass it around from person to person during the course of the seder. This symbolizes the Israelites carrying their packages on their shoulders as they left slavery in Egypt. A question arose from an Ashkenazic man who had married a Sephardic woman. The couple and their children attended the Passover seder at the home of the wife's parents. Being Sephardic, the wife's father conducted the seder according

---

[29] ALR 8:41.
[30] ALR 2:20; 3:2; 8: short answers 5.

to the Sephardic custom – and there was no "stealing" of the *afikoman*. The Ashkenazic son-in-law, though, wanted his children to follow the Ashkenazic custom at the seder. Rabbi Halevy stated that the seder was to follow the custom of the head of the household, not of the guests – including the son-in-law. Guests who had a different custom could explain to their children the various practices among diverse groups of Jews. This would broaden the children's education.[31]

Unnecessary Stringencies

Rabbi Halevy was undoubtedly a genuine pietist who believed that *mitzvot* should be performed with religious devotion and scrupulous attention to detail. He advocated the maintenance of customs, as part of his general devotion to all aspects of the Jewish religious tradition. He was a religious traditionalist, who well understood the tendency of some people to accept stringent halakhic rulings and to adopt pietistic customs. He did not disapprove of this tendency, unless it resulted in behavior that was presumptuous or arrogant, caused controversy, showed disrespect to one's rabbis, or led to leniencies in other aspects of halakhah. If it was essentially a private matter between a person and the Almighty, it was fine to adopt extra stringencies in matters of religious practice. As a rule, though, he opposed adopting stringencies that had not been instituted by the sages of the Talmud.[32]

Rabbi Halevy had an aversion to false or shallow expressions of religious piety. For example, he condemned the practice of brides and grooms who went to the Western Wall in order to have photographs taken of them and their wedding party. Yes, their wedding photographs would show them at this holy site. But this was only for dramatic effect. In fact, their presence at the Western Wall for photographs was a desecration of the holy place. "On the contrary, they should go on the [wedding] day to

---

[31] ALR 6:35. For other responsa relating to Sephardic and Ashkenazic customs, see ALR 2:23; 2:30; 2:34; 5:18; MH 1:4.

[32] ALR 8:21. See also ALR 5:9 and 7:22 where he opposed adding prohibitions that were not specifically prescribed by the sages of the Talmud.

the Western Wall as individuals, not dressed as bride and groom. They should pour out their prayers and supplications to the Divine Presence that hovers in this holy place, praying that they should have the merit to build a home faithful to the nation of God and His Torah, filled with happiness and blessing."[33]

Some rabbinic authorities had ruled that the thirteen praises of God listed in the *yishtabah* prayer should be chanted in one breath. Rabbi Halevy ruled otherwise. These praises should be read *not* in one breath. Rather, they should be chanted sweetly and slowly. They were so important that they deserved to be read nicely – not rushed in one breath.[34]

He was also unhappy with those who suggested unwarranted or farfetched stringencies of observance, who sought to forbid activities which, in fact, were not forbidden by halakhah. A certain Hassidic Rebbe had declared that it was forbidden to hang pictures of non-kosher animals (e.g., dogs, cats, horses) in children's rooms. Parents should not allow their children to play with toys depicting such animals (e.g., teddy bears). Rabbi Halevy pointed out that this ruling was made by the Rebbe specifically for his own followers. It did not apply to anyone else. As to the gist of the issue, there was no halakhic prohibition of looking at non-kosher animals or at pictures of them. The prophet Yehezkel's vision of the heavenly throne included the images of four animals, including a lion and an eagle – both of which are not kosher. Among the flags of the tribes of Israel were images of non-kosher animals, e.g., lion, eagle, wolf, snake. In olden times, it was common to travel by horse or camel; everyone looked at these animals. Why would anyone think such an activity was prohibited? In conclusion, it was certainly permissible to have pictures or toys of such animals in children's rooms or in schools.[35]

---

[33] ALR 6:83; cf. 8:92.

[34] MKH 1:46, p. 177.

[35] ALR 8:60. See ALR 6:54, where he permitted photographing the sun, moon and stars; and ALR 5:22, where he permitted the drawing of angels that were not

Some rabbis expressed concern about the high costs of weddings. A number issued prohibitions, others made strong proclamations urging their followers to make smaller, less expensive weddings. Among their reasons were the halakhic prohibitions of wastefulness and extravagance. Rabbi Halevy believed there was no halakhic prohibition at all in having large weddings. Obviously, one should not take on extraordinary expenses if he felt it would cause him serious financial problems. The halakhah expected guests at weddings to give gifts to the bride and groom in an amount around equal to the cost the host had to pay for each guest. Thus, the wedding was essentially "paid for," in the sense that the parents paid for the wedding celebration and the guests provided that same amount to the bride and groom.

Aside from the halakhic permissibility of large weddings, Rabbi Halevy pointed out that weddings provided a living for many workers – food companies, caterers, waiters, flower companies, etc. "What need is there to cut off this branch of income that grows from day to day? Moreover, without any doubt this festive evening [the wedding celebration] adds great joy to the couple and their family, relatives and friends. Let happy occasions multiply in Israel, especially during this period of tension over security in which we are living."[36]

Rabbi Halevy was asked if it was permissible to write out the plus sign in mathematics, since it was in the form of a cross – the symbol of Christianity. He found no halakhic objection to writing the plus sign, since it was obviously not for religious purposes, and no one would imagine the mathematical symbol to be a religious sign. He pointed out that there are actual crosses on the currency of various countries, and no one had ever suggested that it was forbidden to use such money.[37]

---

depicted as human beings with wings, and permitted drawing human beings and sculpting the form of a human head.

[36] ALR 1:24; see also ALR 4:26, where he finds no halakhic prohibition for celebrating birthdays.

[37] ALR 5:21.

Rabbi Halevy also saw no halakhic prohibition in using the dates of the Christian calendar, when these dates were necessary for dating business documents or government transactions. On personal letters, one should use the Jewish date. But even on such letters, some great rabbis have used the dates of the Christian calendar. This certainly did not represent any acceptance of Christianity, but was simply a matter of general practice and convenience devoid of theological implications.[38]

In his treatment of questions relating to *minhag*, Rabbi Halevy demonstrated his deep-rooted traditionalism, his keen sense of human psychology, his courage to call for changes when changes were justified, and his dislike for needless prohibitions. His erudition went hand in hand with his sensitivity to the feelings of the parties of each case. He was blessed with a gift that is not so common after all: common sense.

---

[38] ALR 6:55.

Chapter Nine

Questions of Faith

Books of rabbinic responsa normally deal with questions in Jewish law: is this permitted or forbidden, am I or my antagonist in the right, what is the halakhically approved way of behaving in specific situations? Rabbi Halevy's responsa certainly reply to many such questions.

Rabbi Halevy's books of responsa cover a broader range of issues as well. He was interested not only in providing proper halakhic guidance governing behavior; he was also vitally concerned with issues of faith. He sought to clarify basic tenets of Judaism, both to strengthen the faith of believers and to win over those who did not view themselves as being religious. His books of responsa are impressive repositories of breathtaking rabbinic wisdom on a wide variety of topics – legal and philosophical.

In volume one of *Asei Lekha Rav*, he began with an extensive discourse on the religious significance of the State of Israel. In volume two, he offered a treatise on life after death. (These two topics will be considered at length in the chapters on *At'halta deGe'ulah* and Metaphysical Issues.) Volume five opened with a monograph on the Divine nature of Torah (*Torah min haShamayim*), while volume seven included a lengthy essay on the reasons of the *mitzvot* (*Kuntres Ta'amei haMitzvot*). He also dealt with theological, philosophical and metaphysical issues in many of his responsa.

Torah from Heaven

Rabbi Halevy wrote his treatise on "Torah from Heaven"[1] as a follow up to his essay on life after death. That earlier work had influenced a large number of readers and inspired many to return to traditional Jewish belief and observance. He had demonstrated from Torah sources as well as from modern medical/psychological research, that the soul continued to live after the death of the body. Evidence showed that the soul was drawn to an eternal spirit, and that it gave an exact accounting of its life on earth.

Yet, the essay on life after death – while attempting to prove the existence of God, life after death, and the soul's accounting for its life on earth – did not address the question of why Jews should observe Torah during their earthly life. While the soul will ultimately stand in judgment for its actions while on earth, how did we know that the accounting would be related to observance of Torah laws? The essay on "Torah from Heaven" was written to answer this question.

Ultimately, the Divine nature of the Torah was verified by a living tradition, from generation to generation, going back to the Revelation at Mount Sinai. That event, witnessed by the entire nation of Israel, was the incontrovertible proof that the Torah was of Divine origin. It was not based on hearsay or on the testimony of a few individuals; it was grounded in the historical experience of hundreds of thousands of Israelites who were actually present at the Divine Revelation at Mount Sinai.[2] Following the line of reasoning of Rabbi Yehudah Halevy in his *Kuzari*, Rabbi Halevy based the veracity of the Divine nature of Torah on direct historical experience, not on metaphysical speculation.[3]

Rabbi Halevy went further. He argued that the most convincing proofs of the Torah's Divine origin were to be found in the Torah itself. For example, the Torah foresaw the future of the people of Israel after the death of Moshe (*Devarim* 31): and subsequent events proved those

---

[1] ALR 5. Page numbers in subsequent notes refer to this essay.

[2] Pp. 18–19.

[3] Pp. 21ff.

prophecies correct. The Torah presented a number of laws that were dependent on Divine intervention. No human author would have or could have made up these laws, because no human being had the power to implement them. For example, the Torah's description of *sotah* (the wife suspected of infidelity, see *Bemidbar* 5) stated that the priest would give bitter waters to the woman. If she were innocent, nothing would happen. But if she were guilty, her belly would swell. This commandment could only have been given by God, who had the power to implement its terms.[4]

Rabbi Halevy also cited laws relating to *tzara'at*, a ritually impure disease that struck houses and clothing, as well as human beings (see *Vayikra* 13–14). These manifestations were clearly supernatural, with no scientific explanation available.[5] No human author would have listed the infliction of *tzara'at*, because no human being had the power to make such a disease appear.

In the Torah's description of the laws of the agricultural sabbatical year, the Torah commanded that the land lay fallow for a full year in each seven-year cycle. It assured the people that God would provide an extra large crop on the sixth year of each cycle, so that there would be no famine (see *Vayikra* 25). Surely, no human being could have made such a guarantee.[6]

The Torah listed rules governing which animals may or may not be eaten (see *Vayikra* 11, *Devarim* 14). The rules were not only specific, but gave extraordinarily accurate descriptions of physical characteristics of animals. The Torah specified that permissible animals had to have split hooves and chew their cud; it also listed the only animals known to have only one of these traits. Which human being at that time could have known these facts that were true of all animals in the entire world? The Torah listed the characteristics of all kosher fish, and enumerated by name

---

[4] Pp. 30–31.
[5] Pp. 31–34.
[6] Pp. 34–35.

all the forbidden birds. Who could possibly have known all this information with such precision? Only God![7]

Rabbi Halevy cited a number of talmudic passages to demonstrate that the Oral Torah, as well as the Written Torah, were rooted in Divine knowledge. In each case, exact and correct information was presented that could not possibly have been known by our sages on their own. They only could have known those things from a Divinely ordained tradition. Rabbi Halevy also provided arguments for the Divine nature of Torah from the exactitude of the way the Hebrew letters were written in the Torah: the spellings and pronunciations of certain words, the sizes of certain letters with some being larger and others being smaller than normal, the usage of the letters *vav* and *yod*. These precise specifications of the Torah text, and their inner meanings, could not have been devised by human intelligence.[8]

In the preface to volume six of *Asei Lekha Rav*, Rabbi Halevy reported that he had received comments from many readers who indicated that the essay had strengthened their faith in Torah from Heaven.[9] This surely was a source of satisfaction to him.

The Reasons for *Mitzvot*

In volume two, Rabbi Halevy's essay on life after death had demonstrated the existence of God, the survival of the soul after the body's death, and the judgment of the soul in the next world. In volume five, his essay on Torah from Heaven had shown that the Torah was Divinely given and was the authentic way of life to be followed by Jews. In volume seven, he added another link in his philosophical essays on the foundations of faith. "All that a human being does or refrains from doing must be understood by him; he wants to know why he should do something or why he should refrain."[10]

---

[7] Pp. 35–36.

[8] Pp. 43–67.

[9] ALR 6, p. 13. He also added another proof that the Oral Law was of Divine origin. See also, NM, pp. 237f.

[10] ALR 7, p. 17. Subsequent notes will refer to this essay.

Surely, no human being could ever totally understand the full extent of the reasons for *mitzvot*, since no human being can fathom the mind of God. The root and ultimate purpose of the *mitzvot* was tied to the supernal world of spirit, far beyond the grasp of earthly beings.[11]

Having said this, though, Rabbi Halevy asserted that it was important for us to try to understand the reasons for *mitzvot* to the best of our ability. We know we cannot achieve full understanding; and we do not base our observance of the *mitzvot* on our ability to understand them. We do them simply because they are the will of God.

Rabbi Halevy presented a listing of all the Torah's commandments, indicating its belonging to one of four categories: 1) where the Torah itself provided a specific reason for the mitzvah, e.g., eat matzot on Passover to remember that your ancestors rushed from Egyptian slavery and had no time to let their dough rise; 2) where the Torah provided a more general reason, e.g., do a particular action or refrain from a particular action because you are to be holy as God is holy; 3) where the Torah gave no reason, but the reason was easily perceived by human beings, e.g., do not murder, do not steal, do not commit adultery; 4) where the Torah offered no reason and where human reason cannot give a full explanation, e.g., the laws of the red heifer, the prohibition of mixing wool and linen, etc. According to Rabbi Halevy's calculation, the Torah gave specific reasons for 147 *mitzvot*; general reasons for 40 *mitzvot*; 207 *mitzvot* whose reasons were obvious without actually having been stated, and 211 with no reason given and not subject to understanding by human reason. He could not decide the categorization of eight *mitzvot*.[12]

Rabbi Halevy offered a parable of three sick people who consulted an expert physician. The doctor prescribed the necessary regimen of medicines. One patient, trusting completely in the doctor's wisdom, followed the instructions and lived. The second patient did a little research about the medicines and his disease; he then decided which medicines to take and which to reject because he did not understand how they worked.

---

[11] P. 38. See also TH 2, *Devarim*, p. 83.
[12] P. 106.

The second patient died. The third patient did careful research into the disease and into the medicines prescribed by the doctor so that he would understand his situation as well as possible. But he followed the doctor's orders exactly – even those that he did not understand – and he lived.

By analogy, the simple pious Jew observes the *mitzvot* because they were commanded by God, who is infinitely wise. He lives. A skeptic follows those *mitzvot* that appear reasonable to him, but rejects those he does not understand. He destroys his soul. The sage tries his best to understand the reasons for the *mitzvot*, but whether he understands them or not, he still fulfills them. He is on the highest level. He has exerted his mind to the maximum human level, but has also come to understand that God's wisdom, as manifested in the *mitzvot*, is far beyond what human beings can fathom.[13]

In the final analysis, we are expected to fulfill the *mitzvot* simply because they are the commandments of Almighty God. But Rabbi Halevy was not entirely comfortable with a blind piety that would agree with the phrase "it is absurd, therefore I believe." No, human beings were to strive to understand the *mitzvot*, even if they knew they would fall far short of genuine understanding. The very process of striving to understand helped a person attain a deeper spirituality, a closer relationship with *mitzvot* and with God. In Rabbi Halevy's view, it was appropriate to ask questions and seek answers; but it was necessary to observe the *mitzvot* even if one did not – and could not ever – fully comprehend their meanings.

The performance of the *mitzvot* improved our souls for life in the world to come. Punctiliousness in fulfilling the *mitzvot* had profound spiritual impact on our souls, beyond anything we can readily understand.

The Midrash taught that our forefathers – Avraham, Yitzhak and Yaakov – fulfilled the *mitzvot*. They lived long before the Torah was given. Yet, accepting this midrash literally, one can presume that through their heightened spiritual wisdom and their intellectual strivings they discovered hidden meanings for *mitzvot*. For example, they ate matzah on Passover,

---

[13] Pp. 110–111.

even though they lived long before the exodus from Egypt. They obviously understood deeper levels in the mitzvah of matzah; they did not eat matzah as a remembrance of the exodus.[14] Thus, intellectual striving can bring human beings to more sophisticated levels of understanding of Torah.

Prayer

Rabbi Halevy received a question from a university student who had begun a process of becoming religious. The student was studying Judaism and was undertaking to observe *mitzvot*. He had begun to say the daily prayers, but felt mixed emotions. On the one hand, he felt that a person could pour out his heart to God. But on the other hand, he did not feel satisfied intellectually with the notion of prayer. Didn't God already know our needs – why was it necessary to relate them to Him? Moreover, did prayer really have the power to change God's will?

Rabbi Halevy noted that this difficult issue had engaged the thought of our great sages over the generations. He found that the best expression of the meaning of prayer was articulated by the medieval Rabbi Bahya.[15] Rabbi Bahya used to conclude his prayers with the following passage: "Lord, I would not have ventured to stand before you, knowing my little worth and little understanding of Your greatness and awesomeness. For You are grand and lofty, and I am too insignificant to ask help from You and to call out to You with praises and sanctifications of Your holy name. But You have permitted me to do this. You have elevated me by commanding me to call out to You, and You have allowed me to praise Your Name most high, according to my understanding of You, though I am fully aware of my smallness before You. You know my lacks and my patterns of behavior. I have not told You my needs in order to inform You of them, but rather so that I may feel the greatness of my lacks before You and express my trust in You. If I ask, in my foolishness, for something that is not good for me or if I seek something that is not to

---

[14] ALR 5:14.
[15] ALR 1:29; see also MKH 1:58, pp. 231–232.

my benefit, Your higher understanding is greater than my understanding. I lay before You all my concerns and I trust Your existing decrees and Your higher providence."

Rabbi Bahya's prayer, framed in honest humility, recognized that we come before God in prayer not through our merit, but because God has ordained that we pray. Our prayers did not inform God of our needs, but reminded us of our dependence upon God. We needed to keep in mind that God's wisdom far transcends our own, and that He alone knows what is best for us. We entrust our lives to His higher wisdom. One who prays with this attitude will come closer to God.

Having received this explanation from Rabbi Halevy, the student was not satisfied that his questions had been adequately addressed. He still wanted to know if our prayers could alter God's will, if God had already decreed something.[16] (For example, if a person were dying, could his prayers change God's mind so that He would give healing, even though His original intention was for the person to die of this illness?)

Rabbi Halevy pointed to examples in the Bible where prayers were offered and God responded by fulfilling the prayers. Nevertheless, it would be wrong to think that God's will changes. So what, then, happened when one prayed?

Rabbi Halevy offered an insightful analogy: "Receiving the Divine influence can be compared to rain. Just as rain cannot make the earth flourish without the earth having been cultivated in advance through plowing and planting, so prayer and the spiritual preparation that goes with it cannot be helpful without prior preparation. A man cannot pray for prosperity while he sits lazily at home; he cannot pray for good health if his actions undermine the rules of hygiene. He cannot pray for wisdom if his mind is not prepared to receive wisdom. Everything depends on God's words: 'And I will bless you in all that you do'."

God's influence of blessing pours on the earth, in His kindness and compassion. It spreads over everyone. Yet, those who are more

---

[16] ALR 2:22.

cultivated spiritually will receive more of God's spirit. Whether we feel God's presence and blessing is less dependent on God than on us. Prayer raises our spiritual sensitivities, thus making us more receptive to God's compassion. Prayer does not change God's will: it changes us.

Rabbi Halevy cited the talmudic passage: "One who elongates in his prayer and analyzes it – in the end he will have a broken heart."[17] Rashi commented that the person who prayed with devotion on the assumption that God would heed his prayers – such a person will have his heart broken since his request will not be fulfilled. Prayer was not a forum for making demands of God and expecting their prompt implementation. Rather, prayer was a framework for a person to come closer to God. The more one prayed, the more he refined his soul to be receptive to God's blessings.

While recognizing that God answered prayers, Rabbi Halevy did not see prayer essentially as a utilitarian means of manipulating God to do what we asked of Him. Rather, he described prayer as a means for a human being to become more receptive to the Divine spirit.

When asked by another questioner why God could possibly need our prayers and performance of *mitzvot*, Rabbi Halevy candidly stated that he had no ready answer for this age-old dilemma. We will not have a clear resolution of this question until messianic times, when the world will be filled with knowledge of the Lord. Nevertheless, our sages have emphasized that God Himself linked the existence of the world to our fulfillment of Torah. Although He did not "need" our prayers and performance of *mitzvot*, He had predicated the existence of the world on our spiritual performance. Instead of our inquiring why this should be so, we should devote ourselves to spiritual improvement whereby we will hasten the arrival of the messianic era.[18]

---

[17] *Berakhot* 25a.
[18] ALR 8:94–95.

When Bad Things Happen

In the mid-1980s, a bus crashed killing twenty-two children from Petah Tikvah. Some rabbis had proclaimed that this tragedy came as punishment for sins. The children's families or the society at large were responsible for evoking God's punishment.

Many people turned to Rabbi Halevy for his views on this topic. He presented biblical and rabbinic sources that shed light on the topic of reward and punishment. Since no human being could possibly know the exact workings of God's mind, no human being could state with certainty whether any particular disaster was a Divine punishment or simply an accident. Rabbi Halevy was clearly troubled by those rabbis who unhesitatingly attributed the bus crash to God's punishment. It was the height of arrogance to make such a statement.

Was it possible that this or other disasters were punishments from God? Yes, of course, it was possible. Whenever tragedy occurred, it was appropriate to review one's behavior and undertake the ways of repentance. But Judaism rejected fatalism. When there were rational explanations of why particular tragedies occurred, one could assume that these were accidents rather than Divine fiats. A parallel can be drawn to human conduct. If one lives an unhealthy lifestyle, he will become ill. This was not a Divine punishment, but a natural consequence of his own irresponsible behavior. Likewise, if a bus crashed, one would need to determine whether the driver was going too fast or too recklessly, or the bus had mechanical flaws, or the weather conditions made driving dangerous. If we could explain the crash logically, then it could be assumed it was an accident – not a punishment.[19]

A question arose: if a soldier were killed in battle, was this a punishment or simply a natural occurrence?[20] Rabbi Halevy answered: it could generally be assumed that death in battle was a natural occurrence.

---

[19] ALR 7:69; See also ALR 8:93.

[20] ALR 7: short answers 78. For further discussion, see the chapter on Dealing With Conflicting Sources.

There was no compelling reason to attribute such a death to Divine punishment.

Rabbi Halevy offered a sophisticated, nuanced discussion of God's providence, eschewing the simplistic pronouncements of popular spokesmen of religion. Human beings were not God's record-keepers and did not know the workings of God's mind. We should use our human intelligence to understand and explain that which can be rationally understood and explicated. And that which is beyond our ken, we should leave to God.

Chapter Ten

METAPHYSICAL ISSUES

In *Dat uMedinah* (p. 75), Rabbi Halevy set out his educational philosophy, to which he adhered meticulously: the way to attract people to Judaism is to teach the essentials of faith first, and to explain specific *mitzvot* later. To this end, he devoted considerable attention to afterlife and other metaphysical issues. He acknowledged that we cannot fully fathom matters pertaining to the soul, dreams, magic, or prayer; but he attempted to guide his readers by appealing to what we could learn from rabbinic and kabbalistic teachings.

Death and Afterlife

Rabbi Halevy fielded numerous questions pertaining to death and afterlife.[1] One of his most significant expositions was a lengthy treatise on afterlife, published in *Asei Lekha Rav* 2:2–19. In this essay, he compared kabbalistic teachings to the findings of Dr. Raymond Moody, a professor of psychology in Virginia who studied near-death experiences. Rabbi Halevy noted a striking resemblance between the respective descriptions of near-death experiences: a dark tunnel; a great light[2]; feelings of love; seeing deceased relatives; vivid images of experiences while alive; ability to

---

[1] Rabbi Halevy noted that so many people had been asking him questions on this subject, that he decided to compose a systematic study of afterlife (ALR 2, p. 17).
[2] In MKH 5:279, p. 355; 290, p. 424, Rabbi Halevy quoted the Zohar, stating that people experience the Divine Presence at the moment of death.

see what was happening "below," near their bodies.[3] Dr. Moody noted that many who revived after clinical death wanted to live more meaningfully lives. This was a relevant lesson for all humans.[4]

Years later, Rabbi Halevy testified to the success of that essay in drawing many Jews closer to their faith.[5] That exposition also elicited several follow up questions, published in later volumes of *Asei Lekha Rav*.

The Soul World

Rabbi Halevy quoted the Zohar, that had Adam not sinned he would have been able to die without any pain of separation. Rabbi Halevy maintained that anyone who lives a holy lifestyle might merit that privilege (*Berakhot* 8a).[6]

In a responsum, Rabbi Halevy referred to a news item in the Israeli daily *Yediot Aharonot* (18 *Tammuz* 5735), where the bodies of two saintly rabbis were found completely intact some thirty years after their deaths.[7] Drawing on rabbinic teachings, he explained that although one's body generally decomposed after the soul left it, there still remained some connection between body and soul. The few physical remains will form the

---

[3] ALR 2, pp. 18, 23–24.

[4] ALR 2, pp. 21, 61–66.

[5] ALR 5, p. 15.

[6] ALR 1:46; see also MKH 5:279, pp. 357–358. Cf. MZR (p. 45), where Rabbi Halevy quoted the Zohar (*Vayhi* 145b): God sends the souls of the righteous to this world, and then takes them back to Heaven, which is why people in this world should be happy for the righteous when they die. It is the King bringing an honored guest back to the palace (cf. p. 167, where the souls of the righteous themselves also look forward to heaven – Zohar *Vayera* 98a). In MZR (p. 106), Rabbi Halevy quoted another passage in the Zohar (*Vayishlah* 168), that the truly righteous do not die at the hand of the angel of death, but rather by a kiss (cf. MZR, p. 143, Zohar *Mishpatim* 124b). Generally, the separation of the soul from the body is the most painful experience (MZR, p. 141, from Zohar *Metzora* 54b; *Vayhi* 145a). See also ALR 1:53, where Rabbi Halevy discussed the issue of non-Jews attaining afterlife.

[7] ALR 1:51.

foundation of a new body at the time of the resurrection.[8] The Talmud (*Bava Batra* 17a) enumerated categories of righteous individuals whose bodies remained intact after death as a result of supernatural protection. Rabbi Halevy saw the news item as concrete proof of Jewish teachings about the afterlife. He then criticized the newspaper: "It is lamentable that this supernatural occurrence…is hidden in an obscure corner of a daily newspaper. It would have been appropriate to give great publicity to this incredible finding, which is reliable testimony to the afterlife."[9]

A non-observant medical student requested more information concerning the connection between the soul world and our earthly world.[10] Rabbi Halevy noted that the Torah prohibited necromancy, but recognized a connection between the two worlds.[11] He then cited the talmudic debate about what souls knew about this world, including the possibility of their returning here for brief visits.

Someone asked if souls interacted in the other world. Rabbi Halevy opened with a disclaimer: we cannot respond to such questions with certainty, but rabbinic literature hinted at answers. A Midrash taught that

---

[8] Cf. ALR 2:6. In MZR (p. 162), however, Rabbi Halevy quoted the Zohar (*Vayhi* 225a), that the body and soul remain connected for twelve months after death, after which the soul departs to its final destination and leaves the body behind.

[9] ALR 1:51, p. 150.

[10] ALR 1:52; see also MKH 5:292, pp. 433–435.

[11] In ALR 5: short answers 69, Rabbi Halevy asserted that contemporary spiritual séances are nonsensical, and also forbidden by the Torah. In ALR 8:51, someone suggested that perhaps séances could increase faith in the afterlife, and therefore should be encouraged. Rabbi Halevy responded that the Torah explicitly prohibited necromancy, and therefore there was no way to permit it. He recommended the study of near-death experiences, which is permissible (and which formed the basis for his own exposition on afterlife in ALR 2:2–19). In MH 2:49, Rabbi Halevy ruled that it is prohibited to ask a non-Jew to conduct a séance to ascertain the identity of a murderer, since we may not ask non-Jews to violate Torah law for us. He expressed skepticism towards the contemporary practice, noting that if the police had thought that there was any validity to this method, they would use it without asking a rabbi. Rabbi Halevy concluded that God had other ways of punishing evildoers, and therefore we should not violate Torah law under the pretense of catching criminals.

souls were placed into different "rooms" in heaven, and could not see each other. But another Midrash taught that as part of their punishment, the souls of the wicked were brought to heaven to witness the reward of the righteous. Rabbi Halevy attempted to reconcile these two sources, suggesting that perhaps there was some general interaction of souls, but not of a deep quality.[12]

Rabbi Halevy appealed to the body-soul connection in his discussions of several halakhic issues. In his ruling on organ transplants, he explained the laws of *bizayon hamet* (showing disrespect to the dead), with the premise that the soul hovered over one's body after death (*Shabbat* 152b).[13] It would cause the *soul* pain were someone to damage the body. If the body could be used to save the life of another person through an organ transplant, however, we may assume that the soul would be happy to assist. Therefore, transplants are permitted when the body is considered dead by halakhah.[14] Elsewhere, Rabbi Halevy ruled that once a person cannot breathe independently (e.g., brain stem death), the respirator could be unplugged. This would keep the person's soul from being held hostage in its body, and free it of torture.[15] The soul benefited from a good eulogy,

---

[12] ALR 5:34; cf. ALR 4:69. In MZR (p. 23), Rabbi Halevy quoted the Zohar (*Vayhi* 135a): the souls of Avraham and Yitzhak came to greet the soul of Yaakov when the latter died. Cf. MZR (pp. 140–141, from Zohar *Vayhi* 217–218), where he states that people are greeted by their own deceased relatives when they die – but they are accompanied by those relatives only until they reach their destination (cf. ALR 2:2; 2:9; also MHK 5:279, p. 353, where Rabbi Halevy quoted the Zohar stating that the outstandingly righteous of each generation are greeted by the Patriarchs as well). In MZR (pp. 161–162), however, Rabbi Halevy discussed other sources in the Zohar that indicate that souls do communicate with one another in heaven.

[13] See also ALR 2:2; 2:10–11.

[14] ALR 4:64.

[15] ALR 5:29; cf. MH 3:34. Rabbi Halevy composed many responsa on topics of medical ethics. He often appealed to metaphysical issues in the course of his halakhic discussions. For some responsa on medical ethics, see ALR 2:56; 3:30; 32; 4:64; 65; 66; 5:29; 6:64; 8:64; 9:22; MH 1:61; 2:62; 3:33; 34; 36. See also Shalom Ratzabi, "Rabbi Haim David Halevy – Halakhah and Philosophy: A Study of the Question of Taking a Terminal Patient Off of a Respirator," in the

since God tells the angels of judgment to see what people are saying about the deceased.[16]

Rabbi Halevy defended a custom that a bride and groom visit the cemetery to invite their deceased parents to their wedding.[17] He then used that question as a springboard to discuss the afterlife.[18] Although the Bible prohibits necromancy, it indicates that this practice could be effective (the biblical story of the Witch of Endor conjuring up the spirit of Shmuel in *I Shmuel* 28 also supports this belief). The Zohar taught that God brought the souls of parents to witness joyous events in the lives of their children. Rabbi Halevy concluded that there was no necessity to invite the souls of one's parents to the wedding, since God would bring them anyway. Rather, this practice developed in order to strengthen belief in afterlife.[19]

Elsewhere, Rabbi Halevy also referred 'to the practice of the bride and groom to visit the cemetery to invite their deceased parents to their wedding. This time, though, he called it an "ostensibly bizarre custom"![20] Although he went on to note that the practice had a basis in kabbalah, his

---

volume of papers about Rabbi Halevy, edited by Zvi Zohar and Avi Sagi. For a more general overview of Rabbi Halevy's interrelating of halakhah and aggadah, see Avinoam Rosenak, "Halakhah, Philosophy, and the Term 'Kedushah' in the Writings of Rabbi Haim David Halevy" in the Zohar-Sagi volume.

[16] MKH 5:283, pp. 376–384.

[17] See discussion in the chapter on The Role of *Minhag*.

[18] ALR 1:50.

[19] In MZR (pp. 84–85, 164), Rabbi Halevy quoted several passages from the Zohar pertaining to the souls of the righteous visiting this world. But see pp. 167–168, where he quoted other passages that appear to contradict this teaching (he discussed the contradiction as well). See also MKH 2:95, pp. 221–232, for an elaborate discussion of the connection between the two worlds as it relates to the practice of praying to God at the graves of righteous individuals or one's own family members. Cf. MKH 4:182, pp. 38–39, where Rabbi Halevy quoted the Zohar (*Balak* 196b), that the souls of the righteous visit especially during the months of *Nisan* and *Tishrei*. See further discussion of the significance of visiting graves in MKH 5:294, p. 441; 295, pp. 445–456. Throughout those discussions, Rabbi Halevy was careful to warn that one always must pray to God, not to the deceased.

[20] MKH 5:236, p. 26; MKH *leHatan veKhallah* 3, p. 26.

presentation of the material is considerably different from that in ALR 1:50, where he defended the practice, and used the question as a springboard to promote faith in afterlife. In ALR 1:50, he was responding to a person who himself considered the practice bizarre, so Rabbi Halevy emphasized the positive elements of this custom.

Rabbi Halevy employed different biblical verses to support the body-soul dichotomy. In ALR 1:50 (and ALR 1:61; 2:2; 2:3), he wrote that *Bereshit* 2:7 ("The Lord God formed man of the dust of the ground, and breathed into his nostrils the breath of life; and man became a living soul") is an explicit Torah reference to the existence of an independent soul. But in ALR 1:51 (the next responsum), he maintained that *Bereshit* 2:7 only *hints* at the soul. He appealed to *Kuzari* I:109 for an explanation of why the Torah never discussed afterlife explicitly.[21] In ALR 1:54, a discussion of *yibbum* (levirate marriage), he considered *Kohelet* 3:21 ("Who knows whether the spirit of man goes upward, and the spirit of the beast goes downward to the earth?") the most explicit biblical reference to afterlife.[22] This particular citation is fascinating, since the simple reading of that verse is a *question*![23]

Once again, it appears that Rabbi Halevy employed sources in a manner that would address his particular questioner in the most effective and appropriate way. In ALR 1:50, when a bride and groom did not perceive the value of inviting their parents' souls to their wedding, Rabbi Halevy wrote that afterlife was an explicit teaching of the Torah. He offered further arguments (dreams, instinct) that the soul's presence can be felt on earth. In ALR 1:54, when discussing *yibbum* (levirate marriage), he

---

[21] See also ALR 2:18, which Rabbi Halevy appended to his excursus on the afterlife. There, he offered an elaborate exposition on Rabbi Yehudah Halevy's answer, concluding that afterlife was an obvious reality to the generation receiving the Torah; therefore, the Torah emphasized how one may attain this eternal life.

[22] Cf. MKH 5, p. 12; introduction to MKH *leHatan veKhallah*, p. 12; ALR 2:18.

[23] For a recent survey and discussion of biblical references to afterlife, see James L. Kugel, *The Great Poems of the Bible: A Reader's Companion with New Translations* (New York: The Free Press, 1999), pp. 192–210.

intended to persuade readers of the connection between our world and the soul world.[24] He therefore stressed that the Bible referred explicitly to afterlife. But when offering a more theoretical exposition of the non-rotting of the bodies of saintly people (ALR 1:51), he did not claim explicit biblical references to the afterlife. He relied on rabbinic and kabbalistic explanations of the phenomenon.

Rabbi Halevy appealed to dreams, intuitions, and related matters in a lecture to police officers.[25] Citing his own exposition on afterlife in *Asei Lekha Rav* 2:2–19, he noted that Dr. Moody's study of near-death experiences confirmed that souls felt shame for immoral earthly deeds. He concluded that we should live holier, more meaningful lifestyles.

Gilgul (Reincarnation)

Rabbi Halevy discussed *yibbum* (levirate marriage), and its dependence on the concept of *gilgul* (reincarnation). The soul of a deceased man who was married could not rest if he died without children. In the event that his widow did not want to marry his brother (or the brother did not want to marry her), the Torah mandated the *halitzah* ceremony in order to free the soul of the deceased (see *Devarim* 25:5–10). To underscore this point, Rabbi Halevy related a dream of a man who did not want to marry his deceased brother's widow, but superstitiously was afraid to perform the *halitzah* ceremony. The deceased brother came to him in a dream, asking why he was preventing his soul from resting in the afterlife.[26] In another responsum, Rabbi Halevy inferred from kabbalistic sources that the soul of the deceased husband entered the first child born from the levirate marriage. "This is why *yibbum* is called an act of lovingkindness for the deceased."[27]

---

[24] He returned to this topic several times in his writings. See ALR 3:33; 4:67; MH 3:44.

[25] ALR 4:69; cf. MKH 5:283, pp. 381–382.

[26] ALR 1:54.

[27] ALR 4:67; cf. MH 3:44. In MZR (pp. 65–66, 102–103, 109–110), Rabbi Halevy quoted extensively from the Zohar on the subjects of *gilgul, halitzah*, and *yibbum*.

Someone asked how resurrection would work if there was *gilgul*, since each soul had multiple bodies associated with it. Rabbi Halevy responded that each root soul had many sparks. In each *gilgul*, a few sparks were active; therefore those sparks can be distributed among the different bodies that had housed that soul. Rabbi Halevy suggested that people who look nearly identical might have souls from the same root.[28]

Do Mentally Retarded People Earn a Share in the World to Come?

Rabbi Halevy addressed a difficult question relating to his exposition on afterlife (ALR 2:2–19). He had written that one's portion in the world to come was proportional to one's spiritual cultivation in this life. What about people who were born mentally retarded, or who lost their thinking ability due to an accident or illness? Were such people deprived of a portion in the world to come? Rabbi Halevy began with his usual disclaimer, that we do not have complete understanding of metaphysical issues. He then cited the Zohar (*Aharei Mot* 61b), that some souls were distanced from God even before they entered this world. Perhaps the souls of mentally deficient humans were in this category. It also was possible that such people are reincarnations of souls that needed to atone for some misdeed done during an earlier lifetime. This particular issue was painful to discuss, and the reader feels Rabbi Halevy's deep sensitivity as he tried to defend the kabbalistic tradition.[29]

Dreams

Rabbi Halevy addressed a variety of questions pertaining to dreams. Rabbinic tradition asserted that some dreams could be "1/60 of prophecy" (*Berakhot* 57b; cf. *Vayikra Rabbah* 32:2), whereas others were pure fantasy

---

[28] ALR 4:68; cf. ALR 2:4–5; MH 2:69. In MZR (pp. 246–248), Rabbi Halevy quoted several passages from the Zohar pertaining to resurrection.

[29] ALR 3:35. Cf. MZR (p. 65), where Rabbi Halevy quoted the Zohar (*Ki Tetzei* 72b) to answer the classical question of when bad things happen to good people. They must be a *gilgul* of someone who had been a sinner in a previous lifetime, so the soul now is being paid back.

(*Berakhot* 55a), or derived primarily from the foods one ate before going to sleep (*Berakhot* 56a).[30]

A woman reported that her first husband had been killed in war. She later married one of his close friends. Her first husband appeared to her in a dream, requesting that she name a child after him. She wanted to know if this was appropriate. Rabbi Halevy responded by citing *halakhot* prohibiting a woman from showing signs of mourning over her first husband in the presence of her second husband. If the second husband genuinely did not mind, though, she may name her son after her first husband. Rabbi Halevy then discussed the possibility of this dream having prophetic value. If so, it would imply that the first husband was approving of her marriage to his friend. Rabbi Halevy suggested that the woman share this interpretation with her new husband, and perhaps he might then agree to name the child after his friend. Whether her dream was prophecy or fantasy, Rabbi Halevy offered an interpretation that would avoid resentment or jealousy.[31]

Another woman wrote Rabbi Halevy that before she was married, she had promised her husband that she would become religiously observant. Though she was observant at home, she still ate non-kosher food and violated Shabbat outside of the home. She began having dreams that she should get divorced, or that she was divorced already. What should she do?[32] Rabbi Halevy praised her: "Before beginning, I want to note that from your letter, it appears that you are an extremely upright person, and your deepest desire is to be straight with others; there is no doubt this is why you have had these dreams."[33] He explained that dreams emanated from one's independent soul (he quoted *Bereshit* 2:7, again as an explicit biblical proof; see discussion above) and confirmed the world of spirit. He then explained that some dreams were 1/60 of prophecy, but

---

[30] In MZR (pp. 101–102), Rabbi Halevy quoted several passages from the Zohar pertaining to the different levels of dreams and their interpretation.

[31] ALR 1:45. See also ALR 7:56.

[32] ALR 1:61.

[33] ALR 1:61, p. 185.

others were psychological manifestations. Since we cannot evaluate our true motives even when awake, how can we possibly evaluate dreams objectively? As a result, Rabbi Halevy suggested that she work hard at keeping her promise of observance, reading a chapter of Tanakh each day, and consulting her local rabbi for guidance. She should not tell her husband about these dreams. Rabbi Halevy thus tried to save the woman's marriage and to bring her closer to Torah and observance.

Rabbi Halevy explained the concept of *ta'anit halom* (a private fast accepted as a result of a bad dream). Regardless of whether the dream was prophetic or psychologically stimulated, one should *view* it as a heavenly call for repentance.[34] However, Rabbi Halevy discouraged the *ta'anit halom* on Shabbat (despite talmudic permission to do so; see *Ta'anit* 12b). Since fasting is generally prohibited on Shabbat, and most people are unable to evaluate their dreams properly, it was better not to become overly distressed by a bad dream.[35]

Occasionally, dreams can have practical halakhic ramifications. A woman reported a dream in which she vowed not to eat meat – did she need to annul this vow, or should she simply ignore the dream?[36] Rabbi Halevy again noted that dreams might or might not have validity. Perhaps she had been contemplating such a vow, and this intention manifested itself in her dream.[37] If the dream actually were a heavenly message, she would need to annul the vow in the presence of a *minyan*. Rabbi Halevy recommended taking the more stringent measure, to avoid even the slightest possibility of violating the biblical rules of vows.

In several responsa, Rabbi Halevy considered dreams as certain prophecy. In one case, a young woman had become religiously observant and subsequently had a dream that her religious grandfather came to her

---

[34] MKH 1:62, pp. 290–292.

[35] MKH 3:133, pp. 181–184.

[36] ALR 7:43.

[37] The *Shulhan Arukh* considered it preferable to be stringent and annul to vow.

and told her to change her name from Berakhah to Leah.[38] Rabbi Halevy assumed that she had not been considering changing her name, and therefore he felt certain that this dream was 1/60 of prophecy: "Your dream appears serious and interesting. It does not appear to me to have emanated from your imagination, because nobody thinks about name changes while awake to such a degree that it would elicit a dream.... Therefore, it is clear to me that your dream contains 1/60 of prophecy."[39] To interpret the dream, Rabbi Halevy quoted the Talmud (*Rosh Hashanah* 16b), that a name change is one of four things that can annul an evil decree. He concluded that her grandfather came to strengthen her own repentance, and possibly to warn her about some decree – maybe barrenness, since God opened Leah's womb. Rabbi Halevy suggested that she add Leah to her name, rather than changing it entirely.

When a brother dreamed that his deceased brother urged him to perform *halitzah*, Rabbi Halevy believed the dream to be true – the message was from the next world. Rabbi Halevy believed that not doing *halitzah* could harm the soul of the deceased brother. He did not raise the possibility of the dream being the result of the living brother's own inner conflicts.[40]

Astrology,[41] Palm Reading, Meditation

Rabbi Halevy walked a fine line between defending what he considered authentic Jewish mystical teaching and rejecting superstition. For example, several traditional Jewish sources considered palm reading a true wisdom. The Zohar taught that one could determine personality from a proper reading of palm lines; another passage in the Zohar stated that were one to repent, one actually could alter the lines on one's palms. After affirming

---

[38] ALR 2:41. Cf. ALR 7:49–52, for an elaborate discussion of the metaphysical impact of a name. See also ALR 6:69; 6: short answers 78.

[39] ALR 2:41, p. 150.

[40] ALR 1:54.

[41] For a survey of rabbinic opinions on astrology, see Rabbi Yaakov Schwartz, "Jewish Implications of Astrology," *Journal of Halacha and Contemporary Society* 16 (Fall, 1988), pp. 6–23.

the general truth of palm reading,[42] Rabbi Halevy asserted that contemporary practitioners of palm reading are unreliable. It is preferable not to consult a palm reader, but rather to rely on our own actions to shape our future. Moreover, there is psychological benefit in not attempting to ascertain the future: one who knew that a disaster is coming will sink into despair. By not consulting a fortune-teller, one may keep matters in one's own hands, and work to create a better future.[43]

Rabbi Halevy adopted a similar approach toward astrological predictions. Many great Jewish thinkers believed that there is truth to astrology; but one could change one's fate by modifying one's own behavior. Although some talmudic Sages accepted the wisdom of astrology, they already were skeptical of people who practiced it in their time (*Sotah* 12b). Rabbi Halevy readily applied this premise to today as well. He noted that Rambam was one of the few medieval Jewish thinkers who denied the validity of this wisdom.[44]

In the above instances, Rabbi Halevy fundamentally believed in the rabbinic sources that acknowledged the validity of palm reading and astrology. Yet, he dismissed those practices today on the grounds that most practitioners are unreliable; people are better off repenting than relying on fortune-tellers, who were probably fraudulent.

In the case of astrology, Rabbi Halevy had no qualms admitting that Rambam held a position at odds with much of rabbinic tradition. Yet, when discussing Rambam's position towards cursing, Rabbi Halevy did not think that Rambam would deny so many talmudic teachings.[45] It seems that context dictated Rabbi Halevy's tone. In the case of astrology, he wanted to discourage people from becoming involved in such pursuits; therefore, he quoted the Sages' skepticism toward the practitioners, as well as Rambam's dissenting opinion. In this manner, he protected the truth of rabbinic teachings, but was able to distinguish between theory and

---

[42] See a similar defense of the concept of the Evil Eye in MH 2:42.

[43] ALR 1:56. See also ALR 7: short answers 54; MH 3:42.

[44] ALR 1:57.

[45] ALR 3:54, see discussion in the chapter on Dealing With Conflicting Sources.

practice. In the case of cursing, he wanted to discourage the questioner from cursing, and also to prevent him from doubting rabbinic teachings. Therefore, Rabbi Halevy did not want to present Rambam as a legitimate dissenter from the talmudic tradition.

Rabbi Halevy was asked whether children's magic shows were included in the halakhic ban on magic. Rabbi Halevy maintained that contemporary magic shows are permissible. The talmudic prohibition referred to placing the audience into a hypnotic trance. Tricks by sleight of hand are allowed; everyone knew that if our eyes were as quick as the magician's hand that we would understand the mechanics of the trick.[46]

Rabbi Halevy had little tolerance for rituals deriving from Eastern religion. A karate student expressed concern that at each session, the group bowed to the original founder of karate, and then to one another. Rabbi Halevy warned that many Eastern practices emanated from genuine idolatry; the student should avoid performing these practices.[47]

Similarly, Rabbi Halevy forbade mantras and other Eastern meditation rituals.[48] Mantras generally were the names of pagan deities, not merely nonsensical syllables. Rabbi Halevy offered a broader discussion of meditation, even were one to strip away the pagan ritual aspects. The goal of meditation is to utilize techniques to clear one's mind of thought, i.e., its goal is to generate emptiness. In contrast, *mitzvot* and prayer embrace reality, rather than trying to escape it. They transform worldly tensions into holiness. "It is tragic that this generation has forsaken the splendor and beauty of God's Torah, with all of its eternal values, in order to dig for itself broken cisterns that hold no water."[49]

---

[46] ALR 2:44. For a survey of rabbinic opinions pertaining to magic shows, see Rabbi Moshe A. Bleich, "Magic Shows," *Journal of Halacha and Contemporary Society* 33 (Spring, 1997), pp. 17–36. Rabbi Bleich (p. 34) asserts that Rabbi Halevy was the only contemporary decisor who reached a clearly permissive ruling on magic shows, while other leading rabbis were inclined either to prohibit, or at least to restrict the permissibility of these shows.

[47] ALR 2:45.

[48] ALR 2:47.

[49] ALR 2:47, p. 180.

Rabbi Halevy's emphasis on combining the realms of halakhah, aggadah, and kabbalah served as a balanced approach to religious life. He recognized that many Jews felt uninspired by the performance of *mitzvot*. In presenting Jewish teaching as an organic whole in *Mekor Hayyim* and his responsa, Rabbi Halevy attempted to restore the original spiritual meaning and context to the normative practices.[50]

Prayer

Prayer is one of the most authentic expressions of Jewish spirituality. Rabbi Halevy sought to reconcile sources proclaiming the efficacy of prayer with other sources that suggested that prayer was not always efficacious. Rabbi Halevy agreed with Rabbi Bahya, who had written that we pray for our own spiritual growth, as a reminder of our dependence on God. Of course, we do not expect to change God's mind. If one genuinely prays with purity and humility, one will come closer to God. Ironically, one is most likely to have one's prayers fulfilled when he or she does not feel worthy of being answered.[51] Rabbi Halevy explained that we are encouraged to sing in prayer (despite the fact that we would not sing our requests to a human king), since music is uplifting. The primary purpose of praying is to deepen our spiritual sensitivities.[52]

Rabbi Halevy discussed the special power of prayer of a sick person who prayed for healing. These prayers were considered more meaningful, because the ill person is much more spiritually aware than usual. One's trust in God eliminated fear. The forces of the spirit exert great spiritual energy on the body, and help in the healing process.[53]

---

[50] See also the article by Yosef Ahituv, "Popular Kabbalah and Modernism in the View of Rabbi Haim David Halevy," in the volume of papers about Rabbi Halevy, edited by Zvi Zohar and Avi Sagi.

[51] ALR 1:29; cf. ALR 2:22; MKH 1:58, pp. 231–234. See further discussion in the chapter on Questions of Faith.

[52] ALR 4:17; cf. ALR 8:94–95.

[53] MKH 1:55, p. 221.

Rabbi Halevy explained that cursing another person could have metaphysical effect.[54] Why should curses work? One deserving of punishment should be punished, anyway; if the person did not deserve punishment God should not allow the curse to be effective. Rabbi Halevy explained that God generally does not punish a person immediately, thereby giving that person the opportunity to repent. If someone cursed another during God's moment of wrath (see *Berakhot* 7a), rightful justice might come.[55] After concluding that cursing can be effective, he advised the questioner not to curse anyone, but rather to study Torah and perform extra *mitzvot*. In this way, his enemies might disappear by themselves (*Gittin* 7a).

Rabbi Halevy discussed the early morning prayer that stated: "Forever should one be God-fearing in secret as in public, admitting truth, and speaking truth to his heart."[56] Only a truly pure and God-fearing person was prepared to accept truth, and admit when he or she was wrong. Rabbi Avraham ben haRambam maintained that Rabbi Yehudah haNasi was called *"Rabbeinu haKadosh"* (the holy rabbi) because of his courage to admit that the words of some non-Jewish scientists of his day had a view preferable to that of the rabbis (*Pesahim* 94b). It is indeed fascinating that Rabbi Halevy – a devotee of kabbalah – quoted Rabbi Avraham ben haRambam's vision of holiness. Normally, the title "Kadosh" was reserved for kabbalists. This citation by Rabbi Halevy is emblematic of his religious worldview. He was deeply steeped in mystical teachings; but he also had a stunning intellectual honesty and a clear recognition of limitations of knowledge. He used rabbinic debates and uncertainties to inspire increased spiritual sensitivity and observance.

In *Mekor Hayyim* volume 5, Rabbi Halevy utilized the Laws of Mourning as an opportunity to discuss the world of the soul. He

---

[54] ALR 3:54.

[55] In MZR (p. 94), Rabbi Halevy quoted the Zohar (*Aharei Mot* 58a), which elaborates on different times of mercy and judgment for seasons, days, and times of the day.

[56] MKH 1:39, p. 143.

enumerated different factors that might encourage souls to visit this world voluntarily. One such incentive is when the Torah insights of the deceased are studied.[57] Perhaps it is a fitting concluding prayer, that by our studying his religious teachings, his soul should derive much benefit and satisfaction.

---

[57] MKH 5:292, p. 434.

Chapter Eleven

RESPECT FOR OTHERS

One of the fundamental Torah values that imbued Rabbi Halevy's worldview is encapsulated in the phrase *kevod haberiyot*, respect for others. *Kevod haberiyot* is not just a matter of good manners or civil behavior; it is a Torah commandment rooted in the words "and you shall love your neighbor as yourself" (*Vayikra* 19:18).[1] It is a vital part of the commandments governing relationships between person and person; and these commandments are essential to righteous living and proper service to God. Indeed, the commandments *bein adam lehaveiro*, relating to interpersonal relationships, are in some ways even more important than the commandments *bein adam laMakom,* between humans and the Almighty.[2]

The halakhah goes to great lengths to protect the self-respect of each individual. It permits "white lies" under certain circumstances, in order to spare embarrassment or bad feelings. The school of Hillel taught that one should praise a bride for her beauty and gracefulness – even if one thought she did not have these qualities in great measure. One should give polite compliments, for the sake of maintaining harmony and good feelings – even if the compliments stretched the truth.[3]

Rabbi Halevy referred to the well-known story of the great eighteenth century sage, Rabbi Yehezkel Landau, author of the *Noda*

---

[1] ALR 7:45.
[2] ALR 3:19; 6:86.
[3] MH 3:56.

beYehudah volumes of responsa. When Rabbi Landau began to serve his congregation in Prague, he saw that the sexton of the synagogue held a plaque on which the blessings for the Torah reading were printed. When learned people were called to read from the Torah, the sexton did not put out the plaque; the learned people, after all, knew the blessings by heart. But when ordinary people were called to the Torah, the sexton put out the plaque before them so that they could read the blessings. This, of course, caused a certain embarrassment to the ordinary people, since they were publicly shown not to know the blessings by heart. When Rabbi Landau was called to the Torah in his new congregation, he whispered to the sexton that he wanted the printed blessings put before him. He then read the blessings from the plaque. He continued this practice all his life, as a means of showing that even the rabbi needed to read the blessings and did not recite them by heart. This was his way of identifying with the ordinary congregants, and removing any shame that they may have felt in needing to read the blessings.[4]

This story about Rabbi Landau is characteristic of the extreme sensitivity of our sages to the feelings of others, especially the common folk who were less educated, less wealthy, and less prominent than others. Over the generations, the rabbis enacted ordinances to protect the honor of such individuals.

Rabbi Halevy was distinguished for his genuine concern for the feelings of others. This quality was manifested in his personal and professional life, and it finds expression in much of his writings.

He was asked a question concerning a young man who wore a toupee.[5] The young man was a student in a religious school where the students prayed together in the morning. He was embarrassed to appear before his fellow students without his toupee. Was it permitted for him to place his *tefillin* atop the toupee? Or was the toupee considered an interposition that invalidated his fulfillment of the mitzvah?

---

4 MH 2:85.
5 ALR 3:3.

Rabbi Halevy noted that the *tefillin* must be placed directly on the head, and that the toupee was in fact an interposition. However, if the student were told to remove his toupee in the presence of the other students, he would not do so; and if he did do so, he would feel terrible embarrassment, "and there is no greater suffering than humiliation." So Rabbi Halevy recommended that the student first pray at home, wearing the *tefillin* properly with the head *tefillin* directly on his head, not on the toupee. He should recite the Shema with the *tefillin* on, thereby fulfilling the mitzvah of *tefillin*. Then, when he later went to school, he could wear the *tefillin* atop his toupee, and pray with the rest of the students. In this way, he would fulfill the mitzvah of praying with a quorum while avoiding feelings of embarrassment.

Rabbi Halevy dealt with another case involving a person who needed a battery-operated machine to keep him from stammering.[6] The question was: could this person use the device on Shabbat? Rabbi Halevy drew an analogy to hearing aids, which were generally considered to be permissible for Shabbat use (assuming the wearers did not have to adjust them on Shabbat). The permissive ruling was based, among other reasons, on the principle of *kevod haberiyot*; the inability to hear and carry on conversations with others was humiliating. The wearing of the hearing aid helped restore a person's sense of honor; he could participate in conversations with others without feeling shamed. Rabbi Halevy ruled that the anti-stammering device was equally permitted, on the same basis.

Rabbi Halevy's sensitivity to the feelings of others was reflected in his ruling that a rabbi who was performing a wedding should not himself taste from the wine cup over which the wedding blessings were recited. Since the bride and groom had to drink from that cup, they might find it unpleasant to drink from the same cup as the rabbi. True, many people were not so fussy and did not mind drinking from the same cup as others. "But aren't we obligated to worry about even the one in a thousand who is particular [about not drinking from the same cup as others], and who will

---

[6] ALR 6:30.

drink this wine [during the wedding] and be hurt?…. I myself once saw a bridegroom, who received the cup of wine from the rabbi [after the rabbi had tasted from it first]. I watched him carefully and saw that he brought the cup near to his lips, but [his lips] did not touch [the cup] and he didn't taste the wine. I understood his inner feeling."[7] Rabbi Halevy stated that in his household, where members of his family did not mind drinking from a shared wine cup, he drank from the kiddush cup on Shabbat and holidays and then passed it to the others. But whenever he had a guest at the table, Rabbi Halevy poured from the kiddush cup into his own separate cup, and then passed the wine to the others, each of whom also had a clean cup at his place.

Rabbi Halevy responded to an agitated man who had visited his office on the following matter. The man had a pacemaker to keep his heart beating at an appropriate rate. The pacemaker was a very sensitive device that would begin sending impulses to the heart whenever the heart's rhythm lagged. The man was afraid that after he died, he would be buried with the pacemaker still in place. The pacemaker might then start to operate, causing him to be revived. If this were to happen when he had already been buried, he would suffer excruciating pain. Others who also had pacemakers shared the man's fears. He asked Rabbi Halevy to issue instructions to all the burial societies that they must remove pacemakers from deceased individuals as part of the preparations for burial. Rabbi Halevy issued these instructions, saying that he wished to be a spokesman for all those with pacemakers who feared what might happen to them after their deaths if their pacemakers re-activated the pumping of the heart. He was concerned that they should live their lives with the secure knowledge that the pacemaker will be removed before burial; thus their minds could be set at ease, and they could live more happily and pleasantly.[8]

The value of *kevod haberiyot* factored into Rabbi Halevy's response to the following case. On a Shabbat, many people had come to a

---

[7] ALR 8:74.
[8] MH 2:66. For other examples of concern for the feelings of others, see ALR 6:8; 6:31; MKH 1:62, p. 273.

synagogue to celebrate with a bridegroom. One of the guests was a young man, whose family asked that he be called to the Torah. This young man was blind, having been injured in battle while serving in the Israel Defense Forces. The rabbi of the synagogue said that the young man may not be called to read from the Torah. The *Shulhan Arukh* ruled that a blind person may not be called to the Torah, since he was unable to read the words in the scroll. Upon being rebuffed, the soldier retorted that he was regularly called to the Torah in the synagogue in which he normally prayed. But the rabbi was not swayed.

The rabbi's decision caused much unpleasantness among the family members of the blind man. Finally, the young man and some members of his family left the synagogue in frustration and embarrassment.[9]

When Rabbi Halevy learned of this case, he was deeply pained. The young soldier, who had lost his eyesight in service to his country, had been treated shabbily; he had been humiliated in public. The rabbi should have heeded the soldier's words that he was called to the Torah in his usual synagogue. He should have assumed that the rabbi of that synagogue had looked into the halakhah before allowing the blind man to receive an *aliyah*. "How careful one must be when it comes to *kevod haberiyot*, who were created in the image of God."

Rabbi Halevy noted that the Sephardic community generally did not accept the ruling of the *Shulhan Arukh* (*Orah Hayyim* 139:3) forbidding the calling of a blind person to the Torah. Leading Sephardic *poskim* allowed an *aliyah* for a blind man, and this had become the normal practice. The rabbi who had prevented the blind soldier from being called to the Torah erred in his halakhic judgment. Through his ignorance of the halakhah, he also caused humiliation to the soldier and his family, and created an embarrassing scene for all those in the synagogue that Shabbat morning. Rabbi Halevy expressed his sorrow that the young soldier had not received the respect and honor that were due him.

---

[9] ALR 6:20.

Although the value of *kevod haberiyot* is very important in halakhah, yet it does not automatically determine the halakhic decision. Rabbi Halevy dealt with another question relating to a blind person: was a blind person permitted to enter the synagogue with a seeing-eye dog? Rabbi Moshe Feinstein had permitted this.[10]

Rabbi Halevy, though, believed that the sanctity of the synagogue precluded bringing a dog into it. In responding to his questioner, who obviously wanted to permit the seeing-eye dog in the synagogue, Rabbi Halevy wrote: "More power to you for upholding the quality of compassion, which is one of the characteristics of the people of Israel. But there are also very holy values that may not be pushed aside due to the quality of compassion, and especially if the quality of compassion is not absolutely necessary [to determine the halakhah, since there are other ways of being compassionate to the blind person while still maintaining the sanctity of the synagogue]."[11]

Rabbi Halevy argued that bringing a dog into the synagogue was inappropriate. It belittled the sanctity of the synagogue. He suggested that the seeing-eye dog be left outside the synagogue. The sexton (or another caring person) could then take the blind person into the synagogue and lead him to a convenient seat. In this way, it was possible both to maintain the sanctity of the synagogue as well as to show kindness to the blind person by enabling him to pray in the synagogue.

Rabbi Halevy wrote several responsa dealing with raising adopted children. Adoptive parents, of course, wanted to raise these children as their own, as all parents raised their children. The halakhah, though, forbade *yihud*, being alone in the same locked room with someone of the opposite sex (except for one's spouse or some immediate blood relations). Since the adopted children were not, in fact, blood relations, did the laws of *yihud* apply? Was it forbidden for adoptive parents to hold, hug and kiss the adopted children after they passed the age of being toddlers? If these

---

[10] *Iggrot Moshe, Orah Hayyim* 1:45.
[11] MH 3:16.

things were forbidden by halakhah, it would create a serious loss of intimacy between the parents and children.

Rabbi Halevy ruled that if the adoptions had taken place when the children were infants, then the parents could treat them exactly as they would have treated their own natural-born children. The laws of *yihud* were set aside, and it was permissible for the parents to embrace their adopted children just as they would have embraced their own genetic children. If, though, the children were adopted when they were no longer infants, then halakhic issues would arise. The reason for leniency when adopting infants was that the parents and children were accustomed to each other and saw each other literally as parents and children. But when the adopted children were older at the time of adoption, there was already a separation between the adoptive parents and children. Therefore, the parents should maintain the laws of *yihud* to the extent possible, and the father's affectionate hugs and kisses should be restricted to the adopted boys, and the mother's to the adopted girls. If the parents adopted both female and male children, the adoptive brothers and sisters could treat each other as natural brothers and sisters until such time as they were informed that they had been adopted. Then, they had to follow the *halakhot* applicable to the relationships between other unrelated males and females.[12]

In dealing with the issues relating to adopted children, Rabbi Halevy demonstrated sensitivity to the needs of the adoptive parents and children. He well understood the importance of natural interaction between them, and respected their feelings and wishes. Yet, his concern for *kevod haberiyot* did not clear the way for a blanket setting aside of the halakhic prohibitions of *yihud* and physical contact between the sexes. As a great *posek,* Rabbi Halevy knew how to maintain the balance between the value of *kevod haberiyot* and the other claims of halakhah.

---

12 ALR 3:39; MH 1:62.

Dealing with Less or Non-Observant Jews

The Torah commands: "and you shall love your neighbor as yourself" (*Vayikra* 19:18). One of the traditional ways of understanding this verse is: you shall love your neighbor – who is your brother in the observance of Torah and *mitzvot*.[13] If a person was religiously observant, then he was considered your "neighbor" whom you must treat with love and respect. Otherwise, you not only did not have to love that person, but you could also feel hatred towards him.

According to this framework of understanding, it would be difficult to imagine a loving, respectful relationship between religiously observant and non-observant Jews. The observant could view the non-observant (or even the less observant) as betrayers of the teachings of the Torah. By rejecting the traditional teachings of Judaism, they forfeited their right to love – and even were worthy of hatred.

Rabbi Halevy eschewed this line of reasoning. On the contrary, he tried to demonstrate that all Jews, religiously observant or not, were deserving of respect. If we were allowed to feel "hatred" towards those who repudiated the Torah, it was only a seeming hatred, more akin to displeasure with their ways.[14] Especially in our times, when so many Jews transgressed the *mitzvot*, the injunction to hate the sinner did not apply.[15] Large numbers of non-observant Jews did not actually reject the Torah on ideological grounds; they simply were careless or ignorant of the laws.[16]

Professor Haim Burgensky, in his study of Rabbi Halevy's halakhic attitude towards "secular" Jews, suggested that Rabbi Halevy remained faithful to the general halakhic constructs relating to the violators of Torah law. Yet, Rabbi Halevy found ways of ruling leniently in matters governing

---

[13] See for example the commentary of Rashbam and the Semag on this verse. See also *Pesahim* 113b, where the Talmud discusses the permissibility of hating one who sinned.

[14] ALR 4:70.

[15] TH 2, *Vayikra*, pp. 66–67.

[16] TH 2, *Vayikra*, p. 130. See also NM, p. 132.

the relations between the observant and the non-observant.[17] He invoked such concepts as *darkhei shalom* (the ways of peace) and *kevod haberiyot*.

Rabbi Halevy revealed his nuanced approach to the non-observant when he wrote: "One whose views are not religious, who does not keep Shabbat, etc., is called in halakhic terminology a *rasha* [a wicked person], with all the desire to avoid ascribing this adjective to any Jew. This [the word *rasha*] is not, Heaven forbid, an antonym for 'good'. A person can have good qualities, be proper and upright in humanistic terms, but [still be] a *rasha* from the point of view of halakhah."[18]

Rabbi Halevy recognized that non-religious people can be fine, ethical human beings. Certainly, he wished that all Jews would be faithful to the age-old traditions of Judaism. They could find true fulfillment in the observance of Torah and *mitzvot*. Until all Jews came around to the religious point of view, though, the religious Jews should live among their less observant neighbors in a spirit of peace and harmony – not antagonism and dissension.[19]

Rabbi Halevy believed that religious Jews should be strong in their beliefs and devoted in their observance of *mitzvot*. However, they should not be disdainful of Jews who did not share their religious commitments. Rather, they should find ways to bring others closer to Torah.

Rabbi Halevy related an incident that had made a deep impact on him. It took place in the year 5709 (1948/49) in Jerusalem. The Chief Rabbis of Israel had called for a major rally to protest the widespread desecration of the Shabbat. Rabbi Uziel made an emotional presentation,

---

[17] H. Burgensky, *"Yahaso haHilkhati shel haRav Haim David Halevy leHilonim,"* in the volume of papers about Rabbi Halevy, edited by Zvi Zohar and Avi Sagi. See also in that volume the article by Ruth Gabizon, *"HaYitakhen Mifgash Amiti Bein Hiloni'im veDati'im beYisrael?"* She suggests that Rabbi Halevy's Sephardic tradition led him to a moderate, tolerant approach to the non-observant Jews.

[18] ALR 1:62.

[19] ALR 6: short answers 89. See also Avi Sagi's article on Rabbi Halevy's philosophy of halakhah in the volume on Rabbi Halevy he edited together with Zvi Zohar. Sagi argues that "the category of ethics precedes the category of religious *mitzvot*, and is a precondition of them."

tearfully reading the biblical words of Nehemiah (chapter 13) about the desecration of Shabbat in Jerusalem in those days.

After the rally concluded, a taxi was called to take Rabbi Uziel to his home. During that period, Israel was suffering from a fuel shortage. As a means of rationing fuel, drivers were allowed to drive six days a week, but one day they were not supposed to use their cars. On the windshield of each car, a letter was affixed indicating which day the driver would not use the car. Religious Jews, naturally, chose not to drive on Saturday, so the sticker on their windshields was the letter "*shin*," standing for Shabbat. The taxi that came to pick up Rabbi Uziel from the rally, though, did not have the letter *"shin"* affixed to its windshield. Thus, the driver was presumably one who drove his car on Saturday, in violation of the laws of Shabbat. Those who were accompanying Rabbi Uziel, still very much moved by the rally against Shabbat desecration, advised the Chief Rabbi not to enter the taxi of a Shabbat violator. After all, Rabbi Uziel had been so eloquent in his condemnation of Shabbat desecration. Rabbi Uziel did not listen to them, and he entered the taxi. He explained to those who surrounded him: "I do not disdain *[ani lo maharim]* any Jew personally, even if he is not a Shabbat observer."[20]

Rabbi Uziel opposed the transgression of Shabbat, but he did not harbor ill will to the particular people who transgressed the Shabbat laws. Rabbi Halevy followed in the footsteps of his revered teacher and mentor. Indeed, Rabbi Halevy stressed the responsibility of religious Jews to interact respectfully with their non-observant or less-observant neighbors. He was asked, for example, if non-observant Jews could participate in the celebration of finishing the writing of a Torah scroll. Usually, a qualified scribe would write the entire Torah, leaving the last few letters to be filled in by the sponsors or donors of the writing of the scroll. Considering the great sanctity of the Torah, was it permissible for non-observant Jews to fill in the concluding letters of the Torah scroll? Rabbi Halevy permitted this, saying that "this is also a matter of giving honor to the Torah, since all

---

[20] ALR 8:97, in the note at the beginning of the responsum.

want to participate in writing a letter. If we prevent them from doing this, there is a fear of complaints, Heaven forbid, since the general practice [was to let non-observant Jews participate]."[21] How embarrassing it would be for the non-observant people to be turned away from participating in this mitzvah. It would be a public humiliation that would only deepen their alienation from religious tradition.

The *Shulhan Arukh* ruled that a kohen who murdered someone, even by accident, was no longer permitted to participate in the priestly blessing. Rabbi Moshe Isserles, though, commented that such a kohen could participate in the priestly blessing, as long as he had repented fully. Although Sephardim generally followed the opinion of the *Shulhan Arukh*, in this case Rabbi Halevy thought that the view of Rabbi Moshe Isserles should be accepted. In our days, argued Rabbi Halevy, we needed to rule leniently in order to keep people from abandoning the synagogue and the ways of the Torah.[22]

An observant Jew raised the question of whether he was allowed to eat in his sister's home. She was generally not observant, but claimed to keep a kosher home. Rabbi Halevy responded that once the questioner had ascertained for himself that the sister's home was *kasher*, he could rely on her *kashrut* even if she were not observant of other *mitzvot*. This was especially so, since the sister had stated outright that she would not maintain *kashrut* in her home if her brother refused to eat there. On the other hand, by maintaining a cordial relationship with the sister, it was possible she might ultimately be brought closer to religious tradition. "And we have been commanded to bring near, not to push away."[23]

Rabbi Halevy wrote that it was permitted to eat in the home of a generally non-observant Jew (who may have been lax in observing the laws of *kashrut*), if the foods consisted only of coffee or tea, fruits, and certain baked goods. The permissive approach was based on the principle of maintaining peace and social harmony. If one were invited to a home, and

---

[21] MH 2:57.

[22] MKH 1:62, pp. 274–275.

[23] ALR 5: short answers 111.

was not sure how strictly the host kept the laws of *kashrut*, one should state his concerns openly, in a nice way, so that the host will be informed of the *kashrut* issues. The host could then prepare food in accordance with proper *kashrut* standards. If, nevertheless, a person were served foods of questionable *kashrut*, he "should try to avoid them with all possible delicacy. And if this can't be done, then you should explain to them with calmness and kind spirit the reason for your avoiding [the food]. On the contrary, perhaps you will succeed on this occasion to influence them to make their kitchen *kasher* and follow carefully the laws of *kashrut*...."[24]

If the host were known to be a really secular Jew who ideologically opposed religious observance, then one should avoid eating anything at all at his home. Concern for social harmony did not justify eating in a home where the host was defiant in violating the laws of *kashrut*. Rabbi Halevy's lenient rulings applied specifically to those individuals who were lax in their religious observance, but who had some sensitivity and positive feelings about the laws of *kashrut*.[25]

It is clear that Rabbi Halevy's concern for maintaining proper relations with non-observant Jews had its limits. While very tolerant towards Jews who were careless in their observance or who were ignorant of the religious laws, he was less conciliatory towards Jews who openly negated the authority of halakhah. He not only was unhappy with secular Jews, but was much opposed to Reform Judaism. He believed that Reform began with minor changes in traditional halakhic patterns, but had moved very far from halakhah. "In the end, it reached the total and decisive destruction of all the belief of the Torah, and the destruction of the holiness of the purity of the Jewish family, causing serious assimilation which approaches today, in certain communities, nearly sixty percent [of

---

[24] ALR 8:47.

[25] ALR 5:19; 9:11; see also ALR 1:37, where Rabbi Halevy advised rabbis to avoid eating at anyone's house except their own. See also MH 3:12, where Rabbi Halevy advised some teachers how to deal with a new teacher who ate non-kosher food in public. He told them that one of the teachers should have called her aside and explained to her the laws of *kashrut*. Certainly, one should avoid embarrassing the teacher.

interfaith marriage]."[26] Although Rabbi Halevy was concerned with the overall need for Jews to be respectful to each other, he was not comfortable with individual contacts with people who blatantly rejected the authority of Torah and halakhah.

Rabbi Halevy was asked a question by a religious young woman who had fallen in love with a non-observant Jew from a secular background. He was a fine person, and she thought that perhaps she would be able to influence him to become religious. Her parents opposed the match. So did Rabbi Halevy. He felt that it was more likely for him to influence her than vice versa, that it was easier for her to fall into the ways of non-observance than for him to accept the ways of observance. Even though we were commanded to love all Jews, nevertheless we were also instructed to keep a distance from those in the category of *rasha*, willful violators of Torah law.[27]

Rabbi Halevy firmly believed that it was essential for the religiously observant community to be respectful to non-observant Jews, to reach out to them in a spirit of kindness and understanding. But this did not mean that one should have close interpersonal relationships with them. Religious Jews had to maintain their own religious standards and commitments; thus, it was important for them to avoid being influenced by those who were careless or antipathetic to religious observance.

Concern for the Honor of Torah

Rabbi Halevy was quite sensitive to issues that cast a bad light on religious Jews. If the society at large viewed religious Jews negatively, then the honor of the Torah was compromised. Non-observant people would be

---

26 MH 3:27. See also ALR 8:72, where Rabbi Halevy wrote to me regarding the status of marriages performed by Reform rabbis.

27 ALR 1:62. See also 1:61. For other responsa dealing with relationships between observant and non-observant Jews, see ALR 1:60; 1:74; 2:41; 3:4; 3:38; 5:30; 6:53; 7:91. For cases dealing with the concept of *lifnei iver lo titen mikhshol*, see ALR 2:29; 4:28; 7: short answers 15; MH 1:64; 2:32; 2:51; 2:70. See also ALR 3:33, where he chastises a father for not having provided a proper religious upbringing to his children.

less likely to be drawn to a Torah lifestyle. In his concern for the religious well-being of all Jews, including the non-observant, Rabbi Halevy demanded the highest standard of behavior from those identified as religious Jews.

He criticized a parochial view of religion that characterized many observant Jews. When they saw people publicly violating the ritual laws, e.g., Shabbat and *kashrut*, they were outraged and called out in angry protest. Yet, "they remain quiet and take things in normal stride when they see social and ethical breakdowns in many areas of our public life, when people swallow each other alive, and the moral thread of our life is broken."[28] Religious Jews should be even more concerned about the general moral well-being of society than they are about the level of public religious ritual observance. When the social and moral fabric of a society are destroyed then the entire society risks collapse.

Religious Jews, through genuine concern for all society, could convey the message of Torah in a kind, thoughtful and meaningful way. But all too often, religious Jews were identified with activities that were hostile and coercive to the non-observant segment of society. They sought to impose ritual restrictions by law and compulsion, rather than by persuasion. Instead of building bridges between the observant and non-observant communities, their behavior tended to create deeper rifts.[29]

Rabbi Halevy expressed his antipathy to coercive techniques in a response to a question from a religious man, one of whose sons had become non-religious. The man was so upset he wanted to write this son out of his will. Rabbi Halevy informed the man that Torah law forbade

---

[28] NM, p. 190.

[29] ALR 8:32–35 about demonstrations in Petah Tikvah against a movie theater that remained open on Friday nights. See also ALR 8:19, where Rabbi Halevy opposed religious factions that were fighting against the imposition of daylight savings time. Daylight savings time was generally popular with the public, and there was no compelling reason for religious Jews to oppose it primarily on religious grounds. This only served to identify religious Jewry with an unpopular, coercive position – one that was not even required by a clear understanding of religious law.

him from disinheriting his son, even if the son was no longer religiously observant. Perhaps the son will one day return to the ways of Torah. Perhaps the son will have children who will become religious. Rabbi Halevy told the man that there was always hope that the wayward son would one day return to the fold. But if the son were cut off from the will, this possibility would diminish greatly. "You should strive always to be in the category of one who pushes away with his left hand, but brings closer with his right hand."[30] In other words, it was appropriate to express one's displeasure in a mild way, but the emphasis (the right hand) should be devoted to bringing the son closer.

The religious community not only had a reputation for parochialism and religious coercion, it also was sometimes stigmatized for not carrying its full share of civic responsibilities. One of the touchiest issues related to the military draft. Students in the *yeshivot hesder*, which fostered religious Zionism, did serve in the Israeli army. Indeed, they have won much praise for their courage and heroism. But students in other *yeshivot* were routinely exempted from military service. Many of these young men remained in their *yeshivot* studying Torah while most of their contemporaries were serving as soldiers in defense of Israel. It was not surprising that the majority of Israelis felt a certain resentment towards those yeshiva students and their supporters in the religious community. The students wanted the benefits of a good life in Israel, but did not do their share to defend their country.

Rabbi Halevy knew that this issue bothered the general public and cast a bad light on the religiously observant community. He pointed out that in a war to defend Israel, all citizens – including yeshiva students – were obligated to fight. While yeshiva students should devote themselves to their Torah studies, in time of emergency they too were obligated to join in the defense of Israel. They could receive military training then. Indeed, a brigade of yeshiva students, including the young Haim David Halevy himself, fought in Israel's War of Independence in 1948.

---

[30] ALR 1:64.

If yeshiva students did not have sufficient time to be prepared for battle, they could be employed in other functions to help the army – as medics, cooks, secretaries, messengers, etc. In time of war, yeshiva students were expected to play a constructive role in the military.

Rabbi Halevy thought that yeshiva students who wished to serve in the army, even when no immediate emergency existed, were free to do so. At root, though, he believed that Torah scholars were to be exempted from military duty; they served their nation by maintaining its moral and spiritual foundations. This was no less important to the survival of Israel than the work of soldiers. Rabbi Halevy insisted that exemptions were only legitimate for true Torah scholars who devoted themselves heart and soul to Torah study. Other yeshiva students, who were not totally engrossed in Torah study, were not worthy of military exemptions.[31] Rabbi Halevy knew that it was difficult for non-religious Jews to realize the true significance and importance of Torah study for the strength of the nation. Yet, he attempted to explain the case for spiritual service to Israel, while at the same time outlining the military roles that could be undertaken by yeshiva students.

The negative image of yeshiva students was reflected in a question Rabbi Halevy received.[32] A yeshiva student was interested in marrying a certain young lady. Both he and his prospective bride were from poor families and lacked the financial resources to get married. The student discussed his dilemma with his friends, and they advised him to do what they had done: get a letter of recommendation from the Rosh Yeshiva and take it around to potential donors who might contribute to the couple's support. The yeshiva student was reluctant to do this, but his friends reminded him that this was a common practice among Torah scholars and students. He felt uncomfortable having to beg for funds; but, without

---

[31] ALR 3:58; 7:72. For problems facing a religious soldier, see ALR 2:29; 7:68. See also ALR 7: short answers 38, where Rabbi Halevy expressed respect for an Israeli soldier who died in defense of Israel. See further discussion in the chapter on *At'halta deGe'ulah*.

[32] ALR 4:50.

funds, he would not be able to afford the expenses of marriage. What should he do?

Rabbi Halevy expressed his sorrow at the predicament of poor yeshiva students. He said that he had received hundreds of such letters requesting funds to support a young couple, but had never gotten used to them. Each such letter caused him deep pain. He felt that this phenomenon was not desirable in itself. Moreover, it led the public to associate Torah students with poverty and beggary, thereby dragging down the honor of Torah. Rabbi Halevy thought that the situation was bad and getting worse. Although he would have preferred to ignore the situation, this young man's letter demanded a serious response.

Rabbi Halevy proceeded to find halakhic basis for taking charity for the sake of marriage. If there was no other way to support oneself, one was permitted to receive charity.

Yet, even though this answer was halakhically correct, it did not deal with the issue at its source. How were we to avoid perpetuating the image of yeshiva students as poor, unproductive people, dependent on charity for survival?

Rabbi Halevy called on the heads of *yeshivot* in Israel to meet to discuss this problem. Rabbi Halevy offered his own suggestion. Next to each yeshiva there should be a factory of some sort. The yeshiva students should spend several hours a day working there; but their pay should not be given to them. Instead, it should be placed in an escrow account in their names. Thus, their earnings would accumulate over the years. When they were ready to get married, they would already have a sum of money that they themselves had earned. In this way, they will have been productive laborers, and will not need to beg for their sustenance. They will be happier and better off financially; and the image of yeshiva students will also rise.

The suggestion was creative and reasonable. But it had little if any impact on the heads of *yeshivot*; and the situation has continued to deteriorate.

For Rabbi Halevy, respectful interaction with others was a basic ethical requirement. *Kevod haberiyot* was a vital ingredient in the halakhic process. This concept governed interpersonal relationships, including those between religious and non-religious Jews. For the religious community to advance the cause of Torah, it needed to be civil and respectful; it had to bring honor to Torah by its words and deeds.

Chapter Twelve

JEWS AND NON-JEWS

Rabbi Halevy was born and raised in a thoroughly Jewish environment in Jerusalem and spent the bulk of his life as a rabbi serving Jewish communities in Israel. His intellectual life was devoted almost exclusively to Torah study. He was a native Hebrew-speaker and did not speak Arabic or other foreign languages. He did not have any close non-Jewish friends; indeed, his interaction with non-Jews was quite limited.

Yet, Rabbi Halevy was not oblivious to the non-Jewish world. He took very seriously the Torah's challenge to the people of Israel to be "a kingdom of priests and a holy nation" (*Shemot* 19:6). By attaining this lofty spiritual level, the people of Israel would be able to influence all the nations of the world to be righteous and God-fearing. Israel was to be an example to others; thus, it was concerned with the religious well being of all human beings. It had a message for humanity.

The Torah was given specifically to the people of Israel. Nevertheless, a large portion of the ethical and theological teachings of the Torah was to be conveyed to humanity as a whole. In fact, the world did learn many great lessons from our Bible and other writings; much of human civilization was built on values and laws derived from our Torah.[1]

Rabbi Halevy's very first book – written only nine years after the conclusion of World War II – was dedicated to the theme of the

---

[1] TH 1, *Shemot*, pp. 90–108. For Rabbi Uziel's views on the Jewish responsibilities towards the non-Jewish world, see my book *Loving Truth and Peace: The Grand Religious Worldview of Rabbi Benzion Uziel,* chapter 3.

relationship between Israel and the nations. In his introduction, he described the chaotic state of world civilization – threats of mass destruction, fear of violence, lack of spiritual direction. Civilization was on the decline. "If there is one teaching, one idea, one clear line that can still bring light into this darkness, it is nothing else than the Torah of Israel and the vision of our true and just prophets. This is the sole source that still has the power to direct and lead, to light in its ethical simplicity the way of the world."[2] The responsibility of the Jewish people was to affirm its allegiance to Torah, deepen its spiritual life, increase its level of religious observance and commitment. In so doing, Israel would have a great positive impact on the nations of the world. The Jewish religious worldview was not insular nor merely inward looking; rather, it called for inner strength and spiritual loneliness as a means to give light and spiritual strength to the nations of the world.

The Torah taught that human beings were created in the image of God. All people – Jewish and non-Jewish – had spiritual worth and dignity. The righteous of the nations had a place in the World to Come.[3]

Responsibilities of Jews Towards Non-Jews

The Talmud (*Gittin* 59b, 61a, 61b) presented guidelines for Jewish behavior towards non-Jews. Poor non-Jews were not to be prevented from gathering the agricultural gifts that the Torah required of Jewish farmers in the land of Israel. Jews were obligated to provide assistance to needy non-Jews, visit their sick, bury their dead, greet them in a friendly way. In explaining these obligations, the Talmud stated that these acts of kindness were due to the principle *mippenei darkhei shalom*, for the sake of maintaining peaceful, harmonious relations.

In codifying these rules, Rambam added the following caveat. "These rules only apply when the people of Israel are exiled among the nations, or when the non-Jews have power over the people of Israel. But

---

[2] BYL, introduction, p. 23.
[3] See ALR 1:52–53.

when Israel has power over them, it is forbidden to let star worshippers [i.e., non-Jews] dwell among us [in the land of Israel]."[4]

According to Rambam, then, compassionate behavior towards non-Jews did not stem from an ethical imperative; rather, it was simply a necessary means of maintaining a civil society. Rabbi Isser Yehudah Unterman, an Ashkenazic Chief Rabbi of Israel and older contemporary of Rabbi Halevy, did not accept Rambam's contention. He argued that the phrase *mippenei darkhei shalom* [for the sake of peace] was not an apologetic explanation for compassionate behavior towards non-Jews, but was a direct mandate. Jews were obligated by the Torah to maintain the ways of peace and harmony, and moral behavior towards non-Jews was included in that ethical responsibility.

Rabbi Halevy took issue with Rabbi Unterman's argument. He pointed out that *mippenei darkhei shalom* could be understood only as an apologetic comment. It was a de facto recognition of the weakness of the people of Israel vis a vis the non-Jewish population. But, in fact, Rambam was entirely correct in his formulation of the laws, i.e., they did not apply when Israel was in a position of strength.[5]

Did this mean that the Jews in Israel had no moral responsibilities towards the non-Jews living in their midst? Not at all. While Rabbi Halevy defended Rambam's understanding of the talmudic text, he concluded that the text was not applicable in the present historical context. The Talmud had been discussing obligations of Jews towards *ovdei kokhavim* (star worshippers). Although the phrase *ovdei kokhavim* could be understood to be a euphemism referring to non-Jews in general, Rabbi Halevy took it quite literally. It referred specifically and exclusively to star (or idol) worshippers, i.e., pagans. Towards pagans, Jews were to be compassionate

---

[4] *Hil. Avodat Kokhavim* 10:5.

[5] See Aviezer Ravitzky's article, including an exchange of letters he had with Rabbi Halevy on this topic, in the volume of essays about Rabbi Halevy, edited by Zvi Zohar and Avi Sagi. See also Ariel Fikker's article in the same volume, dealing with the concept of *darkhei shalom* between Jews and non-Jews. Rabbi Halevy's discussion of this topic is in ALR 9:30 and 9:33.

for the sake of peace. When Jews had the upper hand in Israel, they should drive pagans out of their society. Pagans held primitive beliefs and practiced immorality. They were a bad influence on a society striving to be righteous and God-fearing.

But today, most non-Jews living in Israel were not pagans. They were Christians and Muslims, followers of religions that accepted the divine nature of the Jewish Bible, and which derived many teachings from Judaism. Muslims most certainly were monotheists. Christians, even those who believed in the trinity, essentially accepted the existence of one God. They did not practice idolatry in the same sense as the pagans of antiquity, but simply were following beliefs and practices that had been passed down to them by their ancestors. Rabbi Halevy cited a number of earlier halakhic authorities who had also ruled that Christians were not to be classified as idolaters.[6]

Rabbi Halevy drew the logical conclusion of his line of reasoning: "There is no need to maintain these relationships [with non-Jews] only for the sake of peace. Rather, since they are no longer in the category of idolaters according to halakhic definition, therefore, providing their sustenance, visiting their sick, burying their dead, comforting their mourners (as mentioned in the *Shulhan Arukh*, *Yoreh Deah* 151:12), etc., all are to be performed because of the human ethical imperative, not specifically for the sake of peace."[7] Relationships between Jews and non-Jews, whether in Israel or the Diaspora, were to be governed by moral obligations that bound all human beings.[8]

Was Rabbi Halevy's view derived exclusively from a careful reading of the relevant halakhic texts? It would be difficult to assert this, especially since other halakhists, such as Rabbi Unterman, did not reach the same

---

[6] Rabbi Halevy did distinguish between the pure monotheism of Islam and the Trinitarian and iconic monotheism of Christianity. He permitted Jews to enter mosques but not to enter churches (ALR 9:13; 1:59). See also ALR 2:43 for another halakhic distinction involving Islam and Christianity.

[7] ALR 9:30, p. 73.

[8] ALR 9:33.

conclusion. Indeed, Rambam himself did not choose to veer from the plain meaning of the talmudic text. He could have distinguished between the star worshippers of talmudic times and the Muslims and Christians of his day; but he did not do so. Apparently, these rules applied generally to all non-Jews, not merely to idolaters.

Rabbi Halevy brought his ethical sensitivity into play when he approached the question of the relationship between Jews and non-Jews. For him, it was simply not conceivable to justify discriminatory treatment in our day basing oneself on Torah teachings. This would be a perversion of the very ideals and ethical standards that the Torah espoused. While in talmudic times, pagans were in fact viewed as a serious threat to the fabric of civilized life, we were not dealing with such "pagans" in the modern situation. We were interacting with Christians and Muslims – monotheists who espoused many values learned from the Torah.[9]

Judaism's Rejection of Racism

Rabbi Halevy was an ardent exponent of the universal ethical values taught by the Torah. He was outraged by any aspersion on the Torah's commitment to humanity. In 1986, he gave an interview to the Israeli publication *"Hadfasah"* (3 Adar II, 5746), which he later published also in *Asei Lekha Rav*, on the subject of Judaism's rejection of all vestiges of racism.[10] At the time, members of some religious parties in Israel were advocating legislation declaring that Judaism was not racist. (This was undoubtedly a response to the hideous anti-Semitic resolution passed by the United Nations, and later rescinded, branding Zionism as a form of racism).

Rabbi Halevy was not at all pleased with the proposed legislation. "The nation of Israel is not racist, not it, not its Torah, not its culture; there is no vestige of racism in its history. Therefore, in my opinion the

---

[9] For responsa dealing with halakhic issues relating to non-Jews, see ALR 7:48; 7: short answers 70; 8:38; 9:12; MH 1:50; 1:57–58; 2:79; 3:37.
[10] ALR 8:68.

entire law is extraneous."[11] Indeed, passing such a law would be understood mistakenly as an attempt to defend halakhah, when the halakhah did not need any such defense.

Was the halakhah's prohibition of marriage between Jews and non-Jews a reflection of racism? Not in the least! Judaism valued the harmony of family life; marriage between people who shared the same religious values, observances and worldview created a proper framework for happiness. Moreover, the prohibition against intermarriage was vital to the survival of the Jewish people. Rabbi Halevy wondered why the question of "racism" was raised in connection with the Jewish prohibition of intermarriage: Islam and other religions taught the same thing, forbidding their adherents to marry out of their faith. Did anyone accuse them of being racists on this basis? Why then should critics single out the Jewish people for its prohibition of intermarriage?

Rabbi Halevy was asked about the Kach party founded by Meir Kahane. This party called for the expulsion of Arabs from Israel. Rabbi Halevy said that there was not a scintilla of support for this idea in halakhah. When the Torah commanded the Israelites to conquer the seven nations that then occupied the land of Canaan, that commandment applied to that situation alone. It was God's will that the land be given to the people of Israel. The seven pagan nations were to be destroyed because of their corruption and immorality. The commandments relating to pagans in the land of Canaan in antiquity did not apply to other non-Jews, and certainly not to Muslims and Christians. The Torah itself took for granted that non-Jews would be living in the land of Israel (see, for example, *Devarim* 14:21), and that these non-Jews would be in the category of *ger toshav*, resident aliens, who subscribed to the seven Noahide laws. Thus, the halakhah did not condone expelling non-Jewish residents of Israel who were not idolaters.

Racism implied that one group thought itself genetically superior to others and rejected the possibility of others becoming part of their

---

[11] Ibid., p. 192.

group. Yet, this concept was not applicable to the people of Israel. According to halakhah, non-Jews may convert to Judaism – and many have done so over the course of the centuries. There was no genetic barrier to conversion. People of any nationality or race could become members of the Jewish people if they accepted the teachings of Torah and went through the process of conversion. Indeed, such luminaries as Shemaya and Avtalion were of convert stock, and they became the heads of the Sanhedrin in ancient Israel. Converts have been accepted into the Jewish people and have made important contributions to the history and culture of the Jews.[12]

The notion of the Jews being a chosen people was not racist.[13] First, anyone could join the Jewish people by accepting the ways of Torah. They too could thereby become "chosen." Moreover, the ancestors of the people of Israel going back to Abraham chose to follow the ways of God. The later generations of Jews have received a rich spiritual heritage that, in fact, did distinguish them from all other peoples of the world. Other peoples may have been chosen for other roles in human history; but it was an undeniable historical fact that the Jews were chosen to receive the Torah and spread its teachings. This had nothing whatever to do with racism.

Conversion to Judaism

Non-Jews of any race or nationality could – and did – convert to Judaism. This was a clinching proof of Judaism's openness to all people and its rejection of racism.

Rabbi Halevy pointed out that there had long been a difference of opinion among our sages concerning conversion. Some were very positively inclined towards conversion, while others were quite negative on the topic. Different eras and different locales fostered different approaches. Each case had to be evaluated on the basis of its own particular circumstances. The Torah purposefully left the topic of

---

[12] ALR 8:69.
[13] ALR 8:69.

conversion vague, not spelling out the specific requirements for converts. Instead, the Torah left the final decision up to each rabbi. "The Torah wanted the mitzvah of accepting converts to be always as an ad hoc decision (*hora'at sha'ah*). Each generation and each judge in his place will decide whether or not to receive a convert or converts, according to the exigencies of the time and place. Let me note in conclusion that the rabbinic courts which are lenient in conversion as well as those which are strict – all intend [their decisions to be] for the sake of Heaven, and they act according to their understanding and pure inner feelings."[14]

Whether rabbis were lenient or strict in accepting converts, all agreed to the validity of the halakhic conversion process. The Jewish people was a community that descended from the ancient children of Israel; but that also was joined by righteous proselytes who shared Israel's faith and destiny.

The Arabs Under Israeli Rule

The Declaration of Independence of the State of Israel called for equal rights for all citizens of Israel, regardless of religion or race. Rabbi Halevy believed that this declaration was true to the teachings of Jewish tradition.
A problem arose, though, when trying to apply the noble ideals of Judaism to a complicated political and social reality. Yes, the Arab population in Israel was entitled to respect and rights; but it was no secret that the Arab world was strongly anti-Israel, waging wars and terrorist campaigns against the Jewish State. Some Israeli Arabs, though citizens of Israel, harbored strong anti-Israel sentiments. Many Israeli Jews worried that the Israeli Arabs, protected by Israeli laws, were in fact a danger to Israel. They lived within the borders of Israel while their sympathies were with their Arab brethren who were at war with Israel.

Rabbi Halevy asserted that Arabs had every halakhic right to live in Israel; but they could not be allowed to threaten the lives of Israelis nor

---

[14] ALR 1:23. See his more elaborate discussion of conversion in ALR 3:29. For the convert's obligation to honor his birth parents, see ALR 6:62. For a question relating to the conversion of an adopted child, see ALR 8:71.

undermine the security of the country. He did not have an exact formula for dealing with this problem, but he did offer a general vision: "It is clear that we cannot relate to the minority [Israeli Arabs] with false accusations and the ferocity of hatred. Who knows better than we the taste of persecutions and racist discrimination that spread hatred and poison in the heart. Rather, we go upright in the paths of peace and understanding, for they are the way of Torah whose paths are the paths of pleasantness and all its ways are peace. We must find a just solution in the spirit of the Torah."[15]

In the spring of 1979, Rabbi Halevy answered a series of questions relating to the status of Arabs in Israel. The questioner raised the issue: since the Israeli Arabs were part of the Arab world that hated us, shouldn't we have the right to defend ourselves from them? Didn't they fall into the category of those who threaten our lives? Shouldn't we have a right to suspect them of being deadly enemies, and treat them accordingly?[16]

Rabbi Halevy expressed astonishment that these questions were purported to reflect the concerns of many. The fact was that there were one and a half million Arabs living under Israeli rule; the vast majority of them lived quiet and peaceful lives. A very small minority among them engaged in anti-Israel activity and threatened Jewish lives. Because of the small group of dangerous people, should it be permissible to attack the vast majority of Arabs who were not engaged in dangerous activity? It would be absurd to think so.

The halakhah allowed one to take preemptive action against one who came with the intent of murder. But that applied only when it was certain, or reasonably certain, that the villain came with the intent of murder. One did not have permission to kill preemptively someone whom he only suspected of possibly wanting to murder him. If someone were actually a *rodef*, a person in hot pursuit to murder a victim, then it was a mitzvah to kill the *rodef* before he murdered the victim. If a villain snuck

---

[15] BYL, pp. 49–50.

[16] The interview was published in a pamphlet entitled *Shefihut Damim: Hebeitim Hilkhiyim uMusariyim*, issued by Oz veShalom, pamphlet no. 2.

into one's house illegally, and one suspected that the villain might commit murder, then one could defend himself by killing the intruder. But absent these obviously threatening actions, one was not permitted to kill a person simply on the vague suspicion that the person might pose a threat.

How then could it be imagined that halakhah would permit or condone murdering Arabs who were not actually engaged in activity that threatened life? It was absolutely forbidden to murder individuals just because they were part of a larger group of Israel's enemies. If we were convinced that a particular group was ready to wage war on us, then we certainly had the right to defend ourselves by attacking our enemies. In a state of outright war, it was permitted to kill enemies who were planning to murder us. But there was no formal state of war between Israel and the Arab population living under Israeli rule.

The questions asked to Rabbi Halevy reflected the deep concern of Jewish Israelis about the potential danger posed by the Arab population. Rabbi Halevy did not dismiss these concerns, but cautioned against extreme reactions. It would be morally and halakhically unjustified to assume that every Arab was plotting an attack on Israelis and was in the category of *rodef*, a murderer in hot pursuit of a victim. The ways of the Torah were ways of peace and understanding, and did not condone acts of violence or murder against random individuals. The vast majority of the Arab population in Israel was surely not in the category of *rodef*.

Rabbi Halevy was not a politician nor a communal activist. He was a Torah scholar and a spiritual leader to his people. He eschewed participation in Israeli politics except as a private citizen who cast his votes for those running for office. The worldview he espoused was not shaped by experience in the political, academic or military arenas. It did not grow out of any long-term dialogues with non-Jews. It stemmed from his careful and thoughtful study of the traditional sacred texts of Judaism and from his own inner impulse towards ethical, righteous and peace-loving behavior.

Chapter Thirteen

GOVERNING THE JEWISH STATE

The emergence of a Jewish State in 1948 must be considered one of the most amazing phenomena in human history. After having been exiled by the Babylonians in 586 B.C.E., the Jews returned to their land seventy years later. The second commonwealth lasted until its destruction by the Romans in 70 C.E. At that point, most of the Jews were murdered, enslaved or sent into exile. Only a small number remained in their ancestral land of Israel.

After nearly nineteen centuries, the Jewish people finally had managed to re-establish a Jewish State in their own historic homeland. Those centuries had witnessed terrible outrages against the Jews – deprivation of rights, humiliation, isolation, physical abuse, plunder, murder. From Crusades, to expulsions, to massacres, to the Holocaust – many of the Christian and Muslim nations of the world had stained their reputations with innocent Jewish blood.

During those centuries of exile, the Jewish people never lost hope of returning to their own land where they could live in peace and tranquility. The religious practices of the Jews kept the dream of return alive. The practical political work of the Zionist movement in the nineteenth and twentieth centuries, led by and large by non-religious Jews, laid the foundation for a modern Jewish State.

Rabbi Halevy was convinced that the emergence of Israel was nothing less than the beginning of the flowering of the days of messianic redemption.[1] In this, he shared the views of his mentor, Rabbi Benzion Uziel. Indeed, it was Rabbi Uziel who had composed the official blessing for the State of Israel, recited in synagogues throughout the world, in which he referred to the new Jewish State as *reishit tzemihat ge'ulateinu*, the beginning of the flowering of our redemption.[2]

Religious Zionists, including Rabbi Uziel and Rabbi Halevy, had dreamt that the return of the Jewish people to their ancestral homeland would be accompanied by a spiritual renewal, that the new State would reflect the values and principles of Torah and halakhah. They no doubt realized that these hopes were not likely to be fulfilled soon. The leadership and much of the population of the State of Israel wanted the country to operate as a modern, secular democracy – not as a theocracy governed by rabbis according to the laws of halakhah.[3]

Rabbi Halevy was unflinching in his devotion to the State of Israel, in spite of its general tone of secularity. He devoted much effort to influence Israel to move into a more religious framework.

For Rabbi Halevy, the State was a means to an end. The essence of Judaism was the Torah and its *mitzvot*. The State served to advance the fulfillment of the teachings of Torah.[4] It offered the Jewish people the most positive framework for living religious lives. The hallmark of the Jewish people was *kedushah*, holiness. Territory, a national language, a united culture and way of life – the State provided all of these assets. Yet, its most important role was to enable the citizens to live righteous and holy lives.[5]

---

[1] For further discussion, see the chapter on *At'halta deGe'ulah*.

[2] Rabbi Halevy gave personal testimony that Rabbi Uziel was the author of this blessing. See his note in TH 2, *Devarim*, pp. 8–9.

[3] For a discussion of Rabbi Uziel's thoughts on a halakhic framework for the Jewish State, see my book, *Loving Truth and Peace: The Grand Religious Worldview of Rabbi Benzion Uziel*, chapter 9.

[4] ALR 6:92.

[5] TH 2, *Vayikra*, p. 58. See also BYL, pp. 114–116. See also the article by Avinoam Rosenak on the concept of holiness in the writings of Rabbi Halevy.

Rabbi Halevy dreamed of how the State of Israel would operate if it were governed by Torah. Since everyone would observe the Shabbat, public transportation, except that needed for life-saving activity, would rest. All restaurants would be kosher, and would serve meals on Shabbat only to patrons who had paid in advance of Shabbat. There would be no unseemly places of recreation – everything would be in the spirit of the teachings of the Torah. Many tourists would throng to Israel to see how its society functioned according to the age-old laws. The Israeli ambassadors to the countries of the world and at the United Nations would speak in the spirit of the prophets of Israel, recognizing that they represented the ancient traditions of our people. The Bible would be studied and loved by the people of Israel, and would be cited in its diplomatic negotiations. The verse in *Devarim* (28:10) would be fulfilled: "And the nations of the world will see that the name of God is called upon you, and they will fear you." This fear referred to honor and respect. In such a setting, the people of Israel will dwell securely in their own land.[6]

Rabbi Halevy emphasized that Israel's diplomacy should be guided by its religious teachings. The world knew that the historic claim to the land of Israel was rooted in the Bible – and the nations of the world themselves recognized the importance of the Bible. How appropriate it would be if the diplomats of Israel did not shy away from the biblical claim to the land. Although Jews had been exiled from their land in ancient times, this did not mean that they had given up or lost claim to it.[7]

The above vision of a religiously-run State was articulated by Rabbi Halevy in the last of his books published during his lifetime, *Netzah Moshe*. But he had made the same points in his very first book, *Bein Yisrael laAmmim*. This was a consistent, firmly-held viewpoint that characterized his thinking throughout his life.[8] Israel was to be a distinctive nation

---

The paper is included in the volume of essays on Rabbi Halevy, edited by Zvi Zohar and Avi Sagi.

[6] NM, p. 286.

[7] NM, p. 16–17.

[8] BYL, at the end of his opening comments to the book; pp. 41, 68–71.

characterized by holiness. It was to live its unique Torah way of life, achieving the highest ethical standards of any nation in the world. Through the study of Torah, the Jewish people would safeguard its spiritual well-being. The strength of the nation of Israel will stem from its spiritual greatness.[9]

Rabbi Halevy presented his religious vision of Israel as an ideal for which the society should strive. He was, though, a realist. He knew that the final redemption was not yet realized. Meanwhile, there were certain key areas of Torah law that he felt must be maintained by the State of Israel — even if Israel were to function as a secular, democratic nation: Marriages and divorces should be under religious auspices, in order to maintain the sanctity of the Jewish family.[10] Shabbat and holidays should be observed in the public domain as a means of maintaining the Jewish character of the

---

[9] BYL, p. 94.

[10] In the mid-1980s, at a conference for rabbis held at Bar Ilan University, Rabbi Halevy had entertained the notion of civil marriages in Israel for couples that were not religiously observant. He was widely criticized in rabbinic circles, although many rabbis privately told him that they agreed with him. I discussed this question at length with Rabbi Halevy in a meeting held in his office in Tel Aviv, in the summer of 1987. Rabbi Halevy told me that he was being isolated by elements of the rabbinic leadership in Israel, that they told their followers not to attend Rabbi Halevy's classes and public lectures. He was pained by this attempt at religious coercion. Yet, in spite of the ostracism he suffered, he underscored to me his belief that civil marriages would solve more halakhic problems than they might cause. He specifically discussed a case that came before him involving a non-religious couple, both of whom had been involved in adulterous relationships. Now they had become religious, and wanted to remain married. The problem was that the halakhah forbade a woman who had committed adultery to remain with her husband. If the couple had originally been married civilly, then this problem would more easily be solved, so that the couple could remain together as husband and wife. Also, civil marriages would not require religious divorces, thereby solving a host of other problems caused when couples terminated their marriages out of the country, without having obtained a religious divorce. When the wife remarried in such cases, her children from the second marriage would be considered illegitimate according to halakhah, since halakhah never recognized the termination of her first marriage. Her second marriage is thus an adulterous relationship. As far as I know, Rabbi Halevy never backed down from his suggestion that civil marriages be allowed in Israel.

State. Restaurants and hotels, and government kitchens should observe the laws of *kashrut*, thereby allowing all Jews – religious and non-religious – the opportunity of equal access. Rabbi Halevy, of course, would have liked the society to be religiously observant, both in private and in public spheres. Since that was not the reality, he pointed to these above noted three areas of public life as a way to maintain at least a minimal religious framework for the State.[11]

Judaism and Democracy

The ideal form of government according to the Torah would not be a democracy. Democracy called for rule by the people, where decisions were reached according to the views of the majority. The will of the people was the determinant.

Torah tradition, on the other hand, prescribed rule by a monarchy with the cooperation of the Great Court – later called the Sanhedrin. The king was a descendant of the house of David, not an elected official. The Sanhedrin was composed of the seventy-one greatest sages in Israel. The sages were chosen not by a popular vote, but on the basis of their merit. They were men of outstanding Torah knowledge and wide general knowledge. The Sanhedrin alone had the authority to appoint members to its body to fill vacancies.

The king was to work in concert with the Sanhedrin, so that his government would uphold the laws of the Torah. The people did not elect their officials, nor did the opinion of the majority of the people determine the laws. Rabbi Halevy stated: "It is clear to me, therefore, that there is no point in discussing democracy in a Jewish state. In a state [governed] according to Torah, all are obligated to observe the Torah and *mitzvot* as given at Sinai. Whoever thinks otherwise does not grasp and understand the essence of the acceptance of Torah."[12]

---

[11] BYL, p. 105.

[12] ALR 8:89. See the article by Moshe Helinger, *"Yahadut veDemocratia beMishnatam shel haRav B. Uziel vehaRav H.D. Halevy,"* in the volume of essays on Rabbi Halevy edited by Zvi Zohar and Avi Sagi.

Some had suggested that Jewish communities over the ages had functioned according to democratic principles. Rabbi Halevy generally dismissed these claims as being incorrect. Yes, the majority ruled in the Sanhedrin – but that was because the Torah specified majority rule in that setting. After all, the only ones involved were profound scholars – not the unlettered masses. Among scholars, it was appropriate to follow the majority opinion.

Moreover, even in Jewish communities that ostensibly followed the principle of majority rule, the standard was to limit voters to the sages and to those who paid taxes – not to the ignorant or the poor.[13] The system resembled a benign oligarchy more than a true democracy.

Having said this, Rabbi Halevy conceded that democracy was the best form of government for our times and in our situation. The Torah form of government, though not a democracy, was certainly to be preferred; but it also was not a realistic alternative for Israel at present.[14] Modern Israel must conduct its public life according to the principles of democracy.

In a talk to rabbis in Israel in the spring of 1963, Rabbi Halevy addressed the theme of the role of religion in the modern Jewish State.[15] He noted that the Torah did not govern Israel. Rather, the democratically elected government ruled. The Knesset had the power to pass laws that were in violation of the Torah. It did not have to consult with rabbinic sages before making its decisions. Even the laws of the State that had a religious flavor – e.g., marriages and divorces to be performed by rabbis, Shabbat as the day off, *kashrut* in the armed forces – were not enacted for religious reasons. Rather, they were practical concessions to the political reality that many Israelis wanted these things. The majority of Jews in Israel – including many who were not strictly observant religiously – respected the Torah and the sages of Torah; they did not want the government to trample on religious sensibilities. Moreover, it sometimes

---

[13] Ibid. See also ALR 8:90.

[14] MH 3:52.

[15] DM, pp. 41ff. The following discussion is based on this source.

made sense in a democracy for the majority to make concessions to the minority, for the sake of maintaining harmony. But these concessions were not unlimited, and they were granted by concession, not by right.

Rabbi Halevy distinguished between what he called *medinat hok* (a state governed by elected officials who enacted laws for the good of the people), and *medinat halakhah* (a state governed by the Torah and halakhah). At first glance, it would seem that these alternatives were in diametrical opposition. Yet, Rabbi Halevy thought that the two approaches could be complementary.

Certainly, halakhah should be the authoritative source for a Jewish government. Yet, the halakhah was not a rigid, archaic system. On the contrary, it had the flexibility to adapt to every situation. "The power and strength of the halakhah is in this, that its basic laws were given by the Omniscient God who sees everything to the end of the generations. Therefore, one can find in it [halakhah] solutions to all the questions of life in each generation."[16]

The halakhah did not provide all the specifics for the way a government should operate; it did not establish a fixed economic system. Rather, it provided God-given principles that could be applied to all situations in every era. The halakhah did not change, but historical conditions changed. It was the halakhah's power and responsibility to adapt to new situations. In matters relating to social and political life, the halakhah left much room for the leaders of each generation to decide what was best for their circumstances.[17] The halakhah did not discuss all eventualities; it did not list every possible rule for the proper governance of society; it did give authority to the leaders of each generation to make ordinances for the better functioning of their communities.

The halakhah itself demanded that government legislate for the needs of society; but the legislation should be true to the principles of Torah. Ideally, the Knesset should consult rabbinic sages before passing laws. These sages would inform the Knesset of the relevant halakhic

---

[16] DM, p. 49.
[17] DM, p. 50.

considerations. The Knesset should not rely on the halakhic guidance provided by individuals who were themselves elected members of the Knesset, and who may have had political motives influencing their presentations. Rather, the Knesset should consult sages who devoted their days and nights to Torah study, who were not involved in the political fray. If the Knesset agreed not to pass a law in violation of halakhah, if it consulted sages before passing legislation, if its laws were true to the principles of halakhah – then it was possible to have a democratic state that operated according to halakhah.[18] Such a government should avoid laws that entailed religious coercion or anti-religious coercion. It should attempt to respect the religious nature of the state, while not passing laws relating to the private observance of religion, where such practice did not openly harm society.[19]

Rabbi Halevy felt that living in a democratic state was a challenge to the religious community. Religious Jews should not see the non-religious community as their antagonists, but as people worthy of their love, care and attention. On the other hand, the non-religious community needed to demonstrate more sensitivity to the feelings of the religious community, and should realize the vital importance of maintaining a Jewish framework for the Jewish State. How tragic it would be if religious Jews came to feel that they lived in spiritual exile in the Jewish State.[20]

Decisions of the Government

Rabbi Halevy believed that it was a religious obligation to love the Jewish State, to strengthen it, to avoid doing anything that threatened its peace and its well-being.[21] Even though it was a secular democratic state, it was a manifestation of God's providence and a step towards messianic redemption. He rejected the attitude of those within the religious community who denied the religious significance of the Jewish State.

---

[18] DM, pp. 56–57.
[19] DM, pp. 58–60.
[20] DM, pp. 74–75.
[21] MKH 1:4, p. 37.

Professor Ruth Gabizon has suggested that Rabbi Halevy, while giving highest authority to Torah and halakhah, demonstrated respect for the secular government's role in Israeli life. He recognized the importance of the work done by government and civic institutions. She attributed this attitude to Rabbi Halevy's having grown up in the old Sephardic *yishuv* where tolerance and open-mindedness were characteristic, and where people did not feel threatened by those who believed or acted differently from them. Thus, Rabbi Halevy (and Rabbi Uziel before him) tended to eschew religious stridency in favor of working harmoniously with all elements of the society.[22]

One of the areas of heated controversy within Israel centered on the issue of giving away conquered land. In the Six Day War of June 1967, Israel defended itself from a looming attack from the armies of a number of Arab countries. Through that remarkable war, Israeli forces took control of the Old City of Jerusalem, the West Bank, and the Sinai and Gaza Strip. (East Jerusalem and the West Bank had been controlled by Jordan, while Gaza and the Sinai had been controlled by Egypt.) Israel also wrested control of the Golan Heights from Syria.

The tiny country of Israel saw these conquests of land as a strategic enhancement to its security. The land provided a buffer zone between the main population centers of Israel and the territories of enemy states. It would now take more time for enemies to reach the mainland of Israel, giving Israeli forces more time to mount an effective counter-attack to a possible future invasion.

After the Yom Kippur War of 1973, where Israel once again succeeded in defeating the armies of its Arab enemies, President Sadat of Egypt came to realize that the region should move in the direction of peace rather than continued war. He traveled to Jerusalem where he was greeted warmly and enthusiastically by the Israeli population, led by Prime Minister Menahem Begin. The peace process began.

---

[22] See her paper in the volume of essays about Rabbi Halevy, edited by Zvi Zohar and Avi Sagi. See in the same volume, the essay by Yedidah Stern on Rabbi Halevy's political views.

With the active involvement of the United States, a peace treaty between Israel and Egypt was formalized. In return for this peace, Israel agreed to return to Egypt the Sinai Peninsula Strip. Israel dismantled its settlements in the Sinai, and withdrew its military forces from that strategic area.

While all Israelis surely wanted peace and were delighted to have a treaty with Egypt, not all Israelis were happy about the inordinately high price Israel had to pay for the treaty. Many felt that Israel should not have ceded so much territory, or any territory at all. Within the religious community, leading rabbis expressed the view that the government had violated halakhah by giving land to Egypt; the government had no right to cede the land. Some argued that the government's decision was null and void and that it should be resisted by the settlers living in the Sinai.

Rabbi Halevy was assuredly not happy about Israel's transfer of territory to Egypt. But he argued forcefully that the government of Israel had the halakhic right to make the agreement. It was the responsibility of government to do what it thought best for the survival of Israel. If the government leaders believed that ceding land would better insure the safety of Israelis, then the government was within its rights to do so.[23]

Rabbi Halevy felt that security experts, rather than rabbis, were in a better position to make a decision in the matter of ceding territory. How could rabbis make a competent decision on this issue without the necessary military and diplomatic information? Since this information was not submitted to the rabbis for their consideration, the most rabbis could do was express general principles of halakhah – but not a specific ruling. Ideally, the government officials should have consulted the halakhic authorities. But since they did not do so, the halakhic authorities did not have the requisite information for issuing a halakhic ruling.[24] They had to defer to the decision of the government.

As the years passed, the issue of "land for peace" did not subside. A suggestion was put forth that the government of Israel should not

---

[23] ALR 4, pp. 12–18. See also ALR 3:56 and 3:61.
[24] DM, pp. 29–32.

transfer land without first submitting its proposal as a national referendum. Then, the people as a whole could express its view whether or not Israel should give land away.

Rabbi Halevy noted that halakhah normally gave decision-making rights to the elected officials of the community. But in unusual cases, the halakhah did recognize the right of the community to voice its opinion, even in opposition to the elected officials. Thus, there was a halakhic framework for permitting a referendum in cases of special concern to the community.

Yet, Rabbi Halevy pointed out that the halakhic sources dealt with relatively small matters (e.g., the sale of a synagogue building or religious artifacts of a synagogue) compared to the issue of "land for peace." Rabbi Halevy believed, on practical rather than halakhic grounds, that a national referendum on ceding land would not yield a meaningful result. The issue was quite complex. Was it realistic to expect that the public would be adequately knowledgeable to vote intelligently? Rabbi Halevy believed that a referendum was incapable of yielding a proper result "where the citizen is requested to answer a multi-faceted and complex question, to which he does not have and cannot have full and comprehensive knowledge (likely also involving security secrets); nor even a national question that has security ramifications, that even if the common citizen were given all the required information he would still not have the ability to fathom the depths of the matter and make a decision."[25]

Rabbi Halevy, then, believed the government and military officials were in the best position to make major decisions; that the halakhic authorities lacked the military and diplomatic information; that the public at large, also lacking the relevant information, was not capable of reaching well-reasoned, nuanced decisions. So even while he himself disagreed with the government's decision to yield so much territory to Egypt, he believed that the government had the authority to make the decision.

---

[25] MH 2:87.

Rabbi Halevy dealt with other questions relating to government authority, and as a rule, he vindicated the government's right to conduct its business as it saw necessary for the wellbeing of its citizens. Thus, Rabbi Halevy justified the government's taking a census of the population, even though a long tradition in halakhah opposed the counting of the people.[26] Since a census was needed for proper government planning in a modern state, Rabbi Halevy permitted the census on the grounds that it did not involve an actual head count, but was done by means of people filling out forms.

Rabbi Halevy also found halakhic justification for the Israeli government to allow sale of arms to other countries, even though halakhic sources forbade the sale of weapons to potentially dangerous people. Rabbi Halevy felt that the State had the halakhic right to engage in trade of arms, if it believed this was vital to its own security. "The State of Israel sells weapons only to friendly nations, and there is no doubt that it does so because of security considerations. It factors in the benefit that will conduce to us from this, and therefore it is obvious that [sale of weapons] is permissible."[27] Rabbi Halevy premised his decision on the fact that Israel sold arms only to friendly nations. Presumably, he would not think the halakhah allowed sale of weapons to those who were not allied to Israel.

Rabbi Halevy found halakhic basis for Israel to sign extradition agreements with other countries. Thus, Israel had the right to imprison Jewish criminals from other countries who had fled to Israel for protection. Israel also had the right to extradite such individuals to countries with which it had signed an extradition treaty.[28]

Rabbi Halevy firmly held that Israel's true security was provided by God and was dependent on the study of Torah and fulfillment of *mitzvot*.

---

[26] MH 3:54.

[27] ALR 1:19.

[28] MH 1:67.

But he also believed that it was necessary for Israel to have a strong military. The Almighty helped those who helped themselves.[29]

A religious young man, just drafted into the Israeli army, asked if he was obligated to follow his officers' orders, even if those orders called on him to violate halakhah.[30] Rabbi Halevy began his responsum with a general discussion affirming the obligation to follow orders issued by the government, including the military leaders who were appointed by the government. "There is no doubt that a democratic state, where the government is elected by the nation in general elections, is a government chosen by the nation. It has the status of a monarchy [described in the Torah and halakhah]. Also to it [the democratically elected government] falls the obligation to obey its orders and instructions."

But while the officers of the military had the power to give orders and to punish violators of their orders, a soldier had no obligation to follow orders that were in clear defiance of the laws of the Torah. On the contrary, the soldier was ultimately responsible to the Almighty, and should not act in a way that transgressed God's laws as manifested in Torah and halakhah. If a soldier were asked to perform duties on the Shabbat that violated halakhah, he could refuse to perform them unless these duties were related in some way to saving lives. If a soldier was not sure that the orders really entailed life-saving activities but he did them anyway, any sin involved belonged to the officer and not to the soldier.

---

[29] In 1990, I met with a Chief Rabbi of a major city in Israel, a man who was known for his great erudition and who authored a number of volumes of halakhic responsa. He told me that a military leader of Israel had asked him to encourage yeshiva students to serve in the army. He had responded to the general: instead of getting yeshiva students to serve in the army, all the soldiers should put down their weapons and start studying Torah. Then, God would protect Israel. He quoted a Midrash that God would protect the Jewish people if they all studied Torah. I asked the rabbi if he would risk the security of Israel based on that Midrash. He told me without hesitation: yes, without any doubt whatsoever! We don't need an army, we need everyone to study Torah. Rabbi Halevy's view was very different. See TH 1, Bereishit, p. 70. See also ALR 3:58 for a discussion of war in halakhah.

[30] ALR 7:68.

The soldier could then later determine if the duties had been necessary or not. If they were not related to life-saving activities, he could lodge a complaint with the military authorities so that he should not be put into the same situation in the future.

In this responsum, Rabbi Halevy affirmed the obligation of soldiers to follow orders; but at the same time he underscored the principle that orders should not cause a violation of halakhah. When the possibility of saving life was involved, then the halakhah itself waived Shabbat laws – and indeed most other laws as well.

In his responsa, Rabbi Halevy discussed other areas of government responsibility, e.g., operating a police force, court system, penal system. The halakhah granted wide authority in these areas to a legitimately elected government. He thought that the halakhah, though, frowned on the concept of imprisoning criminals except as a last resort. The Torah, for example, punished thieves by making them pay back what they stole, usually with an extra penalty (i.e., double the value of what they stole). This was more effective and more humane than locking people in prison.[31]

Economic Issues

Rabbi Halevy disagreed with those who thought halakhah was incapable of dealing with the practical issues relating to running a modern state. He argued that the Torah provided necessary guidance for all situations and for all generations. Yet, the Torah was consciously vague when it came to establishing a political and economic system. While giving general guidelines, it left specific decisions to the leaders of each generation.[32]

The Torah did not advocate a specific economic system for several reasons. First, economic conditions changed from era to era. Since the Torah was eternal, it avoided the establishment of a fixed system that

---

[31] See ALR 5:46 on the role of police in halakhah; MH 2:74–77, on halakhic principles governing a court system; ALR 3:57 on the halakhah's negative views on imprisonment. On the latter, see also MH 2:78 and TH 2, *Vayikra*, pp. 118–119.

[32] ALR 3:56; See also TH 2, *Vayikra*, pp. 95ff.

might become outdated or cumbersome over the course of time. Moreover, the Torah wanted to give free choice to the leaders of each generation in matters relating to the secular aspects of life.

The Torah provided laws relating to economics: honest speech and conduct; true weights and measures; gifts to maintain the poor; sabbatical years for the cancellation of debts, etc. The Torah demonstrated tremendous compassion and concern for the widow and orphan, the poor and defenseless. It called for a just and merciful society that protected its residents and provided them with sustenance.

Rabbi Halevy discussed the Torah's laws of sabbatical years, where debts incurred by loans were cancelled. The purpose of this law was to give poor debtors a chance to have their slates cleared so they could start over again without the burden of debt. The Torah foresaw the possibility of lenders holding back on their loans as the sabbatical year approached. After all, why would they want to lend money when the loan would be cancelled by the sabbatical year? The chances of their being repaid diminished as the sabbatical year approached.

In order to encourage lenders, an ordinance known as *prosbul* was instituted. Bills of debt were turned over to the rabbinical court before the sabbatical year began. Such documents were not subject to cancellation by the sabbatical year; only debts directly between individuals were cancelled. By employing the *prosbul*, the lenders did not need to fear losing their money; hence, they would feel free to continue lending to others, even as the sabbatical year approached.

Rabbi Halevy offered a novel explanation of this system. He suggested that the rabbinical courts did not agree to accept the bills of debt in every case. If a person had borrowed money in order to purchase a house or other property, or if the loan were for business purposes – the rabbinical court would not necessarily want these debts to be cancelled by the sabbatical year. Thus, after examining each case, the court would decide if it were appropriate to spare this debt from cancellation. But in cases where loans were given to poor people, specifically as an act of charity and lovingkindness, then the court would not agree to have these debts spared from cancellation. On the contrary, the court would want these debts to be cancelled in order to fulfill the intention of the Torah to help the poor. "Even though I have not found any basis in halakhah for my suggestion, nevertheless my heart tells me that this is how things were arranged originally when the ordinance was instituted."[33]

In a similar vein, Rabbi Halevy theorized about the Torah law forbidding charging interest on loans to fellow Jews. The intent seemed to be to protect poor people from running up huge debts due to ever-increasing interest charges. However, the rule prohibiting the charging of interest was problematic in a dynamic economic system. People needed to borrow money for business purposes and for major purchases. Even middle class and rich people needed to borrow money. But why should someone lend money at no interest, when the borrower himself intended to use the money for investment purposes? In order to facilitate large-scale loans, rabbinical law established a *heter iska*, a document that circumvented the prohibitions of charging or paying interest. The document essentially treated loans as partnerships, where one party (the borrower) agreed to pay the other party (the lender) a certain amount of the profits derived from the money. So the increased amount was not technically interest, but was a percentage of the value of the business paid to a partner.

Rabbi Halevy opined that the *heter iska* could be used only in cases of commercial loans. But when money was lent to help out a poor person, then the *heter iska* did not apply. The poor person was obliged to pay back only the exact amount borrowed, and no more. This maintained the essential concern of the Torah for the welfare of the poor, while not inhibiting the development of commerce.[34]

The State of Israel had an obligation to provide a viable economic system for its citizens. The halakhah provided some of the necessary tools, e.g., *prosbul, heter iska*. But it also left adequate room for the leaders to adopt policies for the benefit of the Israeli economy.[35]

---

[33] ALR 3:56.

[34] MH 3:49.

[35] ALR 7:70–71.

A healthy Israeli economy was not only desirable for the happiness of its citizens; it was also vital for the further development and security of the country. A thriving economy would attract more Jewish immigrants. It might also encourage parents to have more children. A larger population would enhance Israel's strength. Rabbi Halevy believed that the government should promote economic growth through constructive policies, including a revamping of the tax system.[36]

The success of the economy depended not only on government policies, but on the honest conduct in business of employers and employees alike. Employers should pay appropriate wages, and employees should work to the best of their capacities.[37] All workers had the right to go on strike if conditions were unsatisfactory and if all attempts at reaching a fair arrangement with the employers had failed.[38]

One of the recurring economic issues that created conflict between the secular government and the religious community related to the agricultural laws of the sabbatical year. According to the Torah, the land could be cultivated for six years, but on the seventh it was to lay fallow. To implement this rule in a modern economic system was not at all a simple matter. The financial challenges to the farmers and to the food industry of Israel would be significant. Agricultural exports would be vastly reduced. The population of Israel would need to depend almost entirely on imported food for large periods of time. This was not only an inconvenience and expense; but it also could be a serious security issue in case of war or political tensions in the world.

Some religious kibbutzim observed the laws of the sabbatical year, and were supported financially by religious Jews around the world. Others

---

[36] DM, pp. 33–34. Rabbi Halevy thought that the Torah's laws of inheritance, sometimes thought to be unfair to women, should be upheld. He argued that the Torah's laws of inheritance were in fact more advantageous to most women than the modern egalitarian system. See ALR 1:22; MH 3:50. In MH 1:63, he wrote in favor of financial prenuptial agreements.

[37] MH 2:80.

[38] ALR 2:64; 2:67; 3:23; 5:23. For other responsa relating to workers' rights and responsibilities, see ALR 6:77; 6:79; 8:86; 8:88.

tried to sidestep the rules by utilizing hydroponics – where the crops were grown in water rather than in the soil. Most of the Israeli farmers, though, simply ignored the rules of the sabbatical year.

At the beginning of the twentieth century, when Jews were beginning to engage in farming in the land of Israel on a larger scale, a number of rabbis (including Rabbis Yaakov Shaul Elyachar, Rafael Meir Fanajel, Yitzhak Elhanan Spector, and Avraham Yitzhak Kook) approved the "sale" of the land of Israel to non-Jews for the sabbatical year. The argument was that the prohibition to cultivate the soil only applied to land owned by Jews. Land owned by non-Jews was not subject to the laws of the sabbatical year. By arranging a "sale" of the land to non-Jews, albeit a legal fiction, it would then be permitted to engage in agricultural activity in the land of Israel. This has been the policy of the Chief Rabbinate of Israel since the inception of the Jewish State.

Although perhaps technically correct, the "sale" of land to non-Jews was intellectually and emotionally unappealing. It was an obvious subterfuge that brought religious law into disrepute in the minds of the non-religious. Rabbi Halevy understood the halakhic attempt to sidestep the rules of the sabbatical year, but was unhappy with the notion of "selling" the land of Israel to non-Jews for one year of each seven-year cycle.

Rabbi Halevy offered what he thought was a reasonable solution. Before each sabbatical year, a panel of rabbis, agriculturists and economists should meet. These experts should determine, based on the economic conditions then prevailing in Israel, what percentage of the land needed to be cultivated in order to maintain the agriculture industry and the national economy. If, for example, it was determined that seventy percent of the land must be cultivated, then the Chief Rabbinate – on an ad hoc basis – should pronounce that all farmers could cultivate seventy percent of their fields. (There was talmudic precedent for rabbinic cancellation of the rules of the sabbatical year when dire economic conditions demanded such radical measures.[39]) The remaining thirty percent would lay fallow, in fulfillment of the Torah law. While this suggestion surely was not perfect, yet it provided a compromise position: it allowed farmers to cultivate the land needed to provide their livelihoods, and it also left some land entirely fallow in fulfillment of Torah law.[40] Rabbi Halevy's suggestion has not been adopted.

Rabbi Halevy had a vision of a modern democratic state operating in consonance with halakhah. He did not live to see his dream fulfilled. He himself thought that the vision would not be realized until messianic times. Yet, his writings shed important light on how the State of Israel should conduct its political and economic life, remaining true to democratic ideals and the ideals of the Torah.

---

[39] *Sanhedrin* 26a.

[40] MH 2:61. He also discusses other issues related to the sabbatical year. See also MH 3:32.

Chapter Fourteen

AT'HALTA DEGE'ULAH:
THE STATE OF ISRAEL AS PRELUDE TO
THE MESSIANIC ERA

Throughout his writings, Rabbi Halevy expressed unwavering faith that the founding of the State of Israel, and the Six Day War, were overt miracles. Anyone who denied the supernatural nature of these events was spiritually blind.[1] There were two options: to believe that this was the beginning of the messianic era, or to be wrong.[2] He never appears to have doubted this belief.[3]

At the same time, the Sages had debated fundamental aspects of the messianic age. Is redemption contingent on repentance? Will the messianic age be a supernatural era, or completely natural? Will it be a lengthy process with ups and downs, or a consistently ascending path? Rambam concluded from these and related disagreements that there was no single authoritative tradition on the messianic age. We would not know its nature until it arrived.[4] Rabbi Halevy was fully aware of the uncertainties inherent in identifying the messianic period.

---

[1] End MKH 4, pp. 367–368.

[2] Introduction to MKH 2, p. 9.

[3] See MKH 4:205, p.191; MKH 5:310, p. 508, where Rabbi Halevy used the formulation, "it is our hope and belief that this period is the beginning of our final redemption." From his other writings, it is evident that his profound hope led to a complete belief.

[4] *Hil. Melakhim* 12:1–2.

Rabbi Halevy, quoting Rabbi Eliyahu of Vilna, considered two aspects of the modern period as definite signs of the first stages of redemption: the return of agricultural fertility to the Land of Israel (*Sanhedrin* 98a: Rabbi Abba says that there will not be a clearer sign of redemption than this); and the ingathering of exiles.[5] For Rabbi Halevy, it was the responsibility of world Jewry to recognize the miraculous nature of the founding of the State of Israel, make aliyah immediately, repent, cooperate with each other, and live a unique national existence in order to set a religious and moral example for the world to emulate.[6]

Rabbi Halevy conceded that we cannot know how the process of redemption will work until it arrives. He quoted the verse (*Tehillim* 126:1) that during the return to Zion, *hayinu keholmim* (it was as though we were dreaming): when redemption came, it would seem as vague as a dream.[7]

Rabbi Halevy's writings reflect a conflict. On the one hand, he firmly believed that we were at the beginning of redemption. On the other hand, he acknowledged that no one knew for certain how the redemption process would unfold. Rabbi Halevy evaluated sources about messianic calculations, natural vs. supernatural redemption (including the role of peace talks and wars as part of the messianic age), repentance during the period of redemption, and other matters relating to Divine Providence.

---

[5] ALR 1:7–12; 4:6.

[6] Introduction to BYL, p. 23; DM, pp. 21, 34–35. Cf. ALR 4:7, 9, where he added that Israel should emphasize its Divine rights to the Land at the United Nations (cf. DM, pp. 21, 35, 59–60). Aside from the desirability of projecting a religious image for the State, Rabbi Halevy believed that this argument would be effective in the international community. By maintaining a purely secular stance, other nations would likely respond in a secular manner, promoting their own interests, such as oil and strategic alliances with stronger nations. When he wrote these words, Rabbi Halevy noted that there was still time to employ these religious arguments; once Israel officially appeals to secular arguments it will forever squander its opportunity to appeal to divine rights (cf. BYL, p. 89). In BYL (pp. 3–4), he added that Israel's enemies have moved their battlefronts to "diplomacy" at the United Nations. For further discussion, see the chapters on Jews and non-Jews, and Governing the Jewish State.

[7] ALR 1:6.

Messianic Calculations

Confident that we were living in the period of redemption, Rabbi Halevy justified messianic calculations. Although the Talmud (*Sanhedrin* 97a) had criticized such calculations, Rabbi Halevy argued that this caveat applied only if a failed prediction might diminish one's faith in the advent of the Messiah. If one certainly believed that the Messiah will come, and made calculations for the purpose of religious awakening, one did not violate the talmudic injunction.[8] Rabbi Halevy further maintained that talmudic opposition to messianic calculations arose because redemption was so remote from their period; but now that the messianic age had arrived, there was no impediment to trying to determine its precise date.[9] Initially, he proposed 5750/1990 as the deadline for the final redemption; but if people repented, it could come earlier.[10]

In a later responsum, he offered an original interpretation of a talmudic argument about the messianic age, based on events from the past century. In *Sanhedrin* 99a, the Sages debated whether the period of redemption would span forty years, seventy years, or three generations. Rabbi Halevy explained that all three positions turned out to be true. Forty years covered the period from the 1947 U.N. partition plan until 1987; seventy years spanned the Balfour Declaration of 1917 to 1987; and three generations went back to 1897, the year of the first World Zionist Congress. Given the coincidence of those three dates in relation to 1987,

---

[8] ALR 1:2. Rabbi Halevy attributed Rambam's stark formulation of the prohibition against messianic calculations to the difficult plight of Yemenite Jewry during Rambam's lifetime.

[9] In MZR (p. 59), Rabbi Halevy quoted the Zohar (*Vayera* 118): God did not want to reveal the time of the redemption, but when the time approached, even children would be able to calculate properly. Rabbi Halevy noted that in that passage in the Zohar, there are stunningly accurate predictions pertaining to our time period.

[10] ALR 1:2; cf. TH 1, *Bereshit*, pp. 148–156.

Rabbi Halevy predicted the final messianic redemption for 1987, only ten years after he composed the essay.[11]

When his prediction for 1987 proved false (on the contrary, yet another major wave of Arab terrorism had recently begun), Rabbi Halevy did not back away from his prediction, nor did he conclude that the Jews had missed a great opportunity for the final redemption. Rather, he stressed that Arab nations were sitting down with Israel to discuss peace, a major component of redemption.[12] Rabbi Halevy had offered a similar rationale for the Yom Kippur War, which led to peace talks afterwards.[13]

Be'itah, Ahishenah

> R. Alexandri said: R. Yehoshua b. Levi pointed out a contradiction. It is written, in its time [will the Messiah come], but it is also written, I [the Lord] will hasten it! (*Yeshayahu* 60:22). If they are worthy, I will hasten it; if not, [he will come] at the due time. (*Sanhedrin* 98a)

This talmudic passage presented an important resolution to a contradiction within a biblical verse in Yeshayahu: will the messianic age come "on time" (*be'itah*), or will God hasten it (*ahishenah*)? The Talmud answered that the outcome would depend on the merit of Israel.

Rabbi Halevy found different ways of interpreting and applying this passage, depending on the message he was trying to convey and on current political events. For example, in *Dat uMedinah* (p. 26), Rabbi Halevy applied the interpretation of Radak (*Yeshayahu* 60:22): once the proper time for redemption had arrived, then the process will accelerate. Only nineteen years separated the founding of the State in 1948 until the victory of the Six Day War in 1967, demonstrating the imminence of the final redemption.

---

[11] End ALR 2, pp. 253–256.
[12] End ALR 9, pp. 395–396.
[13] ALR 1:6, see further discussion below.

But after the Yom Kippur War in 1973, Rabbi Halevy shifted to a modified reading of the aforementioned talmudic interpretation of *be'itah, ahishenah*: if the messianic age were merited early, it would not be accompanied with suffering. If it came "on time," it would be a natural process, entailing affliction. No longer did Rabbi Halevy think in terms of a quick process; he began to view the prolonged struggle of the State as part of a longer divine plan of redemption.[14]

To explain the prominent role of secular Zionism in the redemption process, Rabbi Halevy wrote that the State of Israel arose as a result of *be'itah*, a natural process. The Talmud (*Megillah* 17b; *Sanhedrin* 97a) stated that wars would precede the final redemption. Historically, Jews had gradually adopted the idea of a supernatural redemption, since they had suffered so much during their exile. "It was understandable to think this way. Was it possible for an oppressed nation – scattered to the corners of the globe, fighting heroically to survive when many branches were cut off in each generation – who, during this time of the sword and destruction, would consider a national revival, return of the exiles, and the founding of a State through natural means?"[15]

Thus, by the time the process of redemption began during the 20th century, most religious Jews *rejected* the possibility of natural redemption. It was specifically the secularists who were able to achieve success. Yes, some religious Jews were involved, but the majority of modern Zionist activists were not religiously observant. In retrospect, it had become obvious that the process of establishing and defending the State had been miraculous.[16] God's plan of redemption was achieved, but most of the religious

---

[14] ALR 1:7–12. In MZR (p. 58) and MHK 4:185, pp. 56–57, Rabbi Halevy quoted the Zohar (*Mishpatim* 94b): the final redemption will not be rushed, unlike the exodus from Egypt. Despite his familiarity with this kabbalistic teaching, Rabbi Halevy obviously preferred his pre-1973 interpretation of *be'itah, ahishenah*. Unfortunately, the Zohar turned out to be correct, and Rabbi Halevy was forced to adopt this teaching out of historical necessity. In ALR 4:6, he adopted the talmudic reading as primary, and Radak's as secondary.

[15] ALR 1:3, p. 18.

[16] ALR 1:3; cf. DM, p. 9.

community had failed to respond. Unwittingly, the secularists became God's agents of redemption.

Rabbi Halevy explained the struggles and wars of Israel not only through *be'itah*, but also with the idea that it would not be dignified were God simply to deliver the Land on a silver platter. Ancient Israel understood this message, evidenced by the way they fought Amalek (*Shemot* 17:8–17). They did not expect supernatural intervention once they had left Egypt. Rabbi Halevy expressed disappointment that many contemporary Jews still had not recognized the messianic potential of today, mistakenly waiting for supernatural miracles. Their error was based on a fundamental misunderstanding of *be'itah*, redemption, and dignity. Rabbi Halevy reiterated that his own interpretation was speculative, since we cannot know how redemption will come until it arrived.[17]

By presenting different interpretations of *be'itah, ahishenah*, Rabbi Halevy reached a composite understanding of the wars following the founding of the State of Israel. Part of his explanation was a concession to natural processes, since we did not merit supernatural intervention.[18] Simultaneously, he found parallels to the exodus, where God intentionally assigned the people of Israel an active role in the process of redemption as an ideal state of affairs.[19] Rabbi Halevy also stressed that war as part of *be'itah* was only the beginning of a theological response.[20]

Rabbi Halevy viewed natural and supernatural as different stages in the messianic process, rather than as alternatives. Mashiah ben Yosef (the first stage of redemption) will be characterized by suffering, whereas

---

[17] ALR 1:4–5.

[18] ALR 1:3.

[19] ALR 1:4–5.

[20] ALR 1:7–12; cf. ALR 4:6; MH 1:26, where he expanded on these ideas. See also MZR (pp. 59–60), where Rabbi Halevy quoted several passages from the Zohar addressing the debate over whether the redemption can come without prior repentance of Israel. On p. 60, he also quoted Zohar (*Vayhi* 215a), that there will be wars. Rabbi Halevy noted that this source demonstrates kabbalistic knowledge that the final redemption would come with wars and sacrifice (cf. p. 153, from Zohar, *Balak* 212b).

Mashiah ben David (the final stage of redemption) will be characterized by a supernatural redemption and the ingathering of the exiles.[21] He thought that the Six Day War completed the first stage in the process of redemption, but we still required national repentance to merit the final redemption.[22] To this end, Rabbi Halevy considered his five-volume series, *Mekor Hayyim*, to have been driven by his passionate desire to hasten the arrival of the messianic age through repentance.[23]

The common denominator of Rabbi Halevy's responses is that we *certainly* were in the early stages of the messianic age. Rather than allowing the Yom Kippur War, Arab terrorism, or other tragedies to negate that belief, Rabbi Halevy offered interpretations that were in tune with unfolding realities. At the same time, he continued to advocate national repentance and unity as the primary catalysts to effect the full redemption.

Rabbi Halevy adopted a finely nuanced position towards military exemptions for yeshiva students. Fundamentally, he favored military exemptions for yeshiva students. Were the entire nation to engage in Torah study, supernatural miracles would occur to protect Israel (see *Sanhedrin* 14b).[24] But after his praise for full-time Torah study, he emphasized that this exemption applied exclusively to those who were truly dedicated to Torah learning. Those who enrolled in *yeshivot* simply to dodge the draft desecrated God's Name. Additionally, *all* yeshiva students must serve in the military during actual wartime. Acknowledging the difficulty of explaining this concept to those not committed to Torah values, he praised *yeshivot hesder*, which combined yeshiva learning with military service, thereby sanctifying God's Name.[25]

---

[21] ALR 4:6; 4:8.

[22] DM, pp. 23–24.

[23] Introduction to MKH 1, pp. 9–14; introduction to MKH 2, pp. 7–10. Already in his first work (BYL, pp. 79–80), Rabbi Halevy stressed the need to connect halakhah with aggadah now that we have entered the fourth and final stage of history – the age of redemption.

[24] For further discussion, see the chapter on Governing the Jewish State.

[25] ALR 1:21; 3:58. See also the chapter on Respect for Others. For a survey of recent rabbinic opinions pertaining to the military exemption of yeshiva students

In a response to pamphlets opposing military service for yeshiva students, Rabbi Halevy defended his position that all yeshiva students must serve in the military during wartime. Training did not take *that* long; and even if the students could not be trained quickly, they could serve in non-combat roles. In this responsum, Rabbi Halevy maintained that those who did not serve at all during wartime were *violating* halakhah, not just giving religion a bad name. He also reiterated his earlier position that any exemption referred exclusively to those who were genuinely engaged in serious Torah study. Insincere students should be drafted to regular military service.[26]

In these discussions, Rabbi Halevy revealed a strong belief in the supernatural powers of Torah, combined with a fervent commitment to the sanctification of God's Name. He also explicated what halakhah really taught about military service for yeshiva students. His deepest desire was for all Jews to be dedicated to Torah study, so as to merit God's miraculous protection, and bring about the full redemption. Until that ideal state was realized, though, Jews would have to maintain military defense forces.

The Yom Kippur War: a Challenge to Redemption?

Rabbi Halevy's earlier writings expressed unreserved enthusiasm about the redemption process. Yet, many of his followers were perplexed by the Yom Kippur War. This war had exposed Israel's vulnerability. No longer did the messianic age appear to be marching forward with increasing brightness.

Rabbi Halevy opened his *Asei Lekha Rav* series with several essays addressing this problem. He paralleled the contemporary situation with the redemption from Egypt. During the exodus, God created a moment of panic at the Red Sea, when the Israelites thought they were doomed. Only when the sea split did the Israelites retrospectively understand God's plan

---

from the Israeli military, see Rabbi Alfred S. Cohen, "On Yeshiva Men Serving in the Army," *Journal of Halacha and Contemporary Society* 23 (Spring, 1992), pp. 5–31.

[26] ALR 7:72.

of redemption. Similarly, the Yom Kippur War initially seemed like a setback, but it resulted in Egypt sitting down to talk peace with Israel for the first time.[27]

Although Rabbi Halevy could have appealed to the principle of *be'itah* (i.e., the natural and painful process of redemption), he chose not to do so. Instead, he stressed the positive outcome of the Yom Kippur War. Rabbi Halevy observed that the Yom Kippur War was not a challenge to one's messianic hopes unless one expected a consistently upward progression in redemption.[28] Since we were not privy to God's plans, we could not assume a trouble-free road to redemption.[29] "Evidently, the nature of redemption includes ups and downs, until it reaches its final stage, the appearance of the Mashiah ben David."[30]

Rabbi Halevy provided a sobering interpretation of the Yom Kippur War as well. Significantly, he suggested that perhaps the Yom Kippur War may have come as a result of our not repenting and acknowledging God's role in the Six Day War – although we cannot know this with certainty. He encouraged repentance and spiritual improvement among the people of Israel. Thus, his discussions took two directions: they maintained belief in the messianic process and they called for a religious revival.

---

[27] ALR 1:6. Cf. DM, p. 27; introduction to MKH 2, pp. 7–10, where Rabbi Halevy made a similar point regarding the Six Day War. Although the period preceding the Six Day War initially was a terrifying time for Israel, it brought about the return of Jerusalem and Hebron, our holiest cities. Rabbi Halevy also highlighted the stunning turnaround in the Yom Kippur War, which was enough to include that war as part of the redemption process, rather than an obstacle (ALR 1:6; 1:7–12).

[28] Prior to the Yom Kippur War, it appears that Rabbi Halevy himself expected this upward progression (see MHK 4, pp. 365–368, where he argued that the founding of the State of Israel would be the final hidden miracle, heralding a new age of revealed miracles). After the Yom Kippur War, Rabbi Halevy needed to incorporate this new development into his general thesis that we still were in the redemption process.

[29] ALR 1:7–12.

[30] ALR 4:6, p. 77.

The Role of Peace Talks in the Redemption Process

Rabbi Halevy suggested that peace talks and recognition by Arab nations were essential to the redemption process.[31] Despite the losses caused by the Yom Kippur War in 1973, and the wave of Arab terrorism in 1987, Rabbi Halevy maintained his belief in the redemption process by appealing to the ensuing peace negotiations.

At the same time, he expressed skepticism about Israel's so-called peace partners. Egypt entered negotiations only because it concluded that it was unable to annihilate Israel in a war, not from a genuine desire for peace. Rabbi Halevy was troubled about Israel being pressured to make land concessions, a process that threatened Israel's security.[32] Additionally, he claimed that "the redemption of Israel will not be complete if the Land of Israel will not be complete."[33]

After expressing his personal reservations about land concessions to Egypt, Rabbi Halevy concluded that the ultimate decision in this matter rested with the Israeli government. Only high officials were expert in the political and security details; they had the halakhic authority to make such

---

[31] See ALR 1:6; end of ALR 9, pp. 395–396.

[32] In his discussions of Sinai concessions, Rabbi Halevy noted that land for peace negotiations would create the dangerous precedent of offering the same for Judea and Samaria. He stated unequivocally that "God forbid" that we should ever reach that state of affairs. See ALR 1:7–12, p. 42.

[33] ALR 1:7–12 (p. 39); cf. ALR 3:62; 4:1. Rabbi Halevy quoted the Zohar, which maintained that full redemption would not occur with non-Jews *living* in the Land of Israel. Elsewhere, though, Rabbi Halevy accepted that Noahides, i.e., those observing a lifestyle of ethical monotheism, could live in the land (see his lengthy halakhic analysis in BYL, pp. 5–71, which addresses the issues of non-Jews living in the land, and making treaties with non-Jewish nations). Here, Rabbi Halevy argued that land concessions are not an impediment to redemption, since in the time of final redemption, Jews will get the land back, whereas now we need security and cannot rely on miracles (cf. DM, pp. 30–33). When discussing the laws of conquest, or Judaism's universalism (see ALR 8:68, 69), Rabbi Halevy invoked the Noahide laws. See further discussion in the chapter on Jews and non-Jews. See also Zvi Zohar, "Religious Zionism and Universal Improvement of the World," in *He'iru Penei haMizrah* (haKibbutz haMe'uhad, 2001), pp. 304–305.

decisions.[34] Although he did not trust Egypt's motives for making peace with Israel, Rabbi Halevy expressed the hope that a new generation would arise in Egypt, accustomed to peace.[35]

Is Redemption Contingent On Repentance?

Rabbi Halevy cited the talmudic debate (*Sanhedrin* 97b) whether repentance is a precondition for redemption or not.[36] He quoted a ruling of Rambam, that repentance was mandatory.[37] But elsewhere, Rambam wrote that the messianic king would encourage repentance, implying that the messianic age could commence prior to a full national repentance.[38] Rabbi Halevy reconciled the two statements by proposing that the messianic process could begin without repentance, but complete redemption required it.[39]

Rabbi Halevy balanced optimism with realism in viewing the religious life of Israel. On the one hand, many Jews were returning to their religious roots; but many others were drifting away from religion. The level of repentance was considerably less impressive than he would have liked. Addressing these concerns, Rabbi Halevy noted that the aliyah movement also started as a trickle. Yet, this trickle led to the creation of the State.

---

[34] ALR 3:62; 4:1; cf. DM, pp. 30–33. Rabbi Halevy made a similar point in ALR 7:53, where he rejected Chief Rabbi Shlomo Goren's criticism of the government's decision to release many Arab prisoners in exchange for only a few Jewish soldiers. Rabbi Halevy noted that this was a difficult security decision; although this release strengthened the ranks of our enemies, it also would strengthen Israeli soldiers' resolve to know that their government will go to great lengths to save them. He also believed that Rabbi Goren should not have criticized the government once it made this decision. In DM, pp. 49–60, Rabbi Halevy developed a more comprehensive halakhic analysis to explain the authority of the government of Israel. See further discussion in the chapter on Old Texts, New Realities.

[35] Rabbi Halevy began ALR volume 4 with a lengthy treatment of the implications of the recently signed peace treaty with Egypt.

[36] ALR 1:7–12.

[37] *Hil. Teshuvah* 7:5. Cf. Rabbi Halevy's further analysis of this ruling and the dissenting opinion in MKH 4:215, pp. 250–251.

[38] *Hil. Melakhim* 12:1–2.

[39] See further discussion in MKH 5:310, pp. 510–511, footnote 16.

Moreover, kabbalists predicted that the messianic age would be a time of religious confusion – many Jews would be religiously involved, but many others would be apathetic.[40] While appealing for more repentance, he still saw the "positive" aspect of non-religious behavior, i.e., it was a characteristic of the early stages of the age of redemption.[41]

Missed Opportunities

> Had you made yourself like a wall and had all come up in the days of Ezra, you would have been compared to silver, which no rottenness can ever affect. Now that you have come up like doors, you are like cedar wood, which rottenness prevails over. (*Yoma* 9b)

> The Sages say: The intention was to perform a miracle for Israel in the days of Ezra, even as it was performed for them in the days of Yehoshua bin Nun, but sin caused [the miracle to be withheld]. (*Berakhot* 4a)

In the above passages, the Talmud taught that messianic opportunities could be squandered if people did not respond appropriately to the initial signs of redemption. The beginning of the Second Temple period could have heralded the messianic age; but since the Jews of the time failed to return to Israel, and otherwise sinned, the redemption was postponed indefinitely.

---

[40] ALR 4:6; cf. DM, p. 87.

[41] In ALR 4:9, Rabbi Halevy expressed a remarkably fatalistic approach to the role of repentance in the redemption: if God gave us the Land of Israel, then it almost does not matter that many people still are sinning; God has revealed His will that the Jews should have their Land again. For a debate over whether the current State of Israel must be guaranteed, or whether it is conditional on Jewish religious conduct, see Uriel Simon, "The Biblical Destinies – Conditional Promises," *Tradition* 17:2 (Spring, 1978), pp. 84–90; and the rejoinder by Leon Stitskin, pp. 91–95.

Rabbi Halevy frequently quoted the *Yoma* passage in his efforts to encourage aliyah. He recognized that most Diaspora Jews remained in exile after the founding of the State and that assimilation among them was rampant. Yet, he never concluded that the current messianic potential was lost – only that we were missing opportunities to achieve gains within this definite period of redemption.[42]

Noting that many Jews were still not making aliyah after the Yom Kippur War, Rabbi Halevy optimistically suggested that perhaps God was giving the Jews living in Israel a chance to establish and consolidate themselves financially. Increased economic stability ultimately would encourage others to come.[43] He further suggested that had the first thirty years of statehood been easier, perhaps the Jewish passion for independence would not have been as strong. Moreover, perhaps the Yom Kippur War would jolt Israelis out of their complacency, and intensify their devotion to the Land of Israel.[44]

Rabbi Halevy halakhically justified ascending the Temple Mount, since we know the precise dimensions of the Temple and we can avoid

---

[42] Zvi Zohar ("Religious Zionism and Universal Improvement of the World," in *He'iru Penei haMizrah* [haKibbutz haMe'uhad, 2001], p. 305) quotes BYL, p. 89, where Rabbi Halevy wrote that "we do not know how much longer the influence of the rise of the State will last...after which this page will be closed in history." But despite this statement, Rabbi Halevy never reached the negative conclusion suggested as possible in BYL. It would appear that Rabbi Halevy appealed to the window of opportunity to inspire others, but he maintained a firm belief that full redemption definitely would occur in our era.

[43] ALR 3:62. In ALR 1:17–18, Rabbi Halevy addressed a student who wanted to make aliyah, but his parents opposed the move. Although Rabbi Halevy could have noted that the laws of honoring parents do not include one's own personal life decisions, he simply ruled that it is against halakhah not to make aliyah, and we are not allowed to listen to our parents when they instruct us to violate halakhah. Rabbi Halevy added that perhaps if the student were to repeat this responsum to his parents nicely, they will come on aliyah also. Cf. DM, p. 11; MKH 5:266, pp. 257–259, where he wrote that all leading *poskim* have ruled that one who can make aliyah but does not violates a positive commandment every day. See also TH 2, *Bemidbar*, pp. 132–140.

[44] ALR 1:7–12.

going to those spots that are ritually forbidden. The rest of the Mount is accessible to Jews who ritually immerse themselves and remove their shoes. He added that rabbis should not prohibit observant Jews from going to the Temple Mount out of concern that non-observant Jews will not follow the proper regulations.[45] He recommended that a synagogue should be built atop the Temple Mount.[46]

Two years after the liberation of the Temple Mount, Rabbi Halevy sadly noted that Israel had squandered the opportunity to build a synagogue there. He expressed anguish that Israel allowed our most sacred site to remain in Arab hands. Jews should have created facts on the ground by building a synagogue when we had the chance.[47]

Rabbi Halevy emphasized that the sanctity of the Land of Israel was not contingent on military conquest, but on settlement.[48] After the Sinai concessions and peace treaty with Egypt, he added that Jews were now forfeiting the opportunity to settle Judea and Samaria.[49] Had a million Jews moved in right after the Six Day War, there would not have been any chance of negotiating its return. Rabbi Halevy quoted *Yoma* 9b, which criticized the Jews' failure to make aliyah during the Second Temple Period. If Jews did not freely come now, perhaps they will be forced to come in order to complete the process of redemption.[50] Elsewhere, Rabbi

---

[45] ALR 1:15; cf. DM, pp. 114–116.

[46] ALR 6:82.

[47] DM, p. 117.

[48] ALR 3:60.

[49] ALR 4:1.

[50] Cf. his fuller discussions in ALR 4:1; 4:8, where he observed that Jews remaining in exile caused the destruction of the Second Temple, rather than the destruction having caused the exile. Full redemption cannot come without a complete return to Israel – this is why God forced many Israelites to leave Egypt against their will (*ki goreshu miMitzrayim*, see *Shemot* 12:39). In ALR 4:7, Rabbi Halevy used the Yaakov-Esav relationship as a model to suggest that Israel remain internationally neutral (cf. DM, pp. 35–40). Rabbi Halevy noted that Yaakov was quite successful in exile, just as Jews have been in more recent history. In the very next responsum (ALR 4:8), however, he discussed exile as a curse, noting that Jews have suffered immeasurably in exile. This is another excellent example of selective citation of sources, depending on his educational

Halevy added a more ominous note to encourage aliyah, observing that neo-Nazi movements continued to thrive all over the world.[51]

Rabbi Halevy thought that Jews had erred in not having made aliyah after the Balfour Declaration in 1917, a time when the Arabs were largely inactive politically. A large influx of Jews would have changed the reality drastically. Since Jews did not come willingly, then, they were compelled to come in the aftermath of the Holocaust. Perhaps the prophetic prediction of a purging nightmare before the final redemption (*Yehezkel* 20) was fulfilled as a result of Jewish reluctance to make aliyah earlier in the 20th century. He again emphasized that we cannot know the workings of God's mind – but we could offer interpretations after the fact, in order to derive religious inspiration and guidance.[52]

Despite his claims of the forfeiture of individual blessings, though, Rabbi Halevy asserted that God never would abandon Israel.[53] He continued to believe that the process of redemption was slowly and irreversibly unfolding, and he interpreted each new event in this light.

Halakhic Rulings

Because of Rabbi Halevy's belief that we were living in the period of redemption, he reached a number of important halakhic conclusions. He believed that Israel Independence Day (5 *Iyyar*) and Jerusalem Reunification Day (28 *Iyyar*) should be observed as formal religious holidays, with Hallel recited.[54] Rabbi Halevy criticized those who opposed celebrating these holidays on the grounds that they were primarily military

---

agenda. For further discussion, see the chapter on Dealing With Conflicting Sources. In 4:7, he noted Jewish success in the non-Jewish world as a result of their isolation; but in 4:8, when trying to encourage aliyah, he focused on the suffering of the Jews throughout their experience in the Diaspora.

[51] DM, p. 15.

[52] ALR 4:6; cf. DM, pp. 12–16.

[53] DM, p. 16.

[54] DM, pp. 88–113. In a footnote in ALR 3:58, Rabbi Halevy quoted Zohar Hadash that says that *Iyyar* is a month of miracles for Israel. Cf. MKH 4:195, pp. 145–146.

victories. Hanukkah also was celebrated because of military victories.[55] He noted that these opponents were driving less observant Jews to view those events in purely secular terms. If *religious* Jews refused to acknowledge God's hand, why should secular Jews?[56]

Rabbi Halevy reevaluated traditional practices pertaining to mourning over the destruction of the Temple. Rabbi Halevy maintained that we still must observe the Fast of the 9th of *Av* until the Temple itself is rebuilt.[57] But after the Six Day War, we should reword parts of the *"nahem"* prayer into the past tense. Since the prayer laments a desolate Jerusalem without any Jewish inhabitants, it simply would be a falsehood to retain the original text of the prayer.[58]

Likewise, he suggested emending a passage in the Grace After Meals, which currently reads, "we thank You, God for the good and ample land that You gave to our ancestors." Now that we are living in the age of redemption, we should say, "...that You gave *to us*." Rabbi Halevy asserted that since Yehoshua instituted this blessing (*Berakhot* 48a), the original text doubtlessly read "to us" as well.[59]

With the settling of the Land, we should again recite the blessing, *"Barukh matziv gevul almanah"* (blessed is He who establishes the borders of a widowed [nation]). Rabbi Halevy was hesitant to rule that one should recite the full blessing with God's Name, although he noted that Rabbi Avraham Yitzhak Kook had done so. Rabbi Halevy agreed with his reasoning.[60]

---

[55] ALR 5:17; cf. MHK 4:226, pp. 315–319.

[56] DM, pp. 86–87.

[57] Cf. MKH 4:202, pp. 179–180.

[58] In ALR 1:13–14; cf. ALR 2:36–39. For other rulings regarding texts of prayers now that we are in the time of redemption, see ALR 4:5; 8:14; MKH 1:62, p. 288; 4:209, p. 214. For further discussion of Rabbi Halevy's ruling on the *nahem* prayer, see the chapter on Old Texts, New Realities. See also ALR 1:18; 8:14; MH 1:9; MKH 1:62, p. 288.

[59] MKH 2:81, p. 97. This argument appears uncompelling; Yehoshua still could have been referring to the initial covenants God made with the Patriarchs.

[60] ALR 4:5.

We still should say *kinot* (prayers of lamentation) on the 9th of *Av*, since the Temple is not yet rebuilt, and the majority of Jews still lived outside of Israel. But we may reduce the number of *kinot*, as he himself did after 1948.[61]

Although the original practice was to tear one's clothing upon seeing the desolate cities in Israel, or the ruins of Jerusalem (*Mo'ed Katan* 26a), Jews now lived in Israel, and the Temple Mount was again under Jewish control. Therefore, one no longer should tear one's garments when going to the Western Wall. However, he thought that the Chief Rabbinate should issue the final ruling on this.[62]

The practice in Jerusalem was to don *tefillin* in the morning of 9th of *Av* at home, and then to come to synagogue for the recitation of *kinot*. Even one who previously did not observe this tradition should accept it, since we were living at the beginning of the redemption.[63]

Rabbi Halevy complained about the prevalent custom at the end of weddings to break a worthless glass rather than something of real value. After concluding that this was not a major issue worth fighting over, he added that especially now, in the age of redemption, we do not have to be as mournful as we had been in the past – and therefore the current practice may be tolerated.[64]

Although Rabbi Halevy allowed some room for leniency as a result of this being the period of redemption, he did not permit choir practice during the three weeks between the 17th of *Tammuz* and the 9th of *Av*. During that period, we should remain mournful.[65]

May we accept converts nowadays, given rabbinic traditions that we will not accept converts in messianic times (*Yevamot* 24b; 76a; *Avodah*

---

[61] ALR 4:34. In MHK 4:205, p. 191, where Rabbi Halevy prefaced his discussion of the customs for the 9th of *Av* (as opposed to the *laws* of that day) by noting that he will be brief, since he hoped and believed that we are in the beginning of the period of redemption.

[62] MKH 2:95, pp. 207–209.

[63] MKH 1:35, p. 131.

[64] MKH 5:237, p. 36; MKH *leHatan veKhallah* 3, p. 36.

[65] MH 1:35.

Zarah 3b)? Rabbi Halevy noted that only a minority of Jews, and very few non-Jews, have appreciated that we now have entered the beginning of the messianic era. Thus, no one would convert to Judaism today merely to join the messianic bandwagon. Additionally, several authorities (Rambam, Rashba, Meiri) ruled according to *Berakhot* 57b, that non-Jews would convert to Judaism even in the messianic age. The Talmud (*Avodah Zarah* 3b) noted that the Messiah would weed out insincere converts, so there was nothing to fear by accepting converts nowadays.[66]

The Talmud (*Berakhot* 54a) stated that one should make the blessing *"Barukh haTov vehaMetiv"* for rainfall, but that practice had fallen out of practice while Jews lived in exile. Rabbi Halevy ruled that since Jews have returned to Israel, they should once again recite this blessing – either after a prolonged drought is ended by rain, or if there is unusually heavy rainfall. The final decision on when the community should make this blessing should be left to the Chief Rabbinate.[67]

Rabbi Halevy discussed whether the original practice of lighting Hanukkah candles outdoors should be restored. He quoted the *Hazon Ish*, who ruled that we still should light indoors, since 1) people might blow the candles out if they were left outdoors; 2) Israel was surrounded by enemies, and there was no guarantee that Israel would survive. Rabbi Halevy emphatically disagreed. Since this is the beginning of the redemption, one in Israel should light Hanukkah candles outdoors, when possible.[68]

Rabbi Halevy opened *Dat uMedinah* (p. 9) with an idea from R. Yehudah Halevy's *Kuzari:* redemption will not come until people desperately wanted it. Rabbi Halevy's life was dedicated to inspire messianic hopes, to encourage people to take an active role in the process

---

[66] ALR 3:29.

[67] MKH 2:92, pp. 181–182.

[68] ALR 7:42. In MZR (p. 59), Rabbi Halevy quoted the Zohar (*Vayera* 114): God swore to rebuild Jerusalem, and it never will be destroyed again, Israel will not be exiled, and the Temple will not be destroyed. Although these aspects of the redemption have not yet been fulfilled, Rabbi Halevy's confidence that we are in the period of redemption allowed him to make this extrapolation.

of redemption, and to promote a religious awakening.[69] He added (p. 26) that the special role of rabbis during this period of redemption was to devote their energy to inspire the hearts of people with an understanding of God's role in history.[70] It comes as no surprise that he concluded his *Mekor Hayyim* series with a chapter on the Messianic age. Although the full redemption has not yet come, Rabbi Halevy did his best to hasten the Messiah's arrival.[71]

---

[69] Cf. ALR 8:94–95.

[70] See also MKH 5:310, p. 507.

[71] For further discussions of aspects of Rabbi Halevy's messianic thought, see Malkah Katz, "Rabbi Haim David Halevy as the Successor of the World and Views of the Sephardic Sages in Israel Who Associated with Religious Zionism in the Days of the Mandate"; Dov Schwartz, "Changes in the Messianic Thought of Rabbi Haim David Halevy," in the volume of papers about Rabbi Halevy, edited by Zvi Zohar and Avi Sagi; Zvi Zohar, "Religious Zionism and Universal Improvement of the World," in *He'iru Penei haMizrah* (haKibbutz haMe'uhad, 2001), pp. 298–311.

Selected Bibliography

Angel, Marc D., "A Study of the Halakhic Approaches of Two Modern Posekim," *Tradition* 23:3 (Spring, 1988), pp. 41–52.

——, *Foundations of Sephardic Spirituality: The Inner Life of Jews of the Ottoman Empire*, Woodstock, Vermont, Jewish Lights, 2006.

——, *Loving Truth and Peace: The Grand Religious Worldview of Rabbi Benzion Uziel*, Northvale: Jason Aronson, 1999.

——, "Rabbi Hayyim David Halevy," *Jewish Book Annual*, vol. 52, New York: Jewish Book Council, 1994, pp. 99–109.

——, *Seeking Good, Speaking Peace: Collected Essays of Rabbi M.D. Angel*, ed. Hayyim Angel, Hoboken: Ktav, 1994.

——, *The Jews of Rhodes*, New York: Sepher-Hermon Press, 1978.

——, *The Rhythms of Jewish Living*, New York: Sepher-Hermon Press, 1986.

——, *Voices in Exile*, Hoboken: Ktav, 1991.

Cardozo, Benjamin N., *The Nature of the Judicial Process*, New Haven: Yale University Press, 1921.

Feinstein, Moshe, *Iggrot Moshe,* 7 vols., New York, 5719–5742.

Halevy, Haim David, *Asei Lekha Rav,* 9 vols., Tel Aviv, 5736–5749.

——, *Bein Yisrael laAmim,* Jerusalem, 5714.

——, *Dat uMedinah,* Tel Aviv, 5729.

——, *Devar haMishpat,* 3 vols., Tel Aviv, 5742.

——, *Mayyim Hayyim,* 3 vols., Tel Aviv, 5751–5759.

——, *Mekor Hayyim haShalem,* 5 vols., Tel Aviv, 5727–5734.

——, *Mekor Hayyim Kitzur Shulhan Arukh*, Tel Aviv, 5735.

——, *Mekor Hayyim leHatan veKhallah*, Tel Aviv, 5739.

——, *Mekor Hayyim Livnot Yisrael*, Tel Aviv, 5737.

——, *Maftehot haZohar veRa'ayonotav*, Tel Aviv, 5731.

——, *Netzah Moshe,* Tel Aviv, 5756.

——, "The Love of Israel as a Factor in Halakhic Decision-making," *Tradition,* 24:3 (Spring 1989), pp. 1–20.

——, *Toledotav uMifalo haSifruti shel Maran haRav Benzion Meir Hai Uziel*, Jerusalem: Imrei Fi Publishers, 5739.

——, *Torat Hayyim,* 5 vols., Tel Aviv, 5752–5753.

——, *Torat Hayyim al haMo'adim,* Tel Aviv, 5763.

Herzog, Yitzhak Halevy, *Tehukah leYisrael*, 3 vols., Jerusalem: Mossad haRav Kook, 1989.

Me'ah Shanah leShekhunat Ohel Moshe beYerushalayim, Jerusalem: Sephardic Community of Jerusalem, 1983.

Uziel, Benzion M.H., *Mishpetei Uziel*, 7 vols., Tel Aviv and Jerusalem, 5695–5724.

Yehoshua, Yaakov, *Shekhunot beYerushalayim haYeshanah*, Jerusalem: Reuven Mass.

Yosef, Ovadya, *Yabia Omer*, 6 vols., Jerusalem, 5746.

Zohar, Zvi, *Halakhah uModernizatziah*, Jerusalem: *Makhon Shalom Hartman*, 5741.

——, *He'iru Penei haMizrah*, HaKibbutz haMe'uhad, 2001.

——, *Masoret uTemurah*, Jerusalem: Makhon Ben Zvi, 5753.

——, "Sephardic Hakhamim, Modernity and the Theology of Haim David Halevy," in *Critical Essays on Israeli Society, Religion and Government*, eds. W. Zenner and K. Avruch, Albany: SUNY Press, 1997, pp. 115–136.

——, "Sephardic Rabbinic Responses to Modernity: Some Central Characteristics," in *Jews Among Muslims*, eds. W. Zenner and S. Deshen, London, 1996, pp. 64–136.

——, "Traditional Flexibility and Modern Strictness: A Comparative Analysis of the Halakhic Positions of Rabbi Kook and Rabbi Uziel on Women's Suffrage," in *Sephardi and Middle Eastern Jewries: History and Culture*, ed. H. Goldberg, Bloomington: Indiana University Press, 1996, pp. 119–133.

Zohar, Zvi, and Sagi, Avi, eds., *Papers on the Teachings of Rabbi H.D. Halevy*, as yet unpublished.

About the Authors

Dr. Marc D. Angel is Senior Rabbi of Congregation Shearith Israel, the historic Spanish and Portuguese Synagogue of New York City (founded 1654). Author and editor of 25 books, his most recent book is *Losing the Rat Race, Winning at Life* (Urim, 2005). He is past President of the Rabbinical Council of America and has won a National Jewish Book Award in the category of Jewish Thought.

Hayyim Angel is Rabbi of Congregation Shearith Israel, where he serves together with his father. He teaches *Tanakh* at Yeshiva University, and has published scholarly articles in journals such as *Tradition, Nahalah, Jewish Thought,* and the *Jewish Bible Quarterly.* His articles have also appeared in several collections of essays.